It Was All in the Cards

To Miller

Share my World
one Love

Michael

It Was All in the Cards

The life and times of

Midtown Mike

Michael Evans

MonteMe

Names of some of the characters have been changed
to protect their identity.

ISBN 13: 978-0-9742775-0-9
ISBN 10: 0-9742775-0-9

Library of Congress Control Number: 2003111264

Fifth printing April 2008

Book production: Tabby House
Final cover design: OspreyDesign
Barbatunde Odesanya, cover design concept
Gibran Brown, cover illustration concept
Lyrics on p. 273 from "Mama—Who Da Man?" written by
Junior/RichardBlackwood/Mickey Power/Lucas

A glossary of street terms is found at the end of the book.

MonteMe
4006 Third Avenue
P.O. Box 570-249
Bronx, NY 10457
www.montemepublishing.com
MidtownMike2002@aol.com

Dedication

This book is dedicated in loving memory of Ma-Ma,
who passed away on January 28, 2004. I love you just because!

Acknowledgments

This book is dedicated to all the people who helped me on my journey to redemption. First, to my ex-wife for helping me to change my life around. I know I did not do it by myself. God put you in my life for a reason. I would also like to thank you for giving birth to our two sons, whom I love more than words can say.

Thank you to the Evans family for being there for me from day one! Love always. And to my publisher and editor, Jim and Linda Salisbury, for their expertise and time helping make my dream become a reality.

And, to my father. Although you were not always physically there, I know you were always watching over me. I'll see you when I get there.

Claude Brown, thank you for giving me the inspiration and the courage to reveal my life to the world. Rest in peace.

Last but not least, I would like to acknowledge my fianceé, Tara, for painstakingly putting up with my obsessive behavior in wanting to get this book done. I know typing and reading all the crazy facets of my life was no easy task. I thank you wholeheartedly. My love for you is no con game.

Introduction

The first time I realized I wanted to write a book was after reading *Manchild in the Promised Land* by Claude Brown. I was only twelve years old and my best friend's sister, whom I always used to hump on, had read the book and recommended it. The reason I think she gave me this book to read was she may have seen a little bit of Claude Brown in me.

I was a little hyper kid who stayed in mischief and was always looking for ways to hustle, scam and get over. She knew I liked to read because she always saw me reading Richie Rich comic books. I loved reading them because they were about the escapades of this little rich white kid with billions of dollars, which fed into my crazy obsession with the almighty dollar.

Whenever a new issue of Richie Rich came out, I would be the first one in line to buy one. I always fantasized that I was Richie Rich (a black version, of course) buying everything I wanted. I guess growing up poor can put anybody in a fantasy world. You know how some people who do not have money always say things like, "If I had money I would buy . . ." Or, 'If I hit the lottery, all of my problems would be solved." Some poor people think money buys happiness.

As a little kid, that was me all the way. I thought money could solve all of my family's problems. My mother was on welfare and my father died when I was nine years old. So, a family living on a welfare budget did not suit me. There were no silver spoons in the Evans' household, no, siree, but we did have a lot of love, drama and chaos.

So, when I read *Manchild in the Promised Land*, I realized I was not the only kid growing up poor and conflicted. Claude Brown's book captured my attention in a way that no other book had ever done. It made me realize there was a whole other world in books and it made me want to learn more about other people's lives.

I also liked reading Donald Goines' fictionalized street tales, which fed my infatuation with the streets. His books were about the lifestyles of drug dealers, pimps and hustlers. But, they were fiction and *Manchild in the Promised Land* was real, which took me to a whole other level.

Claude Brown's book was about his growing up in Harlem. He gave it to readers raw and uncut. He told the good, the bad and the ugly about himself and his life. After I finished reading his story, I was blown away with all the things that happened in his life and how he told everything with complete honesty.

Then and there I knew that one day I wanted to write my own life story. And, I told myself when I did, I would tell the whole truth and nothing but the truth—the good, the bad and the ugly without sugarcoating anything. At the time my whole idea of writing a book was just a passing thought, but the good thing about my idea was, it made me read a lot of other people's autobiographies. I've read about Richard Pryor, Little Richard, The Supremes, Barry White and *Makes Me Wanna Holler,* by Nathan McCall. Reading about these people's lives only intensified my yearning to write about my own life. Every so often I would tell somebody about my plans and they would look at me like I was crazy or just another brother with visions of grandeur. It got to the point that the only person I would talk about it with was China.

She became my girlfriend when I was seventeen years old; I had had a secret crush on her since I was nine. We got together after I was deep into the street lifestyle of being a three-card monte player. The reason I titled my book *It was All in the Cards: The Life and Times of Midtown Mike* is because my story will give you a ringside seat into what can happen to a young fatherless kid who looks for a father figure in all the wrong places. My search led me straight to the streets, which is the wrong place for a curious and impressionable young kid to find a role model. Out on the cruel, take-no-prisoners streets, I did not find what I was looking for. But, what I did find was a hard way to go.

A lot of the men I encountered on the streets did not have the slightest idea about how to properly guide a young kid looking for positive guidance. Most of them had grown up just like me—without a father in their household. Some of the people from whom I sought advice about life were drunks, hustlers, pimps, con men and so-called players. How could they teach me about something they knew nothing about?

My quest brought me to the streets of Midtown Manhattan at age fifteen. This is after years of being involved in different types of petty scams and hustles. Now, I was in the place of bright lights where they say stars are born. No, I did not get my name in the lights, but I did wind up a bona fide three-card monte player on Broadway and all over Midtown.

This book is not fiction or some fairy tale Richie Rich comic book. This is a true-life depiction of a young street hustler caught up in real-life situations. Picture an impressionable fifteen-year-old growing up around real pimps, prostitutes, hustlers and con men on the crazy Midtown streets from 1979 to 1986, where Forty-second Street (aka The Deuce) was in its heyday, with drama and chaos. All while I was caught up in this Midtown lifestyle, little did I know that this type of crazy atmosphere could be a perfect setting for the book I had always envisioned writing. But, talking about writing a book and actually doing it are two different things. Then, add the fact that I wanted to write all aspects of my life story, truthfully telling the good, the bad and the ugly parts, without ever glossing over anything. I knew I had done a lot of unscrupulous things that I never told anyone about— let alone the woman I one day planned to marry.

These were just some of the things I had to deal with before I put pen to paper. On some days writing was very stressful and emotional because I was telling about some crazy situations that had happened. Writing them down was like reliving them. Sometimes it is hard to face the past. Other days I could not wait to start writing because I was so much in a writer's mode that the pen seemed to move itself. I would find myself either laughing real hard or crying. But, I would feel so at peace with myself afterwards because so much had been revealed to me. Writing this book was a very emotional and enlightening experience for me. And, it can only help me on my road to redemption.

So, now that I have finished my part, there is only one thing left to be done and that is for you to read it. I suspect you will not like some of what I have to tell and other things might make you laugh. I do not know how you will feel about everything in this book. But, I do know, if you really get honest with yourself, you might even relate some of the things in my life to your own life.

As I take you on a journey through the eyes of a confused kid, I hope you realize that I never wrote this book so that I could become anyone's friend or role model. I wrote this book honestly because I know there are a lot of kids growing up in the same conditions that I found myself in, or maybe even worse ones. If they can read this and see themselves falling into the same traps I did, then maybe they can change what they are doing and try something different.

Like I tell my two sons, I made mistakes so that you don't have to. If one kid can learn from my mistakes and not fall victim to what I went through, then that is one fewer kid who we all have to worry about. So, here it is, my story, *It Was All in the Cards: The Life and Times of Midtown Mike.*

"The realist shit I ever wrote . . ."
—Tupac Shakur

1

Honeywell Avenue

As I turned over in bed in the middle of the night, I noticed two things: First, my little sister, Carolyn, was not in the bed and second, I was hearing some funny noises, which I knew to be only one thing. Ma-Ma's thirty-three-year-old cousin, Reggie, from Down South, was up to his old tricks in the living room. "Uh-uh-uh," is all I heard as I made my way to the living room.

As soon as I made it to the entrance of the living room, I spotted Cousin Reggie having sex with an old lady who appeared to be in her sixties. My seven-year-old sister, Carolyn, was sitting on the radiator with a ringside seat. So I sat next to her to watch the action.

Cousin Reggie always liked an audience, even though he knew we were too young to be watching someone having sex. He kept on humping and stroking the frail, little old lady, telling her lies.

"Yeah, baby, I'm gonna buy you a house. Yeah, baby, a car, too. What you want, baby, I'll buy it all." These were all lies because Cousin Reggie didn't have a pot to piss in and he lived with us.

As the woman moaned and groaned, he told lie after lie. It was like we were watching a porno movie, but the only thing missing was the popcorn. After we got tired of the action, we got up and went to the back to tell Ma-Ma that Cousin Reggie was in the living room doing the nasty with an old lady. She got up and headed straight to the living room, cursing and hollering.

"Reggie, if you don't get this bitch out of my house, I'll kick her ass and your ass, too! What did I tell you about fucking around these kids?"

He gave Carolyn and me this crazy look, then lied and said, "Oh, Mabel, I'm sorry. I didn't know those kids were up!"

Ma-Ma and Reggie were first cousins and she loved him like a brother. They both were raised in the South and migrated to New York during the late fifties. Cousin Reggie was a tall man about six feet four inches, slim and dark skinned. He was funny, crazy and street smart—all wrapped up in one.

My family consisted of my mother, Mabel, whom I called Ma-Ma, my father, Curtis, sister, Carolyn, whom my uncle Howard always called Redbone because she was light-skinned. I think this saying originated in the South. We all lived in a brown, six-story brick building at 1975 Honeywell Avenue in the Bronx. In the summertime, the sun lit up our apartment like a cornfield in the South on a bright summer day. In the winter, the clouds from the sky cast a dark shade over our apartment. I loved the shiny wooden floors, which were so slippery that Carolyn and I used to slide across them.

These were the same floors that my parents and their friends did their funny dances on, like the jitterbug, funky chicken and the belly-wop. The belly-wop dance was the one we would laugh at the most because all the adults would be moving their bellies while screaming "ah, sooki sooki now" or "watch out now."

We loved our parents' rent and card parties because we would sneak around watching the funny things that went on throughout the night. My parents gave these parties when they just happened to be a little short with the rent money.

The people who came to our parties consisted of some of the tenants that lived in our building as well as people from around the block. These were working people, people on welfare, alcoholics and even drug addicts, who sometimes were the same ones that used to burglarize our apartment. I know you can tell by the Cousin Reggie incident, that a lot of ungodly things went on where I lived. I witnessed many things growing up in this sometimes-crazy atmosphere. Some of the things I learned later guided me, positively or negatively.

My father, Curtis, was a very smart man and had been the valedictorian of his high school Down South. My parents met in New York after moving from the South. They fell in love and were married. I was their firstborn and they named me Michael. In some ways, I was like my mother, and in others, I was like my father. I took personality traits from each of my parents and I resembled both. I have a round face with a light-brown complexion, like my father, and a small nose and brown eyes like my mother. I have my father's small lips and smile, along with his slim physique and broad shoulders. My sister, Carolyn, was their second child. After having us, my parents were both happy until my father started to drink heavily when he did not get the jobs he thought he deserved. I guess he thought a high school valedictorian deserved better. So, when he got drunk, he would get into crazy arguments with Ma-Ma, so there was always lots of drama in our apartment. Later on she also drank. In some ways Ma-Ma understood what he was going through and she really felt for the man whom she married. She knew he really loved his family and he wanted to be a good provider. But, when he was not getting the good jobs, it really stressed him out.

Ma-Ma had two brothers, Howard and Woodrow. Howard owned a roofing business that made him lots of money. He would always pop around our block in his new car and fine threads. Woodrow was an electrician who also made good money. Ma-Ma always bragged to my father and friends about all the money her brothers made.

All of her bragging just ate my father up. I cannot say it was jealousy because he was not a jealous person. I guess when a person is struggling, it is hard to hear about another person doing well. Also, he may have thought she was making fun of him. He once asked me if I loved my uncles more than I loved him. I promptly said, "No." I was shocked when he asked me that. But his mind was so distorted that he did not even pay attention to what I said; he just kept talking. "One day I'm gonna make lots of money and buy us a lot of nice things and a car so we all can go anywhere we want."

My sister and I loved him very much, but we hated the drinking and the fights. One thing I really loved about him was that he never liked to spank us. In fact, he did more talking than hitting. I can only remember one time being hit by him and that was only a few taps. Ma-Ma was the disciplinarian of our household. She knew how to whip some ass.

If she told you to do something and you did not do it, she would yell, "I can show you better than I can tell you." And she would beat the living shit out of us. I can still hear good old Cousin Reggie yelling, "That's right, Mabel, whip their asses! Whip those bad-ass kids' asses!" Then, after our beating, she would start crying and say, "Beating ya'll kids hurts me more than it hurts y'all." I could not believe her because my ass was on fire.

I remember that my parents had a big fight when my father accused Ma-Ma of cheating; he only made these accusations after drinking. At the time, it really hurt her because none of it was true. So, she promptly kicked him out and he went Down South where he stayed for a little while then came back, apologized to Ma-Ma and they made up. This negative cycle went on from time to time until eventually she got tired of the accusations and started to do what he already thought she was doing.

I guess after so many fights, even two people who love each other can grow apart. The last fight they had, she kicked him out and later he came back, begging her to open the door. He was screaming, "Mabel, let me in! Let me in!"

She would not let him in, so I made a move for the door when he started calling for me to open it. She yelled, "Boy, if you open that door I'm gonna beat your ass!"

So, I lay back down. Little did I know how this scene would haunt me; I did not open the door for my father when he needed me. Eventually he left and a few days later went back Down South where he became severely depressed.

He was admitted to a mental ward where they said he later committed suicide. My sister and I were too young to get the full meaning of our father's death. I was nine years old and she was only eight. All I know is that a few days later, we were on a Greyhound bus on our way to his funeral.

During the long ride, Ma-Ma drank vodka, which made her cry. I guess she was thinking about all the memories they shared and how she was going to raise kids on her own. While she cried, my sister and I played in our seats. At the time we did not know that the death of one's parent is maybe one of the most devastating things that can happen to a child. What I do know now is the death of my father affects me deeply today. Maybe by committing suicide, in some odd way, he helped me to not choose suicide as an option no matter what trials or tribulations that I might go through.

After the bus arrived in Thomasville, Alabama, we went to my grandmother's house to wait for the funeral. Thomasville, where Ma-Ma was born and raised, was a beautiful place with a mix of nice big houses, nice little houses, and some shack-like houses. It also had big fields that looked like the plantation fields I had seen in movies. I never liked those plantations because white people always had blacks working in the burning hot sun. But, as soon as I laid my eyes on those fields in Alabama, I just wanted to take my shirt off and run through all the greenery. They had corn, watermelon and lots of other fruits and vegetables. The weather was hot and sticky, which made me very thirsty. So, when we went into my grandmother, Gertrude's, grayish, shack-type house, I ran and hugged her. Then I walked into the kitchen and drank some water. As soon as I tasted it, I spit it out and yelled, "Man, this water tastes like it got salt in it!" My family just laughed as I made a funny face. Then I said, "Grandma, where's the bathroom?"

She replied, "Boy, there ain't no bathroom. You take your butt outside if you gotta go."

I was shocked. As Carolyn and I headed outside, I said, "What type of place is this that don't have no bathroom?"

My sister said, "Grandma must be poor because her house is nothing like those other big houses we saw."

I nodded as my eyes drifted over to a small patched-up, dirty-looking shed. I asked, "Carolyn, that must be where they go to the bathroom."

I opened the little door and *boom!* A stench that smelled like the dead dogs in back of our building hit me. I almost fell out from the nasty odor. My need to go to the bathroom would have to wait. I said, "I can't wait until we get back to New York. This is crazy."

Ma-Ma always said she grew up poor, but she never went hungry. Now I believed her about the poverty. I just wondered how she made it through all of this. After attempting to go to the bathroom, we went back in the house where all through the course of the day lots of cousins, uncles and aunts stopped by the house to offer their condolences. Meanwhile my sister and I acted like we were on a mini vacation, traveling to different relatives' houses.

Ma-Ma's uncle Harvey took a liking to us and he rode us all around in his big black pickup truck. We met his beautiful wife, Sadie, who wanted us to stay and live with them in their big beautiful white and yellow house. When we went shopping with them, I asked if they could buy me a soda in a little grocery store that I saw. They told me that blacks were not allowed in that store. Immediately I had flashbacks of all the bad things I saw happen to black people on television because of racism, like being bitten by dogs and hosed down with water by whites. The feelings of rage that would overtake my body whenever I saw it always made me feel like I was going to explode. Now here I was in the place where a lot of those things happened. In New York we had racism, but it was sugarcoated to the extent that sometimes you were fooled into thinking it did not exist. A lot of white people smiled in your face but called you nigger behind your back. Some of them said, "Man, my best friend is a black guy," even though a black person had never stepped foot in their houses. Or they said, "Man, I got nothing against youse people," but it sounds more like, "I got nothing against *used people*."

In the South, they deal with black people differently. White people will call you nigger to your face, and say it with ease. They let you know right away that they don't give a fuck about you. So when my aunt told me that I could not go in the store, I realized what a beautiful world we make.

The next day it was time for the funeral. Carolyn cried all the way from Grandma's house to the funeral. Ma-Ma and Carolyn had to be comforted throughout the entire service. I remember staring at my father in the coffin and asking, "Ma-Ma, does Daddy have any money in his pockets?" Ma-Ma looked at me and said, "Shut up, boy."

Looking back, I find it very strange that I asked such a stupid question. Here it was my darkest hour, but my little mind was thinking about money. I did not understand death at all because I had never experienced it. Death was just a word to me. For all I knew, my father was going to get out of the casket and come back home with us. Perhaps that question, was a sign of my eventual love of money. After the funeral, we told everyone good-bye and headed back to New York.

My father's death was a major turning point in my life. At my young age, because I was curious and impressionable, I deeply needed a strong father figure. I subconsciously searched for a male to step in and guide me like a father would do. This is when Cousin Reggie started to play a big part in my life, which was not a good thing because he was buck wild. When I was nine, he taught me a lot of things about street life, specifically how to hustle, scam and get over. But I liked the fact that Cousin Reggie took me to places. If Ma-Ma had found out, she would have cursed him out. He was a street-smart guy. He took me to gambling spots, number holes and apartments all over the city, where he had sex with his girlfriends while I watched. We used to go to Harlem where he seemed to know everyone wherever we went. He knew drug dealers, gangsters, pimps—you name it. This was a time when I was very curious and impressionable. I was also very observant. So, I took a whole lot in during these escapades with Cousin Reggie. One time as we got on a bus, Cousin Reggie whispered something to the bus driver and we rode free. I then asked him, "What did you say to the bus driver?"

He answered, "Oh, I told him your mother was in the hospital, sick on her deathbed, and we had no money to go see her."

These were all lies. The real story was Cousin Reggie was taking me with him to the hospital to scam the doctors for pills. He would pretend to be sick with different ailments to get the prescription pills that he wanted. He was a good actor—on the caliber of Marlon Brando. So, after his Oscar-winning performance, the stupid doctors wrote prescriptions. Cousin Reggie then sold all the pills on the streets. This scam was called the pill hustle.

Some of these negative things I learned from him would come in handy later. After he took me all over town, we went home and incurred the wrath of Mabel if she had been drinking. Ma-Ma was the sweetest person in the world when she was sober. But, if she was drunk, watch out!

Ma-Ma was one of the quickest persons I knew when it came to pulling a knife. I don't remember that she ever stabbed my father or Cousin Reggie, but all of her boyfriends who came after my father got stabbed, and even some friends. Ma-Ma once told my sister and me that her father had taught her how to use a knife. A lot of people who grew up Down South carried them. Cousin Reggie's best friend, Clarence, always got on Ma-Ma's nerves when they were drinking.

One time he said something nasty about getting into Ma-Ma's pants and that was all he got to say because in a split-second, she was lunging toward him with a knife. Clarence put his hands up in defense, but she stabbed him real bad in his hand. Emergency 911 was called and luckily for Ma-Ma, Clarence didn't tell them what really happened. He just went to the hospital and got a lot of stitches, then came back to our apartment and continued to drink. At least he wasn't a snitch!

Another time Ma-Ma was drinking with her best friend, Marge, who did not take any shit herself, Cousin Reggie, Clarence, and Ma-Ma's boyfriend, Winchester. All of a sudden, Winchester and Ma-Ma were arguing about all the clothes she bought him, down to his underwear. The day before this argument, she had made him strip down to his underwear in a crowded elevator. This was because she had bought everything that he had on. Ma-Ma had done this to him numerous other times. Next thing you know, she started to kick his ass, like she always did. But this time Winchester wasn't having it. I guess he was tired of Ma-Ma embarrassing him.

This time he decided he wasn't going to take anymore bullshit from her. So, he ran to the back and before you knew it, he pointed a gun at everybody in the kitchen. They yelled, "Put the gun down, Winchester! Put the gun down!" But, he would not listen. It was quite tense, when all of a sudden, Ma-Ma yelled, "I ain't afraid of no gun," as she knocked the gun from his hand. After that everyone proceeded to kick Winchester's ass. After we later found out that the gun he pulled was a fake, we didn't let him live it down.

* * *

"Reggie, what happened to your hand? Why is one of your fingers missing and your thumb so swollen?"

"Well, boy, when I was in the Army fighting for this country, I got shot in the hand and them white motherfuckers kicked me out. They didn't give a fuck about me after I got hurt. Ship 'em in and ship 'em out. That's why I don't give a damn about no crackers. I get over on them any way I can."

"So, is that the reason you don't have a job, 'cause you don't want to work for the white man? Ma-Ma says you ain't got no j-o-b and a woman don't like no broke-ass, I mean no broke man."

"See that's what's wrong with you damn bad-ass kids. Always in grown folk's business. First of all, I'm a jack-of-all-trades and second of all, what your mama needs to do is kick that bum ass Winchester out this house, 'cause I pay the cost to be the boss. Now you get yo' little brown, narrow ass from around me."

I walked off wondering if "paying the cost to be the boss" meant just showing up with sardines and crackers, like he did every other month when he got his SSI check. And, did being a jack-of-all-trades mean someone who steals, scams and messes with a whole lot of women. If so, Cousin Reggie was one. Lying was also one of his trades he used every chance he got. He told me, "Hey, boy, you know I used to sing with the Five Blind Boys from the South," even though his vision was twenty-twenty and he could spot a freaky drunk lady from a mile away. Chasing women was something he did every chance he got. Cousin Reggie was Mr. Fuck 'em blind, crippled, or crazy. Kirk from the TV show, *Star Trek*, who used to have sex with green women from different planets, had nothing on Cousin Reggie.

I once saw him having sex with a lady with a cast on her broken leg. Can you picture some lady having sex on a couch with her cast propped up? Not a pretty sight! He didn't care that her kids and I were watching. I saw him doing things that kids should never bear witness to, like smoke weed, drink alcohol, gamble, curse and of course, have sex. The things that he did around me affected me more than what he told me. Although I liked a lot of the things that I saw, I did not like some of the things he would tell me.

"Boy, your father was smart and crazy all at the same time. Sometimes smart people got too much damn stuff going on in their heads," he told me.

20

I never liked when he said things about my father that I could not quite understand. Whenever he mentioned something about him, I did not know if I should be mad or happy. But that never stopped me from watching Cousin Reggie in action. What curious kid would not like to see an adult doing something that should be done in private? Watching him have sex was better than getting my little hands on a porno tape. Watching him smoke reefer and make funny faces made me laugh. He would say, "Boy, don't tell yo' mama." And, I kept on laughing. No one made me laugh more than Cousin Reggie.

Every time he mentioned wanting to do the nasty with aunt Mamie, I cracked up because I knew if I told my mean uncle about him disrespecting his wife, there would be hell to pay on Cousin Reggie's part. My uncle would have beat the living shit out of him, and Cousin Reggie would have more than a messed-up hand to worry about. In my book, my uncle was tougher than Shaft, badder than Bruce Lee and he had a meaner look than the singer Barry White. Cousin Reggie wasn't scared of many people, but, he was scared of my uncle.

I used to think Cousin Reggie had nine lives. Here was a man who had been beaten, stabbed and shot and still somehow always made it out alive. One time he showed up at our apartment, bleeding, with a bullet in him. Even though he was badly hurt, he told Ma-Ma to just let him sleep and he would go to the hospital in the morning. I guess he knew that the cops would get involved. She called for an ambulance anyway. You never knew what type of drama Cousin Reggie had gotten into on the streets. Being from the South, he may have been slow at the tongue, but he was fast with a knife. The worst thing someone could do was make fun of his Southern accent or his messed-up hand. He already had a complex about people making fun of Vietnam vets. And, because he had injured his hand in the military, he took it personally. Fools do not suffer fools lightly.

I wonder if every family has someone like Cousin Reggie? The one who gives the whole family a bad name by the way he acts and the things he does? The family member who curses like a sailor, shows his ass at family picnics, gets drunk and wants to fight everybody? Or when he's drunk, tries to act smart, talking about things he knows nothing about. Well, that's Reggie and then some.

I knew Ma-Ma really loved her cousin. The fact that she never stabbed him, told me this. But, they did have their arguments, especially when he got his SSI check. He would disappear for three days, then come back with twenty cans of cheap sardines, knowing he would be cursed out. No matter what, she never kicked him out.

Before Ma-Ma met Winchester, and while she put up with Cousin Reggie's crazy shenanigans, she had fallen for Kevin, a short black man. He was the super of our building and he and Ma-Ma got together during one my parents' many breakups. My little brother, Kevin, was born not too long thereafter. My brother looked just like his father. Ma-Ma's friends used to call them black geechies. This is a derogatory term for someone who was real black. My brother's father was a no-good bastard who treated my family like shit. He had women and kids all over the place, and he beat Ma-Ma. Thank God their relationship did not last very long. I was glad when he left. If I were not a kid, I would have kicked his ass.

I loved little Kevin and by the time he turned three, he joined Carolyn and me in the pranks we played on Cousin Reggie. One time Cousin Reggie had a bottle of vodka beside him while he slept on the big blue couch in the living room. We all took the bottle to the bathroom where we poured it out and substituted rubbing alcohol. Then, we returned to the living room and put it right next to Cousin Reggie, who was a hard sleeper. A few hours later, he woke up and the first thing he did was grab for that bottle of vodka to take a long swig, like alcoholics do. Have you ever seen two alcoholics buy a bottle of alcohol from the liquor store and as soon as they get outside, one of them opens the bottle and tries to drink it all with one swallow, but the other guy grabs his hand and stops him? Well, that's the same way Cousin Reggie always drank alcohol—one long swallow. I think he had the longest throat in the Bronx. We knew he was going to do this even before he lifted it to his mouth. So, there he stood, drinking away. As soon as he consumed half the bottle of rubbing alcohol, he gagged and choked and he ran to the bathroom. Ma-Ma hit him on the back until he threw it all up. Cousin Reggie then screamed, "Them bad-ass kids tried to kill me! Mabel, those kids tried to kill me!" Ma-Ma grabbed the belt and gave us the worst beating we ever had. But, the beatings never stopped us because we also messed with Cousin Reggie's food. Anything we could get our little hands on was mixed in it. We put half-boxes of salt, whole bottles of hot sauce, half-boxes of pepper—you name it. He often headed for the refrigerator in the middle of the night, and mixed leftovers all in one big pot. He did this when he was drunk; we were always ready for him. Damn, we were bad-ass kids! But the funny thing about it, he ate all the food mixed with all the stuff we put in it, like it was the best-tasting food in the world. That was something we could never understand. But that never stopped us from creating mischief, day in and day out.

* * *

Living at 1975 Honeywell Avenue was an ongoing learning experience for bad kids looking for guidance. I cannot say Cousin Reggie was a positive role model for me growing up, but he did teach me some things about how to survive on the streets.

Another place where I learned different things, besides my ABCs, was at my elementary school, P.S. 67 on Mohegan Avenue and Crotona Parkway. P.S. 67, a block from my home, was like any other public school in the Bronx. It was a large six-story brick building with a bunch of rooms and windows on every side. There were blacks, Puerto Ricans and a few other minorities. We were all in the same boat—poor, minority and disadvantaged kids, predisposed to get inferior educations from teachers who did not even live in our areas. But, every so often we would get a few teachers who really tried to teach us.

I had one such teacher, Mr. Colbert, who saw something in me that I did not see in myself. He called on me to participate in class. I could never understand why he picked me because I was the kid who always told jokes, made spitballs and humped on the girls in the coat closet. On the days that Ma-Ma would have to come to school because of my bad behavior, I acted like an honor student. I did this because I wanted a favorable report from my teacher. That is how Mr. Colbert found out I was a good reader.

I think my love of reading came from reading the Richie Rich comic books. Reading them catered to my fascination with money. Every time I finished a new issue, I dreamt I was him. I was just a little kid, living in a fantasy world. But, reading those stupid comic books did help me develop the love of reading. So, it was not all bad.

Every time Mr. Colbert called on me to read, I was ready. He once told me, if I did not get an education, I would never be anything in life. But, if I got one, I could be anything I wanted—even president. I always thought he was lying when he said that because all I saw on television was black people being beaten with billy clubs, hosed down with water and bitten by big dogs—just because they were black. So, I just could not picture them letting a black person be president. But, I kept on reading and doing my lessons anyway. I wanted to be something and I loved money.

In some respects I liked school and in other ways I hated it. I noticed that some kids had more than others. Ma-Ma did her best with the little bit she had, which came from welfare. But, you do not fare well with welfare. And, after my father died, she received SSI, which was not much.

I quickly found out that the schoolwork was not a problem and I grasped the lessons rather easily. But, what was a problem for me was not having the nice clothes that some of the other kids had. During the Christmas season, the teacher asked the students to come to the front of the class to tell what they were getting for Christmas. I told all types of lies. I said that Ma-Ma was going to buy me a ten-speed bike, a real car, some new clothes, jewelry and everything that I knew all the other kids wanted. I guess I learned how to tell all those lies from good old Cousin Reggie. The kids looked at me and laughed. They knew that I was the same kid who did not have enough money to buy cookies and pretzels when the cookie cart came around to all the classes.

Boy, do I remember that cookie cart. Here I was, this little kid who loved sweets so much that I went to the store even with just one penny to buy a piece of candy, but I didn't have money to buy anything. When the cookie cart came around, all I could do was watch as it rolled on by as my mouth watered. When the cart left my classroom I wanted to cry. I promised myself after that I was going to get some money—someway, somehow. I decided when I got home that I would have a talk with Cousin Reggie.

I told him that I had no money. He said that when he was a little kid Down South he used to sell newspapers and pick apples. I did not know anything about picking apples, but I did see a kid around my block selling papers. And I saw kids packing bags and carrying people's groceries at the supermarket. So, I headed to the A&P supermarket up the block from my building, where I asked the cashier if I could help her pack the customers' groceries and she said yes. I made enough money to buy all the candy and sweets I wanted: Lemon Heads, Now or Laters, Boston Baked Beans, plus sunflower seeds. After that, I was the envy of all the students at my school. I thanked Cousin Reggie for leading me in this direction and sometimes I gave him money to buy Thunderbird wine.

But, by this time I started doing some other things that were a bit dishonest. My school held cookie and candy sales during the year in which students sold candy to raise money for the school. If you sold a lot you would get a prize. What I quickly found out was the prize was cheap. I decided that the next time they had one of these sales, I would keep the money. Acting like an honest, law-abiding student, I went around my neighborhood taking orders and collecting money. But, when it was time to produce the goods, I told my customers and the school that I had been robbed, which was a lie. I know this was dishonest, but I guess this was just another twist to some of the scams taught to me by Cousin Reggie. I justified my actions by rationalizing that this was sufficient payback to the school for torturing me with that cookie cart. I never even thought about all the innocent people who I scammed. Where's a good father figure when you need one? It was not Cousin Reggie.

I told my best friend, Mike, who lived in my building, all about what I had done and he said it wasn't right. I really liked Mike since the first day I met him; we had many things in common. We both liked to play basketball, baseball and all the other kids' games. We also shared the same name and his father was dead, just like mine. So we clicked. He was concerned about me so I guess that's why he asked me to go with him to the Boys Club on Hoe Avenue. He went there from time to time because it had fun activities for kids. When I asked Ma-Ma if I could go, she said yes. She knew I had too much idle time on my hands and this would give me something positive to do. So, off we went to the Boys Club, Mike and Mike.

I guess the reason they had Boys Clubs in the ghetto neighborhoods was because they knew a lot of kids were growing up in one-parent households. This atmosphere offered some much-needed structure and guidance in our lives. The club kept us off the streets and out of trouble.

I immediately fell in love with the Boys Club. There was a big basketball court, swimming pool, pool tables and Ping-Pong tables—you name it, they had it. Other boys included Andy, who looked like the football player, Lawrence Taylor, who played for the New York Giants; Lloyd Daniels, whose hands were wrinkled like alligator skin; Little Ray, Papito, Alfred, Paul and Rick Vance, whose parents bought him everything he wanted, even 'gator shoes. Just watching him come to the club everyday with new stuff was slowly taking its toll on me. He had all the latest sneakers, like Pumas, Pony's, Converse and fly clothes as soon as they came out. While I, on the other hand, walked around in old Pro-Keds, spanked up with black magic marker and white polish to make them look halfway decent.

Positive individuals worked at the Boys Club. Some taught us the fundamentals of playing basketball and other sports.

I really took a liking to a white man named Bob Caprini, a coordinator and basketball coach who helped me with my dribbling and shooting skills. He always seemed like he truly cared about the kids. Plus, he treated us with the utmost respect. When he thought I was good enough, he put me on the kiddie basketball team. Our teams played other Boys Clubs, such as Columbus Boys Club, Kips Bay Boys Club and teams from other community youth centers.

When we won a championship, Bob took us to celebrate at his house. His wife cooked spaghetti and meat sauce for everyone. This was the first time many of us had ever eaten food in a white person's house. Then, we watched the NBA basketball teams, dreaming of one day playing in the NBA. I really liked Bob and his wife. Bob treated everyone the same, regardless of race, creed or color.

I liked other staff members also, such as Robbie C. and Kenny Carter. They really looked out for me and took me under their wings. The club had something that they called overnights, in which all the boys and coordinators spent the night at the club. We played sports and swam all night long. On these overnights, you had to bring food and all the goodies you wanted to eat. So, I went to the A&P supermarket up the block from my building and hustled all day until I made enough money to buy all the things I needed. The reason I hustled was because I knew Ma-Ma didn't have money to give me. After I finished working, I bought the goodies and showed up with a bigger bag than anybody. I guess the reason I did this was because I wanted all the other kids to think my family had money, which was obviously not true because we were poor.

* * *

One of the things that I have asked myself to this day is why did I have such a preoccupation with money at such an early age? I remember one day I was at the club and I spotted boxes of old raffle tickets. These were tickets we had sold a while back to generate money for our basketball uniforms. All of a sudden I got an idea. I figured I could take the tickets home, change the dates on them, and make a killing selling them around the neighborhood. I also told myself I could make up a story to tell the customers about the date of the drawing having to be changed, but that would be the last time they would hear from me because unbeknownst to them, they were already talking to the winner. I knew they would fall for my story—hook, line and sinker. What adult would not like to help a kid's basketball team? I know this was not an honorable thing to do and the club counselors would not like it one bit, but, I did it anyway. Good old Cousin Reggie's scams were inspiring me. I blame no one at the Boys Club for my acts of deceit and deception. Negative seeds had been planted way before I ever stepped foot in the place. Even though, I always felt something was pulling me away from it, I still loved the Boys Club and all the coordinators, just the same—especially Bob

Caprini. I had so many beautiful and positive experiences while being a member. But, like I said before, something was pulling me away from it. *The streets were calling.*

* * *

Somebody reported Ma-Ma to the welfare bureau. They told them she was collecting Social Security benefits and welfare at the same time, which was illegal. After my father's death, she was given SSI, but never reported it to the welfare bureau. Apparently one of our neighbors was the one who reported her. I suspected, Liza, on the fourth floor, who was jealous of Ma-Ma for some strange reason.

Why is it that when one person gets five cents more than another person, someone gets jealous? Here you had a widow with three kids to raise, trying to feed her family the best way she knows how, and then somebody saw something wrong with that. I guess the person who did the reporting, thought a family was supposed to survive on the few measly dollars that welfare gave it every month. So, because of this so-called law-abiding citizen, who ran a weekend gambling spot in her apartment, Ma-Ma was arrested.

When she got out of jail the next day, we all had to go down to the welfare bureau where Ma-Ma fought hard to keep us. The officials tried to put us in foster care. But, after she cried and pleaded her case all day, finally agreeing to repay the money that they had given her, they let her keep us.

While we waited in a big office that smelled of Cheese Doodles and cigarettes, I noticed that the place was packed with poor black and Hispanic families. One skinny kid, seated directly in front of me on the hard orange chairs, could not stop digging in his nose and eating what he found. I guess he was hungry.

After we left the welfare bureau, Ma-Ma told us it was going to be hard now that our financial situation was changing. I just hoped I did not have to resort to digging for gold in my nose.

* * *

"Ma-Ma, can you buy me a new snorkel coat like the one Rick's mother bought him? It only cost forty-five dollars."

"Boy, that's forty-five dollars I ain't got! And why every time one of your friends gets something you feel you got to get it? You know I don't get my SSI for another two weeks," said my mother.

"But Ma-Ma, didn't you tell Cousin Reggie you hit the number the other day?"

"Boy, you better stay out of grown folks' business. You and your bionic ears are going to get you in trouble. First, I only had a two-

27

dollar hit and, second, that chicken and dumpling you ate was bought with that money, not to mention the box of cereal you and Carolyn ate up in one day. So, Mike, you take your little scrawny ass and get out of my face before I give you forty-five dollars worth of ass whippings."

Well, it was worth the try, even though I knew getting my mother to buy that coat would be harder than parting the Red Sea or walking on water. It's funny how my mind told me to ask for things that I knew my mother couldn't afford and yet still act like I was shocked when she told me no. Lately I had been doing some pretty strange things, such as opening the refrigerator, seeing there was nothing in it, then five minutes later doing it again. I thought to myself that maybe if I kept checking, whatever it is I was looking for would magically appear, like the million roaches that nest in the broken black phone hanging over our yellow, grimy kitchen wall. Carolyn had threatened to tell Ma-Ma about me digging my dirty hands into the cereal boxes that these same roaches get in. She thought I was looking for small prizes, but what she failed to realize was, I hoped maybe this time they put money instead.

My mind had a way of playing tricks on me at times when I wasn't in the mood for tricks. My friend, Mike, once told me if one of my teeth came out, I should place it under my pillow and the Tooth Fairy would come during the night and give me money. When I lost a tooth from biting down on a hard apple Now or Later candy, I couldn't wait to get home to place my tooth under my pillow. I slept with one eye open waiting for the Tooth Fairy, which was wishful thinking on my part. Needless to say, nobody showed up. The next day I ran into Mike at school and I promptly told him never to mention anything about a Tooth Fairy. How could I even expect some fairy-tale character to come in the night and solve my money problems, when no mystical money fairy ever showed up in the daytime to solve my family's financial situation? The only time anybody showed up to our apartment with money was when my mother or Cousin Reggie hit the number, which wasn't often. There were times when Cousin Reggie would sometimes show up with money when he got his SSI. But, most of the time, he arrived broke two days after he received it, with his usual twenty cans of sardines and a box of crackers.

* * *

"If that motherfucker ever even looks at one of my kids, let alone, hits one of them again, it will be the last kid he hits, and he's lucky I only stabbed him in his arm. I was aiming for his heart. Don't no motherfucker put their hands on my kids, but me. I brought them into this world and only God or me can take them out."

Ma-Ma was mad as hell when she found out one of the crazy people who lived in the single-room occupancy across the street, kicked my little brother down a flight of stairs.

Kevin, about five years old, was visiting with Skeeter and his wife, Fannie, in their little room, when they got him drunk and told him to go home. Instead of making it home, he fell asleep on the stairs and a crazy man, who liked throwing knives, spoons and forks out of windows, kicked him down the stairs. Someone found him lying at the bottom of the stairs, picked him up and carried him across the street to our building. When they brought him to our apartment and told Ma-Ma what had happened to her youngest son, she went ballistic.

Kevin had a big lump on his head and he was talking crazy. He was saying stuff like "goo goo, ga, ga," just like a little baby. We did not know if it was from the fall or the alcohol he had been given. After seeing him in this state, Ma-Ma grabbed a big butcher knife and ran across the street in her nightgown, ready to do some serious damage to the person who had hurt her little boy.

One thing about Ma-Ma, she did not mess around when it came to her children. Everyone on our block knew not to mess with Mabel's kids. Plus, when it came to using a knife, some said Ma-Ma's hands were faster than a bullet. Since my father had died, she had to be the man and the woman of the house. Even when she had a boyfriend, she never let him put his hands on us. She did all the whipping and chastising, if our asses needed to get whipped.

Cousin Reggie once tried to play man of the house and tried to whip us. Ma-Ma grabbed the belt out of his hands and started swinging at him. That gave us carte blanche to do anything we wanted around him because he feared the wrath of Mabel. That was his last attempt at trying to be a disciplinarian in our apartment.

The man who kicked my brother down the stairs must not have been thinking. All the crazy people who lived in his building knew about Ma-Ma's reputation with a knife. Everyone on the block had heard about how she stabbed her boyfriend and saved his life at the same time. When she stabbed Winchester and he went to the hospital, the doctors told him, his being stabbed was a blessing in disguise, because had it not happened, he never would have gone to the hospital where they found out about his cirrhosis of the liver. After that, the people around our block thought that Ma-Ma had the ability to take a life or save a life with her knives. But, maybe some of the crazy people across the street had death wishes.

The six-story building where the crazy man lived, was a dirty gray color with green leaves and twigs growing around it, making it resemble a haunted house. It looked real creepy and housed drunks, dope fiends, and all types of low-life degenerates. Word around the block was this was a place where a lot of the crazy patients discharged from Bellevue Hospital lived. Everyone in the neighborhood called it the "funny farm."

We had all different types of names for these tenants, like bag lady; vampire man, who only came out at night with black and white clothes and make up; lump lady, who had little lumps all over her face and body; and knife man, who had kicked Kevin down the stairs.

Ma-Ma always told us, "You stay your little asses outta that crazy building, 'cause if I ever catch you over there, it's going to be hell to pay."

But a threat of another ass-whipping was not enough to keep us curious kids from playing where we were not supposed to play. The quickest way to get a kid to do something is to tell him not to do it. This is why every so often, my brother and I messed around across the street.

On the first of the month, when the tenants got their checks, they paid us to run errands. Sometimes they got so drunk that they paid us twice, and we kept it.

In the summer when the free-lunch program was in effect, I went around to all the places to collect free lunches, then sold them to the tenants across the street. Because I ran my own little free lunch business, I had to take care of my customers, which meant spending time at the so-called funny farm. A lot of kids in the neighborhood were scared to go in there, but not Kevin and I. We were used to seeing misfits up at our apartment when Ma-Ma gave her parties, so weird characters never fazed us.

Someone always acted the fool at these parties and when people got drunk, all hell would break loose. And, let's not forget about good ol' Cousin Reggie who lived with us. He was definitely missing a few marbles. Ma-Ma told us he was kicked out of the Army. I cannot remember the reason for his discharge, but all I know is, it was not honorable whatever he did.

Cousin Reggie was so crazy that once when he was drunk, he pulled his penis out on Ma-Ma. Ma-Ma gave him a Bruce Lee kick of death right in the groin area. He let out a scream that woke up the whole building. Needless to say, that was the last time he got nasty with his first cousin, Mabel.

Cousin Reggie was worse than a dog when it came to sex. I saw him doing the nasty with old ladies, fat ladies, drunk ladies, right in our living room.

So, if my brother and I could deal with the stuff that went on in our apartment, we could deal with a bunch of misfits across the street. But, not being scared of the people across the street left him open to being kicked down the stairs. Even though I know Ma-Ma was mad at him for being over there, that still did not stop her from confronting the knife man. When she finally caught him, she stabbed him, before he could get to his knife. Little did he know he had messed with the wrong kid—the son of the quickest woman with a knife in the Bronx.

* * *

In P.S. 67, we performed a play called Candyland. I was chosen to be the Candy Man because my teacher thought I was a good singer. This was the lead part. I got up on that big stage in the school auditorium, just singing and smiling as I sang "The Candy Man" like Sammy Davis Jr. I had on my red-and-orange costume with silver glitter and white cotton balls all over it. My face was painted yellow and white, and I had on a silver top hat. Around my neck there was a cardboard box with a white strap and lots of candy inside. As I sang, "Oh, the candy man can, the candy man can, 'cause he mixes it with love and makes the world taste good." I threw candy to everybody in the audience. I spotted my mother looking good in her peach dress and new wig, as I acted out my lines. After the show I ran over to her and kissed and hugged her as the audience clapped and cried. My mother could not stop crying; she was so proud of me.

She was with her boyfriend, Winchester, so I told everybody he was my father. I guess that's how badly I wanted a father. Every man she took up with became my "fake" father. I wanted anybody who would listen to know I wasn't a fatherless child.

I once overhead my friend's mother saying that there were too many bastard children being born. Even though I knew this wasn't my mother's case, I still wondered if being fatherless now, in any form or fashion, made me a bastard.

2

Love at First Sight

"Uh-oh, here she comes. Mike, don't start bugging out like you always do," said Bud, my first cousin, son of my uncle Howard. "Man, you stuttering already."

It was now or never because Chrissy, who lived in my cousin's building on 169th Street, was headed straight towards us, with her best friend, China, who I had a crazy crush on. Here I was, nine years old, nervous and stuttering over the prettiest young girl in the neighborhood. She was a beautiful Puerto Rican girl, with chinky eyes, a little nose and lips and long hair down to her waist. China seemed to be about my age. Since the first day I saw her, my heart felt like it had been struck by something. If there is such a thing as love at first sight, that's how I felt. I was head-over-heels for a girl even though I had never spoken with her. The funny thing about it all, is I was not even close to being shy. I was the type of kid who was always in some girl's face, trying to kick some crap to get my hump on. I learned my smooth lines by listening to the older guys kick game to the older girls, who may have gotten their game from listening to Blue Magic, the O'Jays, or Barry White, the king of smooth rap. Whenever I hung around them, I memorized their lines, and used them on the younger girls. Well, it was primetime and here came my chance to kick it headed straight in my direction.

"Hi, Chrissy. Hi, China," said my cousin, Bud.

"How's it going?" said China.

"Oh, hi, Bud," said Christine. And there I stood, looking like a tongue-tied dummy.

"Uh, uh, uh," I stuttered as they walked on by. Bud laughed like he was losing his mind.

"Man, Mike. What is it with you and this girl?

"BBBud, I just don't know. It's just something about he-er."

"Well, you better go drink some water, 'cause you starting to look a little sick."

My thoughts drifted. Was it that I knew deep down in my little heart, she's different from the other girls? Or, was it my conscience telling me, *No Mike, you're not good enough; so don't mess up the mind of a good girl.* Lord knows I was a conflicted child with deep-rooted issues that needed to be worked on, preferably by someone with professional certificates, because Cousin Reggie's guidance had really worked a number on me. There were so many confusing thoughts flowing through my brain, I didn't know if I was coming or going. With time on my hands, I decided to head up the hill with Bud to play basketball. I was feeling stressed out and needed a physical release from the tension. Bud and I sometimes played sports during the day and later got into other activities, including hustling in the supermarkets, so we would have money to gamble with the homeboys.

I loved visiting my cousins on the weekends because there was always so much fun to be had. My uncle's family consists of my aunt, Mamie, and their sons, George, Stan, Bryant, Bud and the youngest, Greg. Whenever I went to their apartment on 169th Street and Third Avenue in the Bronx, I never wanted to go back home. I wished my mother would move us to the 169th Street projects so I could be with my cousins and friends all the time.

Bud and I always tried to stretch my weekend visits by staying up all night talking about girls. Little China always came up in our late-night conversations. Sometimes we laughed so hard about the way she affected me that we risked waking up my mean uncle. Boy, if that ever happened there would be hell to pay. Like Ma-Ma, my uncle knew how to give a good ass-whipping. He used to tell us that he learned how to give a good ass-whipping from getting beatings from his father. Now he was passing down the family tradition to his boys. My cousins never doubted him one bit on that particular subject. They told me his father taught him well.

My uncle never had a chance to whip me because I was too fast for him and I, too, had been taught well. I had become well-versed in the art of dodging my mother's ass-whippings, who had also learned from our grandfather. I think that Ma-Ma had passed a college course: How to Give a Good Ass-Whipping 101.

So, I was well prepared for the strong-arm tactics of my uncle. If I even sensed an ass-whipping was in the making, I cut short my weekend visit. My cousins would say, "Hey, Mike, why are you leaving so soon?" Then I'd say, "Man, I just got this weird premonition that I can't discuss right now, but I'll see you all next week." That's when I always found out about the family beating they received.

I laughed my little head off, as they wondered how I dodged another beating. What my cousins failed to realize is, I had special perceptive powers and those same powers were telling me that little China would one day play a big part in my life.

3

Checking Out the 169 Crew

I met many people hanging around 169th Street. The younger guys were Denny Jackson, who always rubbed wax from his ears onto his shirt collars and Sticky Hines, who liked cracking jokes. His older brothers, Gabby and Skittles were also funny. Then you had Mitchell on the second floor, who laughed at my jokes, even if they were not funny and, Joey on the seventh floor, and the Damon Ruiz' family on the sixteenth floor. I really liked little Damon even though he would tell on us to the adults. Then there was Spence Harry who became my new best friend because we had so much in common.

We were both growing up fatherless, living with alcohol-addicted mothers, and we both had this strong lust for money. I had been taught how to gamble and hustle by Reggie, and Spence was instructed by his big brother, Stewart, and Ernie Bowen, who was like a brother to him. Spence caused a lot of havoc and chaos on 169th Street and I did the same around my block. So, when we met up it was like a marriage made in hell. Butch had finally met Sundance.

Now I had two best friends—my cousin Bud, who was the one who catered to my good side, and Spence, who catered to my devilish side. But, sometimes while hanging with either one of them, the good and bad would intertwine.

Meeting Spence was a defining moment in my life because I learned how to scalp tickets and play three-card monte with him. Monte would later play a major part in my life.

Some of the older guys around 169th Street also influenced me: Mickey Hart, Renny Hart, Mike Downes, the Ruiz brothers. Louie and Jock Ruiz, won the Golden Gloves boxing tournament. Then there was Big Tommy Wise, who was known to knock guys out with just one punch, Skeemo, who resembled me, Joe Mean and the crazy Bowen brothers.

A lot of them were notorious street fighters, who had mastered the "fifty-two block," a style of fighting in which you blocked any punch that was thrown, while at the same time hitting the other person. So, if you wrote a check that your ass could not cash, you would be in big trouble going up against any one of them. I tell you no lies. People were scared to even walk around 169th Street. If they did not have any good reason to be around there, they would stay as far away as possible.

The younger guys and I always emulated the older guys—how they walked, talked, and fought. We looked up to these guys because they were cooler than cool, tougher than tough and got all the girls around the block. These guys were sharp with their white tank tops and new sixty-nine Pro-Ked sneakers. I used to love watching Mickey Hart and Skeemo walk the diddy-bop with one leg cuffed up real high on their Lee jeans. Now you see rappers, like LL Cool Jay doing it. We, the younger guys, learned to play dice and gamble just like the older bucks.

Spence and I hustled in the supermarkets, packing bags and carrying groceries, so we could make enough money to buy dice and cards. All the parents on the block knew we were getting their young kids into gambling because they always used to catch us doing it on the sixteenth floor of the building. Sometimes the elevator would shoot to the top without stopping and the doors would fly open and guess who would always be standing there with the dice and cards in their hands? Yes, Spence or I. It was so bad that one day we were playing cards and Damon messed up and mentioned something about a house party that we weren't invited to because the parents thought we were a bad influence on their kids. I said, "What party?"

Our friend, Denny Jackson, said, "Oh, it ain't no party!"

But I could tell he was lying by the look on his face. So, he had to tell me the truth.

Even though the parents would not let us go to the parties, that did not stop us from going to Fordham summer camp with their kids. All the project kids and I would get up on a bright summer day, get dressed and wait for the big blue 55 bus with our camp counselors, Joe, Jewel, and Barbara Ann Jackson to take us to camp. Jewel and Barbara Ann were Denny Jackson's tough sisters.

When Denny got into trouble, he did not go get his brothers, he got his sisters. I have seen with my own eyes Jewel or Barbara Ann kick many a guy's ass. They fought like men and kicked ass like men. A girl did not stand a chance in a fight with anyone of them. Lord help the girl if she tried to fight with both of them. The Jackson sisters had the demeanor of a mean jail warden. So, this made them a perfect fit when it came to being camp counselors of bad-ass project kids; they took no crap from anyone. When they told you to do something, you did it, and you did it fast. If not, you got your ass whipped. Then they told you, "Go get your daddy and mama and we'll kick everybody's ass."

So, off we all went on that big blue 55 bus headed to Camp Fordham with the Jackson sisters. After taking the short bus ride up to Fordham Road, we got off, with the sun's glare beaming in our ashy faces, then headed across the street to the Fordham University campus. Our little hearts fluttered like butterflies as we envisioned the fun to be had. We could not wait to get through the big black gate. The white security guard looked at us like we ghetto kids did not belong anywhere near a college campus.

The camp coordinators ran down all the activities, such as basketball, football, tennis, and swimming. My cousin, Bud, and I knew we were going to love this place. We always played basketball and football with all of our friends around the projects. Now all of us were going to have the times of our young lives doing all of the things kids love to do, on this huge campus.

The camp coordinators issued everyone camp shirts in blue, green, orange, and yellow. The colors corresponded to assigned groups. Our group from 169th Street received the green ones, which I liked because green is the color of money and you *know* how I liked money.

Camp Fordham was such a nice place; it had beautiful green grass and big apple trees. I fell in love with the campus on the first day. After that, we took full advantage of everything Camp Fordham had to offer.

Sometimes my 169th Street homeboys and I did what our counselor wanted us to do. But, sometimes we snuck off and did our own thing. This was breaking the number one rule at the camp: You must always stay with your counselors. It was hard for the counselors to keep track of everyone. Spence, Bud, Sticky, Damon, and I had a lot of energy and we were too sugar-charged to stay in one place.

The campus buildings included dorms and offices for the students. Sometimes our little campus journeys took us to these places where we laughed and joked with the students who did not go home for the summer. Little did we know that some of us camp kids would never become college students due to various circumstances beyond our control. Some of us would go on to lives of crime and drugs, or would wind up in jail or even dead. You can put Spence and me in the crime category. Although, some kids made it out of the ghetto by getting a higher education and then going on to good jobs, there are those of us who were caught in the mix with all the drugs, crime and violence that we encountered every day.

The kids I knew, who were growing up in the 169th Street projects, had it twice as hard, due to the fact that most of them were part of one-parent households and some had no adult supervision at all. When you lump together that many people in a bunch of sixteen-floor project buildings, in a four- to five-block radius, there's usually bound to be trouble.

Many kinds of people lived in my cousin's building. There were people who held jobs with the city, state or private sector. There were those who didn't work, such as the ones on welfare, and others who were trying get over the hump by any means. Then there were drug dealers, dope fiends, who would steal anything that was not tied down, hustlers and stickup kids.

When I went around 169th Street, I saw a lot of drama that could be detrimental to anyone's mental and physical well-being. On any given day, I might witness someone being stabbed, shot or killed for a number of reasons. Often the violence was over money, respect, infidelity, jealousy, envy or drugs. Sometimes any combination of motivations could lead to a tragic ending.

Take for instance the time I learned about the fierce wrath of a lesbian whose woman had left her. A pretty eighteen-year-old woman was found on one of the project roofs, murdered with her breast and long hair cut off. And, she had been stabbed hundreds of times in her vagina area. Whoever committed the violence inflicted his or her rage ten times over. Rumor around the projects was that it was the lesbian's girlfriend. The girl had decided she had been tricked into the gay lifestyle and returned to her ex-boyfriend.

The first time I ever heard about incest was when one of my friends told some of our homeboys and me that his father was having sex with his sister. We were all sitting on the staircase hanging out when we started making comments on how big his sister's ass was and how we all wanted to get with her. We were just little kids talking a bunch of crap. But, then he shocked us when he blurted out by mistake, "My father fucked her." Then he tried to take it back, but it was too late. We could not believe what we had just heard. I wondered how could a father have sex with his own daughter. If you cannot trust your own parents, who can you trust?

That was not the only sick thing that I learned was going on around in the projects. I also learned people that walked among us raped and sometimes murdered girls on rooftops. What I was finding out about living in the ghetto was some people who didn't have what they wanted, took it. That included the stickup kids and robbers who took money and valuables from anyone that they chose to. Some people took the approach that your money was their money. So, any young kid growing up around this type of madness would need a break.

This is why camp provided a much-needed break for kids growing up in the belly of the beast. Camp gave us the perfect opportunity to have fun and get away from the block for a little while. But, when you are a little kid and you are brought somewhere to have fun, having fun can mean many different things. To my little homeboys and myself, having fun meant going to the college cafeteria and stealing anything we could get our little sticky hands on. Having fun to us also meant sneaking over to the girls' groups to try to get our hump on.

One time a guy from another group tried to hump on a girl and got his ass kicked. She had fighting skills just like the Jackson sisters. One thing you learn in the 'hood is never underestimate the power of a female. Homeboy had to find this out the hard way. I guess he never saw the actress, Pam Grier, kicking ass in her movie *Foxy Brown*. But I had. So, I already knew not to mess with any girl who did not want to get messed with. If a girl liked a guy, she had her ways of letting him know.

So, after we were tired from messing with the girls and roaming around the beautiful campus, we made our way to our assigned group. This was when the real fun began. We played sports on professional-sized courts and fields, and engaged in other camp activities. There was all the space any project kid could ever ask for. The wooden floor on the basketball court was so shiny that it reminded me of the floors in my mother's apartment. The huge football field had never-ending, perfectly groomed green grass. It brought back memories of the large plantations that I had seen Down South when I visited my grandmother. I pictured the other camp kids and myself playing football with rain falling down on our happy little faces.

Life at Camp Fordham turned out to be a pleasant experience for all of us—a change from the streets and school.

The only thing we didn't like was taking tennis lessons. To us, it was a white kid's game. Plus, there were no tennis courts around our blocks, so what was the point in learning the game? Same with hockey. What poor kid growing up in the ghetto had money for tennis or hockey equipment? Our families barely had enough for ten-speed bikes on Christmas. And, if our parents managed to get us one, we were the talk of the 'hood. We learned that we'd better not let it out of our sight, not even for one split-second, because someone would be waiting to steal it. My cousin, Greg, received a ten-speed bike one Christmas and not too long afterwards, a guy with a big hammer took it from him, right in his building. This was double trouble for him because his father didn't like excuses. He still got his ass whipped. So, imagine having tennis or hockey equipment in the 'hood. You would not last a day with it. There were many reasons for us not to like tennis, so, when the counselors took us to the courts, all we would do is hang around cracking jokes, talking to the girls and gambling.

Yes, gambling. Spence and I always kept a deck of cards, as well as dice, on our person. Little Damon, the project snitch, sometimes told Jewel or Barbara Ann what we were doing, and got us into trouble. In turn, we whipped his ass. Damon had a favorite saying, "No nervous, no nervous," which he said with a stupid smirk on his face when he thought somebody was doing something that could make them nervous. I liked Damon a lot even though he was a snitch. He did whatever Spence and I told him to do including stealing in the cafeteria. But, if he got caught, that was another story. One time he did, and he dropped dime on us. Jewel suspended us from the camp for a week. Like Damon always said, "No nervous, no nervous." We were mad at him for squealing, but we always made up, like friends do. After the suspension was up, we returned to camp.

Every so often throughout the summer, the Fordham University basketball and football teams played games against other college teams. Spence and I found out that the public had to pay five or ten dollars to watch. However, the parents of the players received a few free tickets, and all the camp kids were admitted free, too. But, what really caught our attention was when we saw some of the parents tearing up some of their extra tickets because sometimes their invited guest did not show up. Opportunity flashed before our bulging eyes. *These people are throwing away money*, we thought. Being that we were poor, we could not sit there and watch money being wasted. So, with the saddest faces imaginable, we started asking for the extra tickets.

We lied, saying that our counselors left us and we could not get in. What parent could deny two snotty-nosed kids the opportunity to see their own kids play sports? So, they would feel sorry for us and hand over the unwanted tickets. We then sold them to the fans who wanted to see the game. While the fans yelled, "Let's go, Fordham, let's go Fordham" inside, outside we ran the counselor-left-us scam over and over again until we made $150 to $200 dollars every time there was a game. Not bad for ten and eleven-year-old kids.

This was the late 1970s when a dollar was worth a dollar. The money we made was used to gamble, buy Puma sneakers and Pro-Keds. We scalped tickets at summer camp every summer for three years. Hustling was in our blood.

Cousin Reggie was proud of my ticket scam. His star pupil was learning fast. Other campers (Damon may have been the first) became jealous of the money we were making so they told the Jackson sisters who promptly kicked us out.

* * *

Getting kicked out of camp should have been a devastating experience for young kids growing up in the ghetto. Most did not have many other outlets to exert all their energy—but, not these two young hustlers. The ousting was a blessing in disguise. It was our graduation into hustling. No more packing bags, selling newspapers and little scams for us. Our new hustle, scalping tickets, was to be a stepping-stone to bigger and better things. We knew that if we could scalp tickets at Camp Fordham, we could scalp tickets at Yankee Stadium, home of the New York Yankees.

Off we went on the big blue 55 bus headed to Yankee Stadium. When we stepped off the bus, we knew we were in a baseball atmosphere. This was not the first time I had been to Yankee Stadium. I had also been there on class trips and on other occasions. All we heard was, "Get your franks, pretzels here. We also got soda to quench that baseball thirst," and, "Anybody selling tickets" or "Who needs tickets." The noise in the area was deafening, but at the same time pleasant to the ears.

On an earlier visit, Spence, my cousin, Greg, and a few other kids and I went to see the Yankees play the Red Sox with an older guy named Lamont, who had free tickets. Spence and I suspected Lamont was either a homosexual or he was attracted to kids. The first time I had heard about pedophiles was when my sister Carolyn told me that a man in our building, who used to take all the little kids skating, tried to ask her for sex. She was nine years old. This was a man who had little kids of his own. God only knows what he was doing to them. So, I always kept my eyes open for these characters.

Then there was the father of a famous actor who was so-called doing his part by giving back to the ghetto communities, teaching acting skills to my sister and other kids at the church on our block. Instead of using all of his knowledgeable wisdom to accomplish this, he chose to put his body into it. He asked my sister to massage his penis. He was not acting. Perverts rear their heads in the strangest places.

I guess Lamont suspected that we suspected what he was all about, because not too long after getting us into Yankee Stadium, he kicked us out of the stadium.

Now, here we were back at the stadium, but this time it was not to watch baseball players with blue and white striped uniforms. We were there to scalp tickets, so that we could leave with pockets full of money. When I noticed a lot of men walking with little kids, probably their children, I felt bad. I thought, *Why didn't I have a father to take me to a baseball game? Maybe if I had one, I would not be trying to scalp tickets.* But I didn't dwell on that.

Spence and I quickly found out that scalping tickets at Yankee Stadium was done differently than at Camp Fordham. The baseball fans at Yankee Stadium were more sophisticated. They did not go for the counselor-left-us scam. Plus the scalpers wore Yankee jackets and hats, and used fake white-guy voices, as they bought tickets for less and sell them for more. We laughed, like the little kids we were, the first time we heard them. After we learned the proper way to scalp tickets there was no stopping us. The first day we made $250, then we went to the 149th Street and Third Avenue shopping district to buy spanking new blue and white Puma sneakers. Forget about watching the Yankees in uniform. We had our own blue and whites.

While window-shopping, we had visions of buying everything. Little did we know that all we envisioned would come true in due time. When we returned to 169th Street, the younger kids admired our new kicks. I thought, *Now they are looking up to us, just like we looked up to the older guys.* That feeling gave us even more of a reason to want to make more money. After taking in the attention and catching some mothers giving us funny looks, we went to the barbershop and got fresh Caesar haircuts to go along with our new sneakers. The diddy-bop twins were in full effect.

It is such a beautiful feeling when you are looking good and you have money in your pockets. We decided to head for the dice game in the back park of my cousin's building—that's where all the drama went down. One time I saw Tommy Wise have a fight there with a muscle-bound cop, who was always messing with people in the neighborhood. He had unfortunately decided to mess with big Tommy Wise, the neighborhood knockout artist.

Tommy Wise was a guy who knocked out guys who knocked out other guys. When he walked down a block, everybody got out of the way. On the day they fought, everyone who the cop had messed with in the past, was there. They were fighting like they were in the *Thriller of Manila*. I cannot lie; the cop was giving as good as he got. Both had muscles everywhere. Tommy threw a left and a right and the cop buckled. The crowd was yelling, "Tommy kick his ass. Kick his ass. I tell you, kick his ass."

At the end of the fight, I myself, called it a draw, but a lot of others thought Tommy won. Then, the two of them made up and talked like they were best friends. Later we found out that the cop had agreed to stop messing with people for no apparent reason. After the fight, the neighborhood tough guys fought everyday like they were trying to win the neighborhood "Top Tommy Wise Contest." Strangers who came around 169th Street and were knocked out during this period never found out why they were being picked on. But I knew.

So, in the back, where this fight happened, was where we found the older guys deep into a game of ceelo and drinking Old English 800 malt liquor beer, which is called "liquid dust" in the 'hood. If you drink it, you had better have a high tolerance for alcohol. I think the 800 on the bottle may have stood for its ability to get an 800-pounder drunk! The older players did not pay us any mind until we pulled twenty-dollar bills out of our socks. Ernie Bowen said, "Damn, the little shorties got dough. So, give them some room."

We smiled as Mickey Hart, Mike Downes, Skeemo and the others said, "Yeah, let the shorties play; scared money don't make no money."

We were not scared, even though these were the toughest guys around the block. The *Daily News* once featured a story about Ernie Bowen and his brothers—calling them the Notorious Bowen Brothers, who terrorized the whole city with crime. Ernie was like a brother to Spence and Stewart, and he sometimes slept in their mother's apartment. Plus, the older guys always looked out for the younger guys on the block. On 169th Street we were all like one big crazy family, even though sometimes family members don't always get along.

Bugsy, one of the gamblers, was the neighborhood big baller. He had all the fine clothes, gold and diamonds. People in the neighborhood looked up to him, because he had so much money. He was a professional three-card monte player in Midtown, and one of the best. Sometimes he pulled out the three cards and tricked us. Nobody could ever find his red card. He was one smooth brother.

Three-card monte is a street game with a "springer," who tosses three cards, consisting of two black ones of the same kind and one red one, across a box. Someone is asked to find the red card and place a bet. Some call it a con game, but I called it a game of chance.

Just being around him made me daydream about having clothes and jewelry like him. I loved it when he talked about Midtown and everything that went on there: the people, the energetic atmosphere, and most of all, the money to be made. We were blinded by the sparkle of his shiny gold and diamonds. His talk got Spence so excited that he begged Bugsy to take us to Midtown to play three-card monte. Bugsy always told us he would, and this day was no different. But, for now we just gambled and waited for his promise to become a reality.

* * *

Not too long after that, we started scalping at all the Yankees, Mets, and Knicks' games, and even at hockey games—a sport we knew nothing about. Spence and I were like two traveling salesmen. Naturally our scalping skills started getting better. The more money we made, the better we dressed. First we bought some Yankee jackets and hats. If you were a scalper, you had to have that. Then came the latest sneakers and clothes. I remember buying my first pair of Florsheim British Walkers. Those suckers were blue leather with a tassel. Damn they were fly! Spence bought a money-green suede pair. Then we took it to another level and bought some sterling silver house medallions that were popular at the time. You could not tell us shit, as we diddy-bopped with our fly stuff and our new Mike and Spence name buckles.

There we stood on a bright summer day, two snotty-nosed kids, with all the fresh gear and money to spend. My cousin, Bud, and all of our friends around 169th Street told us it was a blessing in disguise when we got kicked out of camp.

* * *

From time to time, Spence, Stewart, and his little brother, Marvin, would be sent Upstate to the Warwick School for Boys. The first time I had ever heard about the place was in a book called *Manchild in the Promised Land* by Claude Brown.

When Claude was little, he was sent to Warwick, a place for wayward boys, because he was bad. But what I could not understand was why my best friend was sent there. Social Services felt that Spence's mother was not taking proper care of them due to her alcohol abuse. Child welfare would make surprise visits and then take them. When Spence had to go to Warwick, it would break my little heart because he was my number one partner in crime. We did everything together and now he was gone.

After about two months, they would come back, making me the happiest thirteen-year-old on 169th Street. I asked Spence about Warwick and he told me its grounds were bigger than that of Fordham University. The difference was it had a gloomy, scary feel. He said there were always fights and stabbings, and thugs from everywhere—Brooklyn, Queens, Harlem, you name it. I knew Spence did not have any problems taking care of himself because if you could make it on 169th Street you could make it anywhere.

After returning, Spence decided that he wanted to chill for a few days before we returned to hustling, so we spent the time causing mischief on the block. We gambled, chased girls, and started a little rap group. I was Mike Nice and Spence was Chilly Spence, Bud was Buddy Love and Marvin was Bogey Dee. We were the wackiest group around.

Our idea for the group came from watching Kool Herc, a DJ who came around our block and outside Claremont Center, a little neighborhood community center. DJ Kool Herc used to play all the fly jams like "Apache," "Dance to the Drummer's Beat," "Parliament Funkadelic," and all the songs everyone loved. He always had a phone by his ear and I could not understand why he was talking on the phone while playing music. I later found out they were headphones.

Spence, Bud, Denny, Sticky, Damon and I danced there. I fancied myself a good dancer, so I danced like I was on Soul Train with my new British Walkers, Oscar de la Renta jeans, and white tank top.

But, no one could dance better than Damon. He did the Hustle better than anyone I knew. The older girls loved dancing with him. Spence would dance sometimes, too, but he thought he was too cool to dance. Tough guys do not dance. He never saw Ernie Bowen dance, so he did not like to do it either

After the jam, we tried to get our hump on with the girls who were partying. I had no problem meeting girls, but all they wanted to do was kiss and hump. I had just dumped my little girlfriend, Gina, for the same reason. I dumped her in a stupid immature way.

I had brought her to my family's apartment when my aunt and uncle were not home. Sometimes they went away on vacation for a few days and my cousins and I took it upon ourselves to throw secret house parties. We were little project kids, freak-dancing to songs like "Flashlight," by George Clinton and the Funkadelics and grinding to slow ones like "Love Won't Let Me Wait" by Major Harris, which to grown folks, was acting a little too grown. They were one hundred percent right, because when the adults were away, the kids did play.

Bass thumps turned into bedroom humps. I got tired of humping and I tried to have real sex with Gina, but she steadily refused. I went in the room and put on a record by the O'Jays called "She Used To Be My Girl," and told her to get out. Boy did I know how to treat the females! Gina was a good shy girl and I should not have done that. But, that was just a sign of where my head was. And I do not mean my top head. I was thirteen years old and I was ready for the real deal—no more humps and kisses for me. Real sex was soon to come, but not how I pictured it.

My homeboys and I spent the rest of the night chasing girls with no luck. The next day I did not see Spence because my family and I went to Great Adventure Amusement Park where we had the time of our lives, riding all the kiddie rides, eating hot dogs and cotton candy. I just loved when my cousins and I all got together to have so much fun.

The next day I ran into Spence and we went to scalp tickets at Yankee Stadium. While we were out there yelling, "Anybody sellin' tickets," with our spanking-new Yankee jackets and hats, Spence told me, Bugsy had taken him downtown the day before to watch out for the cops while he played three-card monte.

He said, "Yo Mike, I made $150 yesterday. Maybe we can go to Midtown tomorrow after scalping tickets."

I said, "Hell yeah, you know I'm with it."

I thought about all the times we had seen the three-card monte games on Thirty-fourth Street when we scalped at the Knicks and hockey games at the Garden. I watched with amazement as the monte players beat everyone out of their money. Those chumps bet forties and hundreds like it was nothing. Now Spence was telling me we had a chance to be a part of the action.

When I got home that night, my mind drifted to the monte player by the Garden and how good he was at flipping those cards. I thought about the bright lights of Midtown and the different types of people who spoke other languages. I thought about the different noises: cars, horns, police sirens, and galloping horses. I loved the whole atmo-sphere whenever I scalped tickets downtown.

Midtown Manhattan was the mecca of New York, and tourists from all over the world wound up there. They came for all the fun and entertainment that the city had to offer, which was everything imaginable—Broadway shows, movie theatres, Empire State Building, Macy's on Thirty-fourth Street, Rockefeller Center on Fifty-second Street, nice restaurants. You name it, New York had it.

I remember the first time I went to Midtown. It was on a trip to the Kodak building with my fifth-grade class. I was the smallest one, so I could barely see the big red Coca-Cola sign in the middle of Broadway. Midtown looked big to me as my little eyes gazed at the tall buildings and billboards on top of them. One billboard caught my attention because it had a man smoking a cigarette with real smoke coming out of his mouth. Everywhere my classmates and I walked, there were brightly lit stores and restaurants, like Nathan's, Howard Johnson's, Orange Julius that sold juice and franks, Playland, and people everywhere. I was immediately hooked on the excitement.

I could hardly sleep in anticipation of the next day's events. After tossing and turning the whole night, I got up at eight in the morning, took a shower and got dressed, then proceeded to pick up Spence on 169th Street.

When I knocked on his door thirty minutes later, all he could do was laugh because he sensed my urgent need for us to get this thing moving. He grabbed his Yankee jacket and we went downstairs to get on the 55 bus.

As we waited, we noticed some of our friends' parents waiting for the bus to take them to work. These were some of the same adults who had caught Spence and me poisoning their kids' minds with dice and cards. Here they stood, with curious eyes, clearly wondering where these two little thugs were headed early Monday morning. Well, they would have to follow us downtown to find out, because these two little businessmen were headed to the big city of dreams where everything in New York ain't always what it seems—Midtown USA, home of the three-card monte players.

After traveling downtown by bus and train, we made our way to Forty-second Street and Sixth Avenue where Spence took me to a donut shop where all the monte players, pimps, prostitutes and con men met up. When we walked in, it was like I had just stepped into the pages of a Donald Goines' street fiction paperback. But this was not fiction. This was real. Sitting at one of the tables was smooth Bugsy, looking sharp in his fly blue jean set, spanking white eggshell Adidas and fancy jewels. Sitting next to him were members of what I assumed was his team. Spence told me the lady's name was Pamela—a tall, pretty dark-skinned woman, who looked and dressed like a model I had seen once in a magazine. I was told, the fat Puerto Rican guy was Saul, who wore the biggest gold-and-diamond medallion that I had ever seen in my life. These were Bugsy's fake betters. They were called "sticks."

Seated at another table with three gorgeous women wearing Spandex and mini skirts, was a tall, handsome mulatto-looking man with jet-black wavy hair. Anyone with eyes could see this guy was a pimp. The other players in the shop called him Chelsea. I was told he wore nothing but two thousand dollar suits and thousand dollar double-striped 'gator shoes. On his fingers were big carat diamonds. This was a boss pimp with fifteen prostitutes working for him: black, white, Asian, you name it. I felt a strong urge to go over to his table and listen to his conversation. I had read how pimps laid their mack down in books, but I wanted to hear a real pimp lay his game down. I knew there was more to pulling hoes than just being handsome, which he was. To pull fifteen hoes, your game has to be tight. So, I could not wait to hear him kick it. Spence could see by the smile on my face and the sweat on my forehead that I was happy to be in this element. But, he told me to calm down because I was getting a little too hyped.

We were hungry so we ate breakfast with Bugsy and his team. By this time I had calmed down and Spence took me around the shop to meet the players. There were Saul's sisters, Jody and Eve, who were both pretty Puerto Rican women. Then there was Lady Day, who was the prettiest light-skinned woman I had ever laid my eyes on. She had beautiful green eyes and the body of a goddess. The reason I say she was the prettiest woman I had ever seen was because China, the girl who had made me nervous since I was nine years old, was a pretty girl, not woman. But, they both are raving beauties.

Bugsy introduced us to the women, and we met players with names like Fronting Cee, Little Bit from Brooklyn, who had a twin brother, Peanut, White Boy Pauley. His choice of name was obvious; he was white. White Boy Sammy, his wife Barbara, Big Burke, who was tall as Julius Erving (Dr. Jay), and Little Clyde who I first observed playing monte on Thirty-fourth Street when we were scalping. He was good. Little Glenda, supposedly the best female three-card-monte player in the world; King, who was Bugsy's brother, Eric, Terry Roth, Skooby, Skeemo, and Mike Soto.

I met many people as I soaked up the energetic atmosphere. I felt their energy flying off the greasy walls in the brightly lit donut shop.

The Indian cook, Ahmed, who ran the shop, was hyper, too. He snapped at everybody and had crazy attitude. He ran the shop like a tyrant and you could tell he was not scared of anybody. I could picture him getting into a beef and pulling a gun from behind the counter. You had to be tough to even hang around a bunch like these players.

But, there we stood, two impressionable kids, ready to embark on something we knew nothing about. Bugsy picked up on this and explained the game of three-card monte. Class was in session, so we could stop guessing.

Bugsy told us we were going to be his lookouts and we had to keep our eyes open at all times. He said the cops would try to bust him by sneaking on the block while people walked by. Our job was to spot them before they accomplished this. I knew this would not be a problem because all we did when we were scalping was dodge cops. The only difference now is we would have to yell, "Slide 'em up" real loudly when we saw them. Then, when the cops left we had to set up the game again so Bugsy could beat all the chumps.

The first place we went was to Fifth Avenue and Forty-third Street. There were so many people I felt like a tiny ant. We set up shop in front of a bank. *No better place than this place*, I thought. Spence was on one corner and I stood on the opposite side. We had the block covered from every angle. At first I had problems seeing through all the people because I was so short and the area was so congested. But soon everything on the block came into focus as my eyes shifted everywhere on the block. I knew if Bugsy got busted, we would not get paid. Our mentors, Uncle Reggie, and Ernie Bowen, would be proud of us. Just look at the shorties go!

As soon as Bugsy started playing, a crowd gathered around him and he proceeded to beat everybody. Within forty-five minutes, Bugsy won $800. We then headed to Forty-eighth Street and Broadway where he won $650 in about a half hour.

Many people walked the streets of Midtown and a lot of the tourists carried thousands of dollars when they did. They walked around with their money because they feared it would be stolen if they left it in the hotel. This left them at the mercy of the monte players. And, like they say, there's a sucker born every minute.

The thrill of being a part of this atmosphere is something that I cannot describe. And it felt like a deja-vu experience. While we were on Broadway playing, I spotted Little Bit and his twin, Peanut, playing up the block. Little Bit's crowd was so big you could not see him, but you could hear him yelling, " . . . one hundred more. I raise you one hundred more. If I can bluff you, I can beat you. Put it up. Black you lose . . ."

The more vics who tried to win at monte, the more vics got beat. Spence was up on the corner holding Bugsy down like his life depended on it. I never saw him this focused before.

Meanwhile, I was looking out for cops and trying to pay attention to the monte games at the same time. *I had plans, big plans.* One day it was going to be me behind one of those boxes, with my hat turned backwards, taking all comers. I would be the black Richie Rich of three-card monte.

The reason I knew this was because I always called the shots with my little homeboys. Whenever I thought up something crazy for us to do, they did it. I was the kid who told his other little friends, "Let's have a biscuit party. You steal the syrup. You steal the biscuits. You steal the orange juice."

And, then I was the one to turn around and draw the map outlining where everything we were going to steal in the supermarket was located, and also detailing how we were going to pull it all off without being detected by the store security guard. After our mission was accomplished, I had everybody singing stupid songs I would make up like, *"We steal, we squeal, we do it all day at Food Way where everything is free."*

I don't know if there was Ritalin to slow kids down when I was little, but boy I needed some in the worst way! I had enough energy for ten kids and this energy had me showing them how to sneak on buses and trains, and into movie theaters. Picture this scenario: "Hey, y'all. Let's go to the movies to see *Enter the Dragon with Bruce Lee.*"

"Mike, how are we going to go to the movies without money?"

"Oh, that's no problem. Let me show you how."

My brain was always at work when there was something I wanted to do or make happen. If I was in school and I wanted to hump on a girl, I made sure I was seated in the back of the classroom out of the teacher's sight. I never had problems finding some girl to go with me in the closet. After learning how to hustle and sell free lunches to the older people for twenty-five cents and packing bags in the supermarkets, I always had money for that extra pack of Lemon Heads or sunflower seeds to bribe them with. "Hey girl, you want some candy? Let's make a deal."

I was "Mr. John Bargain" in the flesh. If I saw an opening, my brain immediately started working overtime, while the other kids were preoccupied with watching cartoons and eating cereal. I, on the other hand, was thinking about ways to earn a fast buck. I figured if I did not have any money to buy the things that I wanted, there was really no reason to go outside.

That is why I could never understand folks who lay on their asses waiting for someone to give them something. They need to get up, get out and do something. No one will give you anything. Now, if you are someone walking around with a death wish, there is always someone out there to grant your wishes. But, if you are someone who wants something more out of life, you have to make your aspirations materialize. I learned that I didn't like the taste of being poor, drinking sugar water, and eating cereal without milk. Just reaching into my pants pockets and finding nothing convinced me that I needed to make something happen. I was not one of those people who has to be stranded in the desert to realize that I am thirsty. Reality slapped me in the face every day and I was tired of it. The Bible says, "Ask and you shall receive," but I was tired of asking and waiting to receive my blessing. I wanted it all now.

Every time my mother caught me lying or doing something wrong, she said, "One thing I hate is a liar and a thief." Well, Ma-Ma, your boy, Michael, was about to turn over a new leaf. I was destined to become a con man, and, one of the best three-card monte players to ever play the game.

As I stood on the corner daydreaming, we played monte for another two hours until Bugsy got tired. The total take for a few hours of work (I mean, con) was $2,300.

After leaving the block we went to Nathan's Restaurant where Bugsy split the money with me, Saul, Pamela and Spence. We were like kids in a candy store, but with a few hundreds in our pockets. The rest of the day we walked around Midtown laughing and getting reacquainted with the players. We eventually left Midtown and went back to 169th Street, counting all our money. *Bulletin! Bulletin! Tell the mothers on the block that the two little businessmen are back from work. I mean hustling, and we're ready to get the dice game started, so hide your kids.*

* * *

The future was looking brighter now that we had two hustles—scalping tickets and playing three-card monte. I looked forward to going back downtown, just like a kid looks forward to opening presents on Christmas. I could not wait to see the bright lights again.

The next morning I picked up Spence and on the train ride downtown, I told him about my big plans. I expressed the fact that I was going to learn everything there was to learn about the game of three-card monte. Then I was going to become a "springer," that is the guy who throws the cards. Spence looked at me kind of funny, like he was thinking the same thing.

When the No. 2 train pulled into the Forty-second Street station, we got off and headed to the meeting place at the donut shop. The first guy I spotted in the shop was Clyde.

He noticed me staring at him and said, "What's up shorty? My name is Clyde."

"Oh, what's up? I'm Mike. I saw you a while back playing cards on Thirty-fourth Street when I was scalping tickets. Man you're good."

"Thanks, shorty. Man, you're an all-right dude."

Then I said, "I'll check you out later."

I slowly made my way into the shop and spotted pimp Chelsea holding court with about nine of his whores. He had an audience of other pimps and players who were drinking coffee and reading newspapers. He told Jackie, one of his whores, to put his goddamn money on the table because all he wanted to see in the morning was green money, eggs and ham. Everybody in the donut shop laughed.

Spence and I walked around the shop meeting our new family in crime, such as Cuban Joe. An old man, he had played monte for more than forty years. He owned a lot of Cuchi Frito restaurants uptown in Spanish Harlem and he drove a new 1979 burgundy Cadillac with vogue tires. I told myself that I would have a talk with him. I knew I could learn a lot from his knowledge and wisdom of the game. I had *big plans*, big plans. I was focused, just like when I was in school and wanted to learn something that interested me. If the players were willing to teach me the game, I was willing to learn.

I was getting hungry so I sat down at a table with Bugsy, Pamela and Saul. Spence said he had already eaten so he went outside. When I finished, I headed outside where I ran into Little Bit's brother, Peanut.

"Yo Peanut, what's up man?"

He said, "Oh, what's up, Mike. Oh, by the way, I want to school you on a little something, but don't get mad. I just wanted to tell you I saw you holding Bugsy down yesterday on Broadway and I noticed sometimes you were paying too much attention to the game and not enough attention to holding your man down."

He continued, "The reason I'm telling you this is I used to do the same thing. I was so anxious to be the man behind the box that I could not wait to get my chance to spring 'em. But as time went on, I learned everything happens in its proper time. But first you got to keep your man out of jail. You know. First things first."

"Thanks, Peanut, for schooling me because I know I'm speeding a little bit."

"Oh, Mike you'll be all right. I'm just another player schoolin' another player. Just take it easy and you will be all right."

I said, "Thanks P."

Bugsy and the rest of the team came outside and we headed to Fifth Avenue. Saul and Pamela asked us about where we were from and if we went to school. I told them I was in the ninth grade at Junior High School 98 in the Bronx. Spence acted like he did not hear them because he rarely went to school.

Saul said, "Well, shorties, if y'all gonna play with us, y'all better stay y'all little asses in school and I'd better not hear y'all niggas is gettin' high."

I said, "Nah, Saul, it's all about rest, dress and progress."

"That's good, shorty. Stay focused."

Pamela smiled like a satisfied parent. As soon as we got to Fifth Avenue, we set up the boxes and I went to one corner and Spence to the other. Immediately a crowd gathered around the game. There was much excitement on Fifth Avenue and many people were headed in different directions. The people in Midtown Manhattan seemed to move at a faster pace than the people uptown. So, while I held Bugsy down, I took Peanut's advice and did my job, which was to keep Bugsy out of jail.

After standing on the corner for about twenty minutes, I saw a police car heading our way.

So, I yelled, "Slide 'em up! Slide 'em up!" to let everyone know that the cops were coming. The crowd broke up and Bugsy said, "Good looking out, shorty. You doing a good job!"

The police car quickly went by so Bugsy returned to the game. As soon as he got back down, another crowd gathered around. All I could hear was Bugsy yelling, "Forty more, forty more." And, Saul yelling, "You got it! You got it!"

I heard the same things over and over, so I assumed while I was holding them down, the vics' bets were being raised. I had an adrenaline rush seeing the cops coming and knowing the vics were betting at the same time.

We stayed on Fifth Avenue about an hour with vics betting and an occasional slide. Then Bugsy decided to go to Thirty-fourth Street near the Empire State Building. We had already won $940 and the day was still young. As we walked to Thirty-fourth Street, I looked at all the ladies' asses on Fifth Avenue. Boy was I a horny little bastard with hormones raging. I was still considered a virgin because humping on girls and kissing was not real sex. Spence always lied about fucking CeeCee, a girl on our block. But, he told the story differently each time, so I knew he was lying. Every time I told Spence I was going to get with that pretty girl, China on 169th Street, he just laughed and said, "Shut up Mike! You're too scared to even talk to her."

Then he said, "No nervous, no nervous" and we both laughed.

* * *

It was a nice August day and people were sitting outside on the steps of the Forty-second Street library on Fifth Avenue, eating lunch, talking and reading, as they watched a street performer with a painted white face, wearing a white T-shirt and black pants with suspenders and acting like a mummy in a scary movie. One thing I liked about Midtown was there were street performers wherever we went. There were also tap dancers, magicians, musical performers, break dancers, comics and even a ventriloquist with a doll on his arm. Spence and I stopped for a little while to watch the mummy guy in white face. Then we headed to Thirty-fourth Street. When we got there, we set up the boxes and we took our positions on the corners.

I loved Thirty-fourth Street because many tourists came to visit the Empire State Building. I knew we could make a lot of money there. Thirty-fourth Street also had more pretty women than the 149th Street and Third Avenue shopping district in the Bronx. But, I knew I had to keep my mind off of the girls or else I would wind up getting Bugsy busted; I had to keep my eyes out for cops. There were a couple of other games going on at the same time as ours. I spotted Little Glenda behind the box with a big crowd around her.

Every so often I stole a quick glance at her and was amazed at how good she was. She moved the cards faster than Little Clyde. This led me to believe what they said about her being the best female monte player in the world. Vics came into her game thinking they could beat her because she was a lady. Little did they know that they were in for a big surprise. Never underestimate the power of a woman.

A few stores down, Little Clyde was doing his thing, with more gold on his neck and hands than the Forty-seventh Street jewelry stores on Sixth Avenue. The pretty women on Thirty-fourth Street loved Little Clyde. He was good and he had the gift of gab.

I envisioned myself behind that box, tossing those three cards just like him, with all the vics and lovely ladies under my complete control. I could see it all. The streets were calling me. Not only did you have monte players in Midtown, you also had pickpockets, con men running every con imaginable, transvestites, perverts, stickup artists and drug dealers. I was drawn to this place where stars were born and dreams were made. *New York, New York, big city of dreams. Everything in New York ain't always what it seems.* I was determined to make my dreams materialize.

Bugsy decided to quit for the day after winning $1,840. One tourist lost $1,100. After Bugsy split up the money, everybody headed back to the donut shop. I noticed a guy wearing a top-of-the-line blue linen suit and snake-skinned boots standing in front of a brand-new '79 blue Seville with vogue tires. The car was shiny as the bright sun beamed on it.

I said, "Hey, Saul, who's that guy standing in front of that fly car?"

"Oh, that's pimp Honey Combs. He's got about eight hoes in his stable."

"Man, Saul, that dude seems like he's really doing it. One day I'm gonna get me a fly car just like that and a big Mike nameplate with gold and diamonds all over it, just like yours. By the way, how much did you pay for your medallion?"

"Shorty, I only paid $3,000, but don't worry, you're gonna get yours but first you gotta slow your roll. You're speeding too fast. There's more money to be made in Midtown than you could ever dream of."

Boy did I hope so, because I wanted my share of it all—every last dime. I knew when I was finally behind that box, the vics were going to leave my game broke.

Saul could tell by the way I looked at Honey Combs and his car that I wanted to meet him. So, he introduced Spence and me to him.

Honey Combs was one cool brother. He told us he was from St. Louis, home of all the boss pimps. His favorite saying seemed to be "understand me." He added, "understand me" to everything he said. I liked his funny accent, like mine. Everyone said that I sounded like I was from the South, even though I was born and raised in New York. I guess the accent came from my mother, who was from Alabama.

Honey Combs talked about how he started pimping and hustling at twelve years old. He told us one of his hoes bought the new Seville he was in front of. I knew he was an all-right brother when he told me one day he was going to take me for a ride in it. Boy, I could not wait to ride in a Seville with a real pimp.

While talking to Honey, we ran into Little Bit, who was hanging with his homeboys from Brooklyn. Little Bit was a nice guy, but you could tell by his demeanor that he did not take any shit from anyone. He was like a little Napoleon. All of his homeboys from Brooklyn looked like they would kill for him. He asked if Spence and I were all right, and he told us if anyone fucked with us, he had our backs.

Even though he did not know us real well, he acted like he had known us all of our lives. Little Bit spotted a guy named Bones who had a big B with diamonds in it. He yelled for him to come over, so that he could introduce us. I found out that Bones was a pimp and his big B medallion cost $15,000. He reminded me of the singer Bootsy from the funk group Parliament Funkadelics. He was tall with long Jheri curls and he had on burgundy, tailored pants, a burgundy silk shirt and a pair of gray 'gator shoes. This was one fly dude. Just looking at him made me want to take my money and go shopping for some nice threads. Plus, seeing Honey Combs's new Seville and all of the nice clothes and jewelry had my eyes bulging as I thought about how these players and hustlers were doing it in Midtown. Saul noticed how I was looking and he said, "Slow down, shorty. Slow down." We laughed.

We spent the day hanging out with Saul. Then he told us we should go uptown because after dark it got really crazy here. Telling us that only got us more interested in what went down at night. Could it be, the freaks come out at night?

* * *

As the days turned into months, I learned more and more about three-card monte and the streets of Midtown. I also noticed when you made money, your friends and other people treated you differently. I also learned that money gets things done.

What's that song by the O'Jays, "For the Love of Money." "Some people got to have it. Some people really need it."

I was making money with my two hustles—scalping tickets and playing monte. Both were very profitable for a fifteen-year-old kid. Now that my homeboy and I had money, we could buy the latest clothes, shoes and sneakers. These were things other kids on our block could not afford; their families were struggling to make ends meet. That's why parents looked at us funny. First they saw us wearing average kid attire, then as time passed, they noticed us wearing all this new stuff. Their curious stares eventually turned into nods of approval. I had so much nice stuff that I had to hide it from my mother in one of my friends' apartments. Even though I had more than the other kids, I never acted like I was better than they were, because I was not. My mother always said, "Money don't make the man, the man makes the money." So, I tried not to walk around with a big ego.

But, I did have my vices, and one was girls. I loved girls, especially the pretty ones. Between the ages of nine and twelve, I had my little experiences of kissing and humping on girls. I even humped on my female cousins when they spent the night at our apartment. So, by this time, I was ready, willing and able for some real sex. I had my first real sexual experience at age fifteen.

It all happened one night in Midtown where Saul had already warned me about how crazy it got at night. I was standing in front of a Carvel ice cream shop on Forty-third Street and Broadway when a mixed-black and Chinese woman lost all of her money playing monte. She was a tourist and she did not have any money left to get back to Florida. So, she told the monte player she would do anything to get it back. He said no problem, but first she had to fuck him and all of his friends. So, we took her to this seedy hotel on Forty-second Street, right around the corner from Playland. I was the fifth person in a six-man train. After having real sex for the first time, I went around telling all the other players about what had happened. (I guess that was the start of my warped sense of what sex and women were all about.) My virginity was lost in the sickest of ways—a gang bang. The negative seed was planted. (Where's a father figure when you need one?) Growing up around pimps, prostitutes and con men is not the best environment to find positive role models, for a little impressionable kid. If you hang around negative things, negative things happen. If you hang around positive things, positive things happen.

4

The Deuce

Sometimes after playing monte, I walked to Forty-second Street between Broadway and Eighth Avenue. We called it The Deuce. This
was the seedy part of Midtown, where all the cheap movie theaters
that showed everything from porno to regular movies were located.
This block also had the x-rated peep shows, where anything could be
bought as long as you had money. The difference between the movie
houses on The Deuce and the ones on Broadway were that on The
Deuce you might find rats and cats running by your feet. And, if you
found yourself in the porno movie theaters, you might find out that
strange people might ask to suck your dick for a fee or maybe even
for free. Anything was game. You had drug dealers, street gangs,
pimps, perverts, prostitutes, low-life degenerates, regular moviego-
ers and runaways up and down The Deuce.

Every so often I found myself hanging with some of the guys
who sold drugs to people walking by. Some of them were the funniest characters you could ever meet. Most of the things they sold were
not real drugs. They would sell Comfrey tea as reefer and Tylenol or
aspirin as uppers and downers. Once they balled up regular tissue
and passed it to a white boy who thought the drugs he had paid for
were wrapped in it. They told him to keep it moving because the cops
were coming. That was just one of the many scams they ran. I could
not understand how some people could be so stupid. My homeboy,
Gumbo, who was really funny, was good at these little scams. He
walked through the block saying, "Smoke, smoke. I got that good
smoke," which was all fake marijuana. He was so good at making
these chumps believe that his smoke was real, he even had regular
customers.

When I was younger, we had a saying: "If you get caught cheating, you get a beating." But, on The Deuce, it went the other way around. If the guy found out that he was sold fake drugs and he wanted his money back, the only thing he got back was an ass-whipping.

Gumbo and the other hustlers bought incense stuff called coco snow from some of its little stores because it looked and tasted like cocaine. If you put it in your mouth, it froze your face. This stuff sold like hot cakes and people came from all around to buy it. One day a regular customer of Gumbo's bought a kilo of the so-called cocaine from him. The guy claimed that his friends from Jersey loved Gumbo's top-of-the-line cocaine. Like they say, a sucker is born every minute. Three-card monte had its victims and The Deuce had its, too.

Sometimes some stupid trick would find himself looking to buy sex on The Deuce. One of the so-called drug dealers would tell a guy that he knew where to find hot and juicy Jezebels of his liking. The trick would fall for the bait, and then the dealer would gain his confidence by smoking a little reefer with him as they walked to where the hoes supposedly were. After arriving at a building, the trick would be told that the lovely lady who was going to fuck the shit out of him could not be trusted. So, it was best to leave his money and valuables with the guy. The trick would give it to him for safekeeping then head upstairs for some serious sex—so he thought. But when he got upstairs there would be no hoe and his "good friend" would be gone. But, at least all was not lost because his money was going to help his newfound friend feed his family. After all, what are friends for?

As I watched these types of scenarios play out on The Deuce, it always made for lively entertainment. I laughed harder on The Deuce than pimp Honey Combs and I did when we watched the karate movies in the theaters in Times Square.

One night I ran into Honey Combs, who took me around in his new Seville as he picked up money from his whores on Eighth Avenue. I could not believe I was finally riding in a fly car with a real pimp. While sitting on the plush leather seats, he told me all about the pimp game.

He said, "Yo Mike, women have been doing their own type of pimping from day one. Understand me? It's called take me to dinner, take me to a show, give me some money all with the promise of some kitty kat, that you might not even get. Understand me? All men have been pimped by a woman one way or another. Understand me? So, what makes it so wrong when we flip it and make the woman give us something? Understand me? You see, I'm the ruler of my hoes' universe. Hoes need guidance and I'm here to guide. I tell them when to eat, shit, sleep and make money. My hoes know the sun don't shine unless I say so. They also know that I can be sweet like candy or I can turn into poison and kill. I ain't never hit no bitch that didn't deserve it. You see a hoe will test a nigga in a minute and if the pimp don't pass the test, she's off to the next motherfucker. I might not be good at nothing else, but I'm one helluva pimp and as long as my papers' right, I'm all right. A hoe's job is to serve and my job is to protect. And, if anybody fucks with my hoes when they serving their master, they get stitches or bullets—no in-between. You see, shorty, I was born to pimp and I'm gon' pimp until I die. I'll pimp Mona Lisa if she could just jump out of that damn picture. Understand me?"

We both laughed as I pictured that crazy scenario.

As he schooled me on the pimp game, "Olivia" a song by the Whispers came on the radio. It's about a girl buying a guy a new Seville. I could tell Honey loved the song by the way he bobbed his head.

I remembered the time he told Spence and me that one of his hoes had bought the Seville we were riding in. I told him one day I was going to buy me a fly car, too. (My prediction eventually came true.) He said I had better give him the first ride when I got it. Then I joked that I would give all of his hoes the first ride.

I liked hanging with Honey Combs because even though he was a pimp, he did not act any different than any of the other guys I knew. Honey Combs had taken a liking to me because he liked the fact that I always had my school bookbag with me, so he knew I was still in school. He and the other players told me to stay in school and get my education. Most of them had not even graduated from high school.

Even though I played monte, I went to school everyday so that I could get my high school diploma. I never missed a day. I had school pulling me one way, and the streets pulling me another. I was a fairly good student in school and my average grades were 80s and 90s. I always had the love of reading, ever since I was in elementary school.

I found another world in books. I liked reading Donald Goines' fictionalized street tales. He really captured the true essence of the streets in all of his books about pimps, prostitutes, hustlers and con men. These were the things that amazed me.

I guess the streets captured my attention more so than school did. Maybe I was drawn to the excitement and chaos. I saw people stabbed, shot and beat down all the time. When hanging in the streets you never knew what was going to happen on any given day.

* * *

One day in Midtown, we saw cops chase a Dominican guy with a knife in his hand down The Deuce. The cops finally caught up to him and said, "Drop the knife." For some reason, he didn't drop it. So, they started to shoot. The guy died right in front of my eyes. This made me think back to when I was eight years old and I saw a little kid run into the street. A cab driving by struck the kid who flew up in the air, came down, and died right before my eyes. The eerie thing about it was that kid was wearing a suit as if he was already dressed for his own funeral. I can still picture him lying there dead, as his mother let out screams I had never heard before.

Yes, Midtown was a place like no other. I saw prostitutes in broad daylight having sex on the streets of Eighth Avenue. Sometimes I played pinball games in Playland, the Forty-second Street arcade. There were so many perverts lurking around, preying on little kids, you would think it was legal. They approached kids and offered them money for sex. A lot of these perverts wore suits and carried brief-cases.

Some of the kids they preyed upon came from the Martinique Hotel on Thirty-fourth Street. This was a welfare hotel with a lot of poor, minority families living in it. Some were kicked out of their apartments for not paying rent, while others were burned out and the city put them there until they could find them housing. Every time I played the games in Playland, I watched these scum of the earth conduct their sick transactions. I was even approached sometimes while playing pinball. Whenever that happened, I cursed like a sailor to draw the attention of one of the workers in the arcade who knew I was a monte player. Then he would come over and kick the guy out.

Midtown was one strange place, but I still loved it.

5

Money Gus and Johnnie Ranks

One day while I was standing in front of the donut shop, fresh out of school and with my school knapsack on my back, I spotted a big muscle-bound dude wearing a green nylon boxer set with some baggy jeans and timberland boots, who was headed toward the shop. Something about him captured my attention. He wore expensive-looking, gray designer frames with no lenses and had more waves in his Caesar haircut than an ocean in sunny California. Next thing you know he was standing across from me talking to Johnny Ranks, Fronting Cee and other players. My instincts told me that he was a monte player. I noticed by his movements and demeanor that this was a guy who did not take any shit. Plus he seemed hyper and energetic like me.

We eventually made eye contact and he said, "What's up, shorty? Want to hold me down?" This meant did I want to slide for him. I said, "Yeah," with no hesitation, even though I did not know anything about this guy. I gathered information from some of the players that his name was Money Gus and he was one of the best monte players. I found this odd because I had never seen him before. Little Bit's brother, Peanut, told me I could learn from him. I had already learned a lot from Saul, Cuban Joe, Pamela and a player by the name of Doug. But, I needed to learn more before I could actually become a springer. My player's intuition told me I needed to get with him.

As Money Gus assembled his team, he asked me, "What's up with the knapsack, shorty?"

I said, "Oh, I just got out of school."

He said, "Man, that's good. I thought you was gonna hold me down with a shotgun in your bag."

I said nah, and we laughed.

After a few minutes he got a team together consisting of Johnny Ranks, a stick and a springer, pretty Lady Day, whom I met on my first day downtown, Spence and I. Gus asked me if I had any cards and I nodded yes. So, we headed to the D-train where I proceeded to sneak on. Spence was scared so he paid his fare. Money Gus looked at Johnny Ranks and said, "Damn. Shorty's got heart. I like that."

Lady Day and Johnny Ranks smiled. When we got on the train, I thought, *Maybe Gus always played on Fourteenth Street, that's why I never seen him before.* But, when I asked him about it he said, "Nah, I just got out of jail from Rikers Island, doing a ninety-day skid bid for some warrants I had."

I guessed that explained all the muscles, and waves in his hair. In jail he had a lot of time to lift weights and brush his hair.

While sitting in the train, he told us about his jail stay. Then he explained to Spence and me, that we had to hold him down good because he did not want to go back to jail. This was no problem to us because we were becoming two of the best lookouts out there. We also knew if Gus got busted we would not get paid.

The D-train finally pulled into the crowded station and we got off and headed to Fourteenth Street. We saw people everywhere. Gus yelled out, "Man, these vics is in trouble. Boy are they gonna pay for that vacation that the judge gave me. I couldn't wait to get out. Now I'm back."

Then he yelled to anyone who could hear him, "Yeah, motherfuckers. The king of New York is back!"

Spence and I looked at each other and said at the same time, "Man, this nigga is ill!" But something told us it was on. We finally made it to a spot on Fourteenth Street where I found out rather quickly after we set up shop, that Gus was good at this game of monte, real good. As soon as we set up, before I could make it up the block, Gus was screaming, "Hey, New York, New York, I'm back, I'm back." He was telling the truth. "Who saw the red card?" Just like that, he was fast. Next thing, I knew, before I even made it to the corner, a big crowd had gathered. I heard Gus yelling, "If I can bluff you, I can beat you. One hundred more, one hundred more . . ."

I could tell the vics were losing left and right because every few minutes a vic would walk past me cursing "that black bastard" or saying "Damn, that brother's good, I thought I had it." The vics just kept coming out of the woodwork. I guess they were all just like me—drawn to his magnetism.

After a few slides, Lady Day told us that Gus beat one guy out of $700 on one shot and the total after an hour was $1,600. I looked to my right and Gus yelled for us to meet him at the McDonald's.

While walking to McDonald's with Lady Day, I could not help but be hypnotized by her beauty. She had the smallest waist imaginable, with a little cute belly button. The ass and thighs on this woman would drive any man wild, let alone a kid like me. The actress, Halle Berry, has nothing on this woman. I pictured Lady Day and myself buck naked doing the nasty and I do not mean humping. Lady Day noticed I was checking her out, so she decided to tease me. She said, "You know, Mike, when I was listening to the weather yesterday, and they said it was going to be a hot day, you know what I did?"

"Nah, what did you do?"

"Well, I cut all of the hair off of my armpits and my, you know what."

I acted stupid, and she said, "You know," as she pointed to her you know what. Talk about hormones raging!

Spence said, "Damn, Lady Day, you got a nigga fucked up."

She said, "Don't worry. With the money you two shorties gonna make out here, females are going to be the easiest thing for y'all to get."

I was two minutes from telling her about my earlier episode with the tourist, but I decided not to.

When we made it to the McDonald's, Johnny Ranks and Gus were already eating. The rest of us ordered food and sat down. Johnny Ranks was not much of a talker, but he seemed to be a good listener. He came across as one calm, laid-back brother. I had met his type before—the ones who never messed with anybody, but when you fucked with them, you quickly found out it was the worst mistake you ever made.

While sitting at the table, I told Gus he was the best monte player that I had ever played with. He just smiled with his green eyes glowing through his designer frames with no lenses.

"Yo shorty, one day I am going to teach you how to throw the cards."

My eyes lit up because everyday I was practicing monte on all my friends uptown and in the school lunchroom. I had even beaten a few students out of their lunch money. My hands were getting faster but I knew there was still much to learn. Before I could get behind the box, I had to learn how to sell the game to the vics. Throwing the cards was just one aspect of the game. Selling the game was another;

that's when the con kicks in. They say practice makes perfect, so, I continued to practice my skills. A few times during the course of my being downtown, I had beaten a few people by tapping them while they were in some of the monte players' crowded games. Sometimes the games got so crowded, the team didn't notice me pulling their vics to the side. Then I would pull out my three cards and start playing in the corner with a wad of twenties in my hand, saying, "Find that red card." The victims would be thinking, *This little punk does not know what he's doing.* So, they bet. But, what they found out was the little punk had enough skills to take them for every dime.

But, that was nothing compared to the adrenaline rush I got when I watched the other three-card monte players do their thing behind the box. I had plans, *big* plans. And, Gus was going to be one of the players to guide me to my dream.

After lunch we headed to Thirty-fourth Street. Money Gus let Johnny Ranks spring 'em while he played the stickman. Johnny Ranks was good at three-card monte and the ladies downtown liked him because he was a brown-skinned handsome dude with a nice physique. He was also known to knock a nigga out. I learned from Money Gus that Johnny lived down the block from Spence and me in the Webster projects. Boy, what a small world. Johnny Ranks played and after forty minutes made $1,120, which was not bad at all.

Then they switched and Gus sprung 'em again. There were always more vics on Thirty-fourth Street. The tourists and pretty women were everywhere.

While I was holding Gus down, I decided to play a trick on the vics. I put a twenty dollar bill at the tip of my sneaker, and then I stepped on it. The people walking by noticed that my foot was on a twenty-dollar bill. So, some of them waited around hoping I would move my foot. As I looked out for the cops, I acted like the twenty wasn't there, but I never moved my foot. It was so funny watching the vics hang around waiting for the chance to get at that twenty-dollar bill. Eventually I looked down and acted totally surprised about finding twenty dollars. Then I heard somebody say "damn." I guess the reason I did this was because I knew suckers went for anything. I could just imagine when I got behind the box how many tricks I was gonna play on the vics. But, for now, I would play my little mind tricks on them.

As I stood on the wall, I could still hear loud-ass Gus, yelling, "Hey, New York, New York. I'm back. I'm back, Cherry, cherry like in strawberry. Find the red. Get the bread."

Little did the vics know they were in the presence of one of the best monte players out there. You could hear Gus two blocks away as he beat vic after vic. At the end of the day, Gus and Johnny's total count was $3,240—a nice take for a guy who just got out of jail. I guess Gus was right. The vics owed him.

After we divided the money, we headed back to the donut shop, where all the monte players were bragging about what they had won during the day. Players were counting off numbers like $3,600, $3,200, $2,800, $1,900 and the day was not even over. Monte was not only played in the daytime, but also at night. So, they all were talking about playing later. Gus said, "Yo shorty, y'all want to play tonight?"

Spence and I said, "Yeah," real fast.

Then Gus said, "Okay, but first me and Johnny have to go up-town to pick up something. Y'all want to come?"

I said, "Yeah, we with it." I knew Spence was down for whatever.

When we got to Harlem, we found out that Money Gus and Johnny Ranks were buying cocaine and marijuana, which did not shock me. I already knew a lot of players got high.

It was a warm November night, like summer. The leaves on the trees had not even turned colors yet to signify fall. There was some-thing about Harlem that made me feel I was among my people. Harlem was ours and no one could take it from us. Harlem was the black mecca of the universe for many people. Even though I was from the Bronx, I still felt Harlem's energy cutting through my bones.

Spence and I were born and raised in the Bronx and we thought of ourselves as some real street-smart dudes. But, little did we know, Harlem dudes were a little bit faster with theirs. If you grew up in Harlem, you saw drugs and everything else sold right in front of your eyes. If you went on Eighth Avenue, you would see drug dealers ply-ing their trade, dope fiends with big arms and hands from shooting drugs nodding on the streets. Sometimes you would see them nod-ding and holding a cup of chili. They would nod real low but never fall or drop the chili. Then, all of a sudden, they would pop back up and repeat the same routine over and over.

Harlem was a place that never slept. People stayed outside all day and all night. Kids in Harlem saw so many things going on that they had to quickly adapt to their surroundings. Harlem had fast men, fast women, working people, poor people, drug addicts, drug deal-ers, bums, winos, churchgoers—you name it. People there had every materialistic item you could think of: expensive cars, jewelry, and designer clothes. It was nothing to see a little sixteen-year-old kid driving a BMW. I could only imagine how Spence and I would have turned out growing up there. We were some fast kids, but Harlem was faster.

The Bronx had a lot going on, too, but it was a little bit more hidden, rather than dead in your face. Walking through some blocks in the Bronx, you might get tricked into believing that everything was lovely and serene. Then *boom*, before you knew it, somebody had a knife in your back. If you were black, you had better not go to Belmont Avenue. Those white guys over there would beat the living shit out of what they call "moolies," a negative term they call blacks. One time I was riding on the outside of the back of a bus, passing through their area and it hit a bump. I fell off and some white boys beat the living shit out of me. I thought I was in the South somewhere being beaten by white guys for not tap dancing right.

But, in Harlem, the tables were turned. If you were a white boy hanging after dark in Harlem, you would definitely get robbed and beaten. But at least they had the courtesy of being robbed first. When a white boy was robbed and beaten, he knew it was more about the money than his white skin. Gus told us while walking to Eighth Avenue that a son of one of the Kennedy brothers used to buy drugs on Eighth Avenue. No one messed with him because the blacks treated him like one of their own. A lot of people in Harlem knew the Kennedys always tried to help black people. And, Lord knows how much we blacks have had to put up with because of racism.

When we got to Eighth Avenue, Johnny Ranks pointed to a dope fiend named Claw. His arms and hands were the size of a big bear because of the heroin he was shooting up. Johnny told us that some doctors had offered him a lot of money for one of his arms. They wanted to use it for tests. But Claw had refused to have it cut off. I could not believe how big they were. There were a million puss blisters all over them. They looked so nasty that I felt I had to throw up. Gus saw me looking at the guy and said, "Shorty, I know Claw scares the fuck out of y'all, but that's a good thing 'cause I don't never want to hear that you and your homeboy are fucking with no get high."

Johnny said, "Man, radar, radar. Gus, stop preaching to them kids, when you and I know we're gonna get higher than a motherfucker." We all laughed.

Then Gus said, "Man, I ain't trying to come across like no Rev. Ike, but I wish somebody would have schooled me about the power of this bullshit I got in my pocket. Maybe then I wouldn't be looking to fly away."

"Well, my man, being that you got our tickets to fly, let's go in this building right here and get us a seat next to the clouds," said Johnny.

"Okay, Mr. Flight Attendant, let's do this," said Gus.

We chuckled as I thought about their funny metaphor.

Then we climbed stairs leading into a gloomy, gray, five-story building. As soon as we got inside, I noticed a few shady characters, who looked like drug addicts. One, in a red and white sweat suit, whose complexion was so black he looked blue, was scratching his bald head and nose all at the same time. Another guy was sitting on the steps, nodding and talking to himself. Then, there was a big fat Spanish girl under the staircase, taking a piss.

Gus said, "Look at that nasty, mcnasty fat bitch, fucking up a good building."

Everybody laughed, including the dope fiends, because the building was so dirty with piss and roaches everywhere, you could tell it had not been cleaned in about a month.

When we made it to the fifth floor, Gus and Johnny told us to go up the last little flight of stairs leading to the roof and chill while they got high. As we sat down on the stairs, Gus went into his pocket and pulled out a big bag of white powder, and four bags of skunk marijuana. Skunk is one of the most potent brands of smoke. Johnny rolled it up as Gus put the cocaine in a hundred dollar bill.

I thought I heard someone on the roof. So, I tuned in to voices that seemed to be coming from the direction of the roof door. I heard someone say, "Yeah, baby, suck that dick. Suck that dick. Whoa, baby, no teeth, no teeth."

Spence and I could not believe what we were hearing. Someone was getting his dick sucked right behind the door. While Spence and I sat there shocked, Gus and Johnny acted like it was an everyday occurrence.

Gus said, "Y'all little niggas want y'all dicks sucked?"

I said nah, but, Spence got up like he was ready for some head.

I then said, "Spence, sit your ass down, you horny bastard."

My telling Spence to chill out was ironic, being that I was the hornier of the two of us. My mind was on sex fifty percent of the day and the other fifty percent it was on money. But, my real priority was money first, and pleasure second, which was why I calmed Spence down. Rest, dress, progress. One of the things I learned while running the streets is when a hustler has money in his pockets, pretty girls are not hard to get.

Johnny liked what I did because he looked at Gus and said, "Man, I'm starting to like little shorty. That's right, shorty, stay focused." Gus took a hit of the powder and nodded his head in approval.

The odor of the skunkweed they were smoking started flowing upstairs in our direction. Immediately, I started getting a contact from the potent smoke. Spence giggled and said, "Man, Mike, that's some good shit. I feel real funny."

I said, "Me too."

"Well, if you're feeling funny, let's go get some head to make us feel better."

Everybody laughed at Spence's stupid comment as Gus put away their stuff and we headed down the stairs. Once outside, Gus tried to talk to every girl who walked by. He said to one, "Hey, baby, you dropped something."

Then she turned around and he started up a conversation. She was dark-skinned with a nice ass and a beautiful smile. I could tell she liked him just by the way she looked at him. As we stood by, Gus went into kick mode and got the girl's phone number. This was his first day out of jail, so we all knew he was real horny and ready for some poon-tang. Sex is the first thing on the agenda of most guys who get out of jail. After enduring the stress of lockdown, they need a sexual release—sort of like a boxer who has been training for months for a fight, without sex. After the fight, he wants to have sex to release all that built-up tension. So, Gus fit into this same type of scenario—horny as hell.

Gus was one wild dude, while on the other hand, Johnny was the smooth and laid-back one. All the women we ran across in Harlem liked both of them. One of the things I was learning about females is that they like the thug types and also the smooth types. Both these hustlers fit those criteria. My homeboy and I were a lot like them in personality.

After Money Gus talked to every female in Harlem, we eventually made it to the 116th Street and Lenox train station and went downstairs. This time all of us snuck on the train, which was crazy, being that we all had pockets full of money. The mind-set of a street hustler was to get over any way he could.

The No. 2 train pulled into the dirty station that smelled like somebody had just thrown up. When the train doors opened, we got on.

Johnny said, "Yo, Gus, you better get yo' ass some pussy fast. You was bugging out there. You kicked it to every bum bitch you saw."

69

Gus said, "Yeah, Johnny, you're right. But, I ain't had no pussy since I got out of jail. Beating my meat on Rikers Island got a nigga fucked up. But, I ain't worried. My girl, Pinky, will take care of a nigga when I see her tonight."

I wondered who Pinky was, so I asked him. "Yo Gus, who's this girl, Pinky?"

"Well, shorty, she's the flyest girl in town and she's my woman. She got my back to the fullest and will kick any nigga's or bitch's ass for me."

Johnny said, "Yeah," with a funny look like he knew something we didn't know. This made me even more curious about Pinky.

As the train moved from station to station, my mind drifted back to the hallway where I had watched them do drugs. I thought about Gus telling us not to get involved in drugs. He did not have to tell me twice. I was already scared of drugs, way before I ever stepped foot in Midtown. Johnny and Gus were not the only players I had seen doing drugs. Drugs were prevalent on the streets of Midtown.

Sometimes I walked the streets with some of the players and they schooled me about what I needed to know to survive there. One player was Bugsy's brother, King, who was one of the best monte players until drugs messed him up. He always told me never to get caught up in the drug lifestyle because drugs would take over your mind, body and soul. I made a pact with him to never mess with drugs. He made me say, "Word is bond," and I did. As for alcohol, I only drank beer sometimes because of what I saw alcohol do to my parents.

One Easter when I was about thirteen years old, I got dressed up, along with my cousins and all of the other kids around 169th Street. To ghetto kids, Easter is like Cinderella day. You got dressed up, then the next day you went back to being bummy.

I was sharp and my pockets were full of money from scalping tickets. It was a bright sunny day and we went to Coney Island and had a good time. When we came back, some of us went to the corner store and bought Old English 800 Malt Liquor beer. Bud, Mitchell, Spence, Damon and I headed to our building and went to the six-teenth floor to get drunk. The beer had me so messed up that I started acting like an asshole, talking bo-coo shit. Spence threw up and ev-erybody could not stop laughing from the effects of the alcohol. When all the beer was finished, we went downstairs and I talked shit to the girls outside. The alcohol gave me false courage.

A pretty girl named Cita, whom I liked a lot, happened to be outside chilling with some of the girls from our building. So, I went over to them, piss drunk to the next level and flashed my money. I told Cita and all of her friends, "I buys my pussy." When I said it, they all walked away with tense, shocked looks on their faces.

The next day all my homeboys told me how stupid I had acted. I felt ashamed because I did not remember anything. So, that episode, along with all I had been through with my parents, helped me not to get caught up in addictions.

From the time I was a little kid, my mother used to tell me that I was "a man amongst men." Back then, when she said this, I did not have the slightest idea what she was talking about. But, now I know she meant that even though I was a little kid, I was my own man. And, one thing I did know about myself was that I never go into anything totally blind. I always, from a man-child sort of way, knew what I was getting into, even if I did not realize the ramifications of all of my actions.

So, as we sat on the No. 2 train headed downtown, although I was in deep thought, I still observed how getting high made Gus even more hyper than he was before taking the drugs. He broke my chain of thought and asked me, "Yo shorty, y'all two little motherfuckers ever get any pussy?"

I told him, "Yeah. I fucked a mixed black-and-Chinese girl in Midtown and now I want to fuck Lady Day."

He said, "Well, shorty, you'd better get in line. Everybody wants to fuck her. Plus, she's Little Clyde's woman."

When he said this I knew I did not have a shot because Clyde was doing his thing downtown, and I was just a little squirrel trying to get a nut.

"But, don't worry, shorty. I'm going to get you some pussy."

Johnny said, "Yeah, Gus, but first you gotta get yourself some pussy." We could not stop laughing. I told myself one day I would have to show and prove, just like in elementary school when we had show and tell, and I tried to prove something by telling lies. Only, this time lies would not work. I was going to have to show Gus that I know how to lay some pipe.

After the train pulled into the crowded Forty-second Street train station, we got off. Gus flew up the stairs like he could not wait to beat those vics. I was right behind him, because I knew the feeling.

The pimp named Bones and some other players were hanging in the donut shop, talking. Bones was the type of pimp who would shoot anybody who messed with his hoes. He was ruthless. His eyes told you to proceed with caution.

After talking with him and all the other players for a little while, Johnny got White Boy Petey to stick for us, then we headed to Broadway.

It was a beautiful night and Midtown was busting at the seams with people as we made our way over there. Every time I stepped foot there, it put me in another state of mind. It was like I transformed from Regular Mike to Midtown Mike. I discovered that more people roamed the streets at night, than during the day. That was saying a lot when I think about all the people who frequented the place in the daytime.

As always, the streets were bustling with more people, more street entertainers, and more monte games. The Coca-Cola sign, along with the other lightings and billboards, lit up the whole area like a baseball field. I felt like I was back at Yankee Stadium scalping tickets when I smelled the pretzels, shish kebabs, franks and smoke. Midtown had its own distinctive smell and feel. You would have to go there to get the full feel of what I am talking about.

I pictured Frank Sinatra singing "New York, New York." *If I could make it there, I'll make it anywhere, New York, New York.* The feeling I got in this electrifying atmosphere made me feel right at home. It was like none other. It was like the feeling a kid gets when he goes to Disneyland. Forget the Bronx, or anywhere else, nothing compares with Midtown.

So, as Spence and I set up the monte game, and Johnny got behind the box, I went to hold him down and take in the scenery. While standing there I knew without a doubt, Midtown was the place where I belonged. Destiny had brought me here. This was the place where many things in my life would be revealed. As I held Johnny down, every so often I glanced at our monte game. It seemed they played monte even better when they were high. The more the vics bet, the more hyper and animated Gus got. One time he came up the block and told me, "Hold us down, shorty. We already took about 1,800."

My eyes lit up and the first thing I thought about was that my day was coming. One day it would be me taking hundred dollar bets, with the vics and other people looking with amazement. One day I would be the star attraction and no one would be able to find my red card. One day even all the monte players and hustlers would be mesmerized by my superb monte skills. But for now, I had to earn my stripes by being a lookout man.

While standing on the corner with my mind occupied by visions of grandeur, I noticed there were pickpockets jostling in the crowds.

I spotted a pretty light-skinned girl with a little Cuban guy, one of the best pickpockets in Midtown. I often saw him picking pockets, and he always came up with somebody's wallet.

He was even better than the jostlers who plied their trade at the baseball and basketball events when I scalped tickets. I saw him go into a white woman's pocketbook and come out with her wallet. Then he passed it to the girl who walked past me and gave me a sly wink. I was captivated by her smile and big butt. They say, never trust a big butt and a smile, but I definitely trusted this one.

If I could have stopped playing monte, I would have gone with her, even though I believed money should come first, then the pretty girls. Boy, the power of that second head is strong, though. But, I kept telling myself, *Money over girls, Mike; Money over girls*, as I tried to get my mind right.

At the same time, I could not take my eyes off her as she headed towards the Howard Johnson's restaurant on Forty-sixth Street and Broadway. A street entertainer named Jesse with a white shirt, black pants, black penny loafer shoes and his hair done up in Jheri curls was doing a great Michael Jackson imitation. No one did Michael Jackson better. Jesse eventually went on to be part of the singing group Force MDs. Yes, Midtown was the place where stars are born.

Across the street from him was Tee, also playing monte, with a huge crowd around him. Not too far from him, by the Bowery, was Little Bit, his brother Peanut, and their team. Everywhere I looked, I could spot a monte game. All the players were out there: Johnny, Big Burke, Jeff Redd, Saul and his sisters, Jody, Eve and Little Skooby, King, everybody. It was like a big three-card monte family reunion, where everyone showed up, including the high ones. But, what was different about this family reunion was you either went home with money or straight to jail. There were no in-betweens.

After Johnny and Gus took turns springing them, they decided to call it a night. Their total take for two hours and twenty minutes was $2,360. Spence and I threw the boxes to the side, then we went upstairs in the Burger King restaurant and split up the money. Afterwards, everyone said they would be back downtown tomorrow. Spence and I felt so good that we called the OJ luxury car service to take us uptown. A shiny burgundy Lincoln Continental cab picked us up on Forty-third Street and Seventh Avenue right by Nathan's.

As we jumped in the car, Gus yelled out, "Look at the little shorties flossing big time." Johnny just laughed. On our way uptown, the cab driver thought he was Mr. Cool, as he lied about the nice car being his. We paid him no mind as our minds drifted off thinking about the many possibilities that lay ahead. The future seemed bright for the two little businessmen from the Bronx.

* * *

During my first year, my mind was like a sponge absorbing everything. My street skills were getting better and better. I was growing up fast, real fast. One day in Midtown was like a whole lifetime, such as the time Money Gus and I boned a girl together. Like I said before, my negative seed had already been planted inside my brain from the last scenario with the tourist.

Gus and I were standing on The Deuce with some other players, just kicking the breeze by a porno movie theater, when all of a sudden a gorgeous, brown-skinned girl with a nice ass walked by. So, like the players we were, we both talked to her. I was looking sharp in a blue Paris nylon tank top and boxer set from AJ Lester, with blue Oscar de la Renta jeans, a pair of burgundy British Walker shoes and my Mike name belt. Money Gus had on a red Paris nylon set with red and white Adidas sweat pants and new red and white eggshell Adidas sneakers. We were fly and anyone could see we were hustlers.

I noticed the girl was picking up on this fact just by the way she was looking at us. After we made small talk, we asked if she wanted to hang out and she quickly answered yes. Something was telling me this was going to be a wild night. I showed her my sinister smile and stared her up and down. *Take a look at these pearly whites, baby!*

We walked to a grocery store on The Deuce and Gus bought beer for everyone making sure the girl saw his hundred dollar bills. I caught the girl staring like she had never seen c-notes before.

Then we caught a cab up to Harlem. When we made it to 116th Street and Lenox, Gus paid the driver as we got out. I knew if the girl had not been with us, we would have jumped out of that Yellow Cab without paying. Being hustlers, you always try to get over in any and every way you can. And, if that means stiffing a cab driver, so be it.

Gus went into a building to buy some drugs. While he was handling his business, I noticed how pretty this girl was.

She reminded me of a young Pam Grier, a beautiful, voluptuous black actress I fell in love with when I was about ten years old. I watched her black exploitation movies in the early seventies. Her movies included *Sheba Baby*, and *Foxy Brown*. When I made money hustling in the supermarkets, I would go to see all her movies. I would sit there by myself with popcorn in one hand and a soda in the other, watching her movies all day. Her beauty had me so captivated that not even the rats and cats running by my feet could make me take my eyes off her.

Now, here right before my horny eyes, stood a young Pam Grier look-alike. I told myself that I knew I could not have the real thing, but this would do.

The girl said, "You and your homeboy are some big time money makers, ain't y'all? I seen all the money he had."

"Well, baby, we do what we gotta do to get some paper."

"I knew both of y'all were hustlers as soon as y'all started talking to me."

When she said this I knew she was materialistic-simplistic, which made me even hornier. I could not keep my horny little eyes off of her chest and ass.

She caught me staring and said, "You look like you wanna touch something. Do you see something you like?"

"Yeah, I can't lie. You look so soft."

Then Gus jetted out of the building. So, I let my eyes do the talking for me.

There was a liquor store across the street, so we headed there and bought two bottles of Moet champagne.

Then the girl said, "Boy, I just love me some sham-pang. Plus, I'm thirsty."

Gus said, "We *thirsty*, too."

He looked at me and winked, and I knew exactly what he meant. After we made the purchase, we walked six blocks to Central Park and sat on a park bench where homegirl proceeded to drink and sniff coke with Gus. I just had some of the Moet and watched them get high from cocaine. The higher they got, the freakier the girl acted. Money Gus slapped her on her big ass as she rubbed on his big muscles and wavy hair.

I was getting hornier by the minute. My dick was talking to me saying, *Get that pussy, Mike, get that pussy.* At fifteen years old, my dick got hard whenever the wind blew. And, here was the chance I had been waiting for—to show Gus all I'd learned on the streets of Midtown.

I had already been with a lot of girls, due to the fact that I was a young moneymaking hustler. Pretty girls loved hustlers. I always stayed fly with all the latest clothes and material things. I kept a fly Caesar haircut and the pimps, hoes, and other hustlers schooled me on the rules of the streets. Pimps Chelsea and Honey Combs always told me to stay fly and keep my game tight at all times. Then all the bitches would flock like flies to shit. What a perfect analogy. They also said, "Never take no as an answer. No, is just a slow yes."

I was a good listener and student of the game. And, now it was time to show my street mentors what I could do. Money Gus was already showing the Pam Grier look-alike what he could do with his hands. And, I was going to show her what I could do with the throbbing thing in my pants.

After about an hour of sitting in the park, we caught a cab and went to the Bronx Park Motel on Fordham Road. This was a seedy motel where a lot of players and hustlers from all over took their hot women. The room we rented smelled like a waterbed had busted and saturated the carpet. On one of the walls someone had written: "I fucked my homeboy, Jerry's, bitch here." Well, I didn't know who's girl this was, but she's gonna get fucked, too.

Gus took off his clothes except for his red nylon set. The girl, who seemed freakier than us, took off her pants and shirt. She had a body to die for and her big breasts were round like melons and her thighs and ass looked softer than tissue. I envisioned a naked model having her type of body. Money Gus led her to the big bed and they fucked like their lives depended on it. There was more sucking and fucking going on in that room than a porno movie. When it was my turn, Gus could not believe how long I could go without coming. I really was putting on an Oscar-winning performance. Even though they did not give Oscar's for porno, I should have won something.

The student was showing the teacher what new things he had learned. And, one of the things I learned was to spray my penis with stuff called Stud 100. This spray prevented premature ejaculation. Throughout the course of my experiences with girls, I had learned that sometimes I would come too fast, so I solved the problem with my reliable Stud 100, that a player named Kendall had schooled me about. Gus could not believe a little kid could have so much stamina. But, he did not know about my little secret. Whenever I used it, other girls thought I was a macho man.

While I was having sex with her, Gus looked on with glowing approval. He was like a proud father watching his son do a good deed. After fucking the Pam Grier look-alike, Gus and I fucked girls, whenever the opportunity presented itself. We saw nothing wrong with a little bump and grind. What we failed to realize is, if you go around bumping and grinding too much, bad things can happen to you. Somebody once said, "When you do dirt, you get dirt." Gus and I failed to realize we were both in for a rude awakening.

6

Crawl, Then Walk

I was waiting in Playland on Forty-eighth Street and Broadway for my monte team when I spotted a pretty redbone girl whispering something to a guy playing pinball. Whatever she was telling him, he was shaking his head no. After she finished, I walked over to kick it with her. I was horny and I considered myself to be a game-tight player.

I nonchalantly walked up and asked her, "What did you ask that guy?" She did not reply, but smiled and asked my name. I answered and she told me her name was Debbie.

After exchanging pleasantries, I got straight to the point and I told her that I liked what I was seeing and I wanted to take her to the hotel. I believed in taking my time! She agreed to my indecent proposal and off we went to a hotel on Forty-seventh Street.

As we walked to the hotel, I was getting hornier by the minute as I admired her voluptuous body and good-looking face. I thought, *Man I cannot wait to tell all my homeboys about this one, after I fuck the shit out of her.* I had my bottle of Stud 100, so I was ready to do some serious stroking.

Once we got in the room she told me she had to go to the bathroom in the outside hallway. So, I said, "No problem," as I undressed and waited for the big throw down. As I lay there in bed, ten minutes went by and the girl had not come back. So, I put back on my clothes and went to the hallway.

I looked in the bathroom and she was not there. So, I went downstairs and asked the receptionist if she had seen a light-skinned girl come this way. She said, "Yes, the girl left about ten minutes ago."

I yelled, "That stupid bitch!" The receptionist looked at me like I was crazy. I told her I was sorry for cursing and left the hotel.

Mr. Game-Tight had been played for a fool, Midtown-style. I guess the reason she did what she did, was to let me know to mind my own business. I should have listened to my mother when she used to say, "Stay out of grown folks' business."

I was discovering rather quickly that in Midtown, game is learned. You could not just go out there thinking you were game-tight without getting some experience. Even a wiseman must learn by experience before he got to be wise. I was only downtown a hot minute and I was caught up into thinking I was already a bona fide player, without even learning the rules of the game. On these mean streets, I had to learn to be quick on my feet or else get caught in the mix.

As I thought back to how that girl played me for a fool, I realized that it made me feel just like a vic feels when he loses his money— stupid. But, I could not expect anyone to pity this fool who plays people for fools everyday. I was not looking for sympathy, but I needed another person's opinion about what I had just gone through. So, when I made it back to Playland, I decided to tell Lady Day what had happened to me.

Lady Day was the one who told Spence and I that all the women would be easy to get, now that we were moneymaking hustlers. Now I was seriously doubting what she said. When I spotted her standing by the arcade with a bunch of other monte players, I told her I needed to talk with her. We went over to the side and I ran down what happened to me. As soon as I told her she laughed, which made me mad.

Then she said, "Mike, I'm sorry for laughing, but I am not laughing at you, I'm laughing because what you told me brought back memories of when I first came to New York from Baltimore. I was fresh off the bus and I let this lame-ass-wanna-be-pimp, talk me into selling my ass for him. He ran down some bullshit about making me a star because I was so beautiful. I had come to New York looking for work as a model and I ran into him hanging by a modeling agency. He said he had big-time connections with modeling agents. So, I fell for his lame game. Next thing I knew he had me selling ass on Eighth Avenue to make money for the supposed modeling agent's fee. After I turned tricks on the stroll a few days, some of the whores out there told me the guy did not have any connections and he had ran that same scam on a few of them. They told me the only connections he had was the connection his hands made to crack pipes."

We both laughed, then she said, "So, you see Mike, you are not the only one to fall victim to the new jack swing. We all get tossed around and played with when we first come down here. You just live and you learn. Down here you first start off as a victim, then you become the victimizer. That's why we call people vics, because they are all victims to our scams."

I said, "Boy, Lady Day, you are so damn intelligent. Plus you got it going on. I just love women like you."

She said, "Mike, are you trying to game me with your flattery? Because you know I can take you to a hotel and leave you there."

As we cracked up at her joke, I wondered if I was trying to laugh my way into Lady Day's tight pants.

Talking to Lady Day made me feel better. She made me see that I had something in common with all the other players. It also made me realize, sometimes you have to crawl before you can walk. One thing I did know about people was that a lot of them thought they were smarter than they actually were. I once read in a book that we only use a very small percentage of our brain capacity. Some use more than others. That's why you have some people who are smarter than others. If what I read is true, then I was going to have to use a little bit more of my brain, because right now I was stuck on "stupid."

The situation with the girl was not my only learning experience in Midtown. Another time, while hanging in Playland, a lady tried to run a Murphy scam on me when she noticed my diamond Mike ring as I was playing one of the games. After she ran down her scam, I told her, "Do I look like a motherfucking chump to you?" She just smiled and kept it moving. I was starting to think that maybe I looked like a vic who was ready to be victimized. Maybe that's how I looked to the hustlers who had been out there for a long time—like a new jack fresh out of the boondocks. But, at least I knew this was a learning experience and it was going to take time to get my stripes. Sacrifice makes everything precise, meaning, if you sacrifice to get whatever it is you want, in due time, you will get precisely what you want.

As I kept going to Midtown, my street skills improved. When I was a full-fledged hustler with the necessary acquired skills, about a year later I ran into the same girl who left me in the hotel. But, this time she could tell by the way I talked and carried myself that I was not going to go for the okey doke. This scenario played itself out with some serious sex; boy was she worth the wait. Homegirl made me come four times. Sometime later I would run into her again.

It started on Thirty-fourth Street where Gus and I happened to be after a long day of playing monte. Earlier in the day, I noticed a girl watching him beat all the vics out of their money. While she stood there in awe, I realized I knew her. This was the same girl who had played me for a fool and left me in a hotel. Then, I met her a year later and fucked the shit out of her. When I looked at her I told myself, "Tonight's the night we get into some shit."

After we finished playing, the girl hung around and Gus talked with her. When I walked up, she said, "Hi, Mike. Long time no see."

I said, "What's up Debbie? How you been doing?"

Gus said, "Mike you know this girl?"

"Yeah, Gus. I know her real well."

When I said it, he knew exactly what I was talking about. Gus asked her if she wanted to hang out and Debbie said, "Sure. We can do that. I was just out here shopping and I'm finished."

I knew this was a lie because she had no bags. Just by the way she was looking at Gus like he was some sort of celebrity told me we were going to fuck her.

She was still looking good with her hazel eyes, like Lady Day's, and her ass and tits seemed like they were even bigger than the last time. As we headed to Tad's Steakhouse on the west side of Thirty-fourth Street, I flashed my sinister smile. Even though I had fucked her, that was a while ago. So, it was going to be like fucking her for the first time.

Gus filled her up with steak and bullshit and ordered a big bottle of champagne. I guess he bought it so we could celebrate the new arrival of our sexual prospect. The pretty redbone kept asking Gus stupid questions like how did he learn to play three-card monte and would he show her how to do it. Gus just laughed and said, "I would like to show you how to do a lot of things before this night is over." Debbie laughed with a stupid *he, he, he, he*, that reminded me of one of those dumb blond broads in a gangster movie.

Homegirl could not keep her hands off of his muscles. I knew the champagne was taking effect because she had a stupid grin on her face. Her eyes told me she would be down for anything. And this made three of us.

As the three of us headed uptown on the No. 2 train, Gus kept touching her on the ass and pulling her close to him as she massaged his muscles. My hormones were raging so fast that I could not wait to get her into a hotel and fuck the shit out of her; I was getting harder by the minute.

I sensed everybody in the last car knew what we were up to. I caught redbone staring at the imprint of my hard penis pressing against the fabric of my Adidas sweatpants. Money Gus asked her if she got high and redbone said, "Sometimes." He suggested that we get off at

116th and Lenox. I knew right then that Gus wanted to get her nice and high before we fucked her.

Gus bought five bags of angel dust called Now or Later, along with two hundred dollars worth of cocaine and another bottle of champagne from the liquor store. Afterwards, we went over and sat on some park benches in the Taft Housing Projects, notorious projects where a lot of big-time drug dealers come from.

Gus and redbone smoked the two bags of the angel dust and we all drank champagne. The angel dust and alcohol had her acting real freaky. I knew she was high when she touched Gus' dick and started licking in his ear.

Money Gus said, "Shorty, what you know about this type of shit. Money and bitches?"

I said, "I know a lot, Gus, and I already fucked her before. Right Debbie?"

"Yeah, Mike, and I made your ass come four times."

I said, "I can't lie, Debbie, you got skills."

As we left the park, Gus said, "Well, shorty, I just got to show her all my skills."

When we got on Lenox Avenue, we tried to catch a cab and all the while I could not take my eyes off of her big ass. A black cab pulled up and we headed to the Bronx Park Motel.

While sitting in the cab, Gus pulled out his cocaine and they sniffed some. Money was the only thing that made me high. So, I was in complete control as I observed the action from the front seat. Redbone tried to kiss him and he quickly turned away, because he did not know where her lips had been. Rule number one on the street: Never kiss a strange girl. You never know whose cock she's been sucking.

She was so high, she did not even notice it. I noticed Gus was starting to get high, too, because he pulled out knots of money from both pockets, counting it over and over. My friend, Spence, would do the same thing. Every time he was around people, he flashed his money. But, I always kept mine in my sock. (No nervous, no nervous.) As Gus continued to count his money, the girl smiled like she had an inside joke that we were not in on.

When we got to the hotel, everyone stripped down to underwear. She had on black lace bikini panties with a matching bra. She was looking good as her fat jelly ass burst through her skimpy bikini panties. I could see her beautiful pubic hair through the lace. She had some nice small titties with big nipples. She pranced around the room dancing like a stripper in a club. She smiled as she put on the show and we acted like we were put on this earth to live the lifestyles of players. Watching her dance and take off her bra and panties had me hornier than ten men. I told myself I had to calm down if I was going to please her. Gus and the girl got on the big bed and fucked in all types of awkward positions.

Gus said, "You see shorty, I don't give a fuck about these hoes," as he slapped her on the ass.

Every time I looked at her, she still had a stupid grin on her face. Gus continued talking, "You see how this bitch is loving how I'm manhandling and treating her like shit. Bitches like thugs. Right baby?"

She kept smiling and laughing.

Then he said, "Shorty, if you keep listening to me, you might just learn something."

She just kept laughing and smiling. I did not know what was so funny, but all I wanted was my shot to ride her big ass. So, after I got tired of watching, I headed to the bathroom and sprayed some Stud 100 on my penis. All while I was thinking, *Damn, if Cousin Reggie was alive, he would be proud of his little star pupil, who had finally made it to the big time.* Then I headed towards the bed to handle my business.

"Yo Gus, let a brother get a nut."

"Okay, shorty. Ride that ass cause she got some good pussy."

First I fucked her doggie-style as she gave Gus oral sex. After a few minutes, I laid her on her back then threw up her legs and went into slam mode. Redbone was loving it. She started moaning and screaming my name. She screamed, "Oh Mikeness. Oh Mikeness."

Money Gus looked at me and smiled. He said, "Damn, little shorty is coming into his own."

We had sex all night until we all eventually fell asleep, like a nice little threesome. When we woke up the next morning for round two, Gus's money was missing and redbone was gone. She stole $1,300 from him. He was mad as hell and he was finding it hard to believe that the bitch had not robbed both of us. He kept asking me a million questions like he thought I had set him up. But, the only reason I had not gotten robbed, too, was because I had hidden my money in my sock. (No nervous, no nervous.) This was something I always did, being that I did not trust anybody. But, Gus had flashed his money all night, and he paid dearly for his mistake. He had broken rule numero uno—never trust a big butt and a smile.

I realized that I now knew what her inside joke was.

7

Tap Dancing Roscoe

"Hey, Mike. Look Cisco just got off the D-train wearing nylon underwear and lizard shoes," Spence said. "He's bugging out."

Spence, Saul, Money Gus, Jody, Pamela, the other players and I were near the donut shop getting ready to go play monte. And there was Cisco, getting off the D-train on this early Saturday morning in his underwear. He had a glassy-eyed look about him that told me he was higher than a kite. Money Gus, Saul and Big-Head Louie walked up to him to find out what the hell was going on. Cisco babbled about how today he was going to make a million dollars and then he was going to Africa to be with the black kings and queens.

Gus told him, "You can go to Africa right now if you want, but first you're gonna need some clothes for the long trip."

Then he and Big-Head Louie walked him to Modell's department store to get some pants and a shirt. As they shopped, I spotted females looking to see how big his penis was.

Jody told Pamela, "Damn, Pamela, that nigga Cisco got a big dick. Maybe he needs a woman to take him home and help him sweat out those drugs in his system with some good loving."

Pamela, and all of us who heard what she said, laughed.

When I first came downtown, I used to find myself staring at some player under the influence of drugs. My reasons for staring were totally different from Jody's. When I stared, it was because I was trying to look into their eyes to see if I could find the answers to why a person would choose to mess his life up with drugs.

My staring started long before I ever made it to Midtown. I used to stare at my mother when she was under the influence of alcohol. I could not understand how something in a bottle could transform my mother from the sweetest woman in the world into the meanest woman. Sometimes when she would be sitting in the kitchen in a drunken stupor, I would go in there and pretend like I was cleaning up, but what I really would be doing was staring in her eyes. But the alcohol had her so drunk she never noticed me. Sometimes I stared so hard into my mother's eyes that I felt myself mentally making some connection with her drunken mental state. I visualized myself turning into her while she was drunk, sort of like how a little kid gets so caught up watching a cartoon that his mind puts him inside the television with all the cartoon characters. He gets so connected to what he is watching that he cannot even hear his mother calling him. That is how deep I would get into this mind-set.

This trance-like-state took me to some pretty strange situations. One minute it would have my mind, body, and soul dancing in the living room, having a good time with friends. We would be laughing, drinking and eating soul food. I would feel so good from the first drink, that I needed another drink, then another and another. The next thing I knew, I would have a knife in my hand threatening to stab somebody, or holding a pot of lye getting ready to throw it on somebody. The alcohol was giving me a false sense of courage to do the craziest things. But, just before I acted on it, I would hear somebody yelling, "What the hell are you staring at, boy!" It was my mother waking me up out of my trance. "I don't know what the hell is wrong with you, but you better take yo' little ass outside!"

My mother failed to realize that I was trying to find out what the hell was up with her and the alcohol. Little did she know that by sending me outside, I was forced to find the answers to my questions about alcohol and other substances by looking into the eyes of strangers. And boy did I learn a lot! By the time I made it to Midtown, my vision was 20/20 with a zoom lens.

So, I was good at detecting what I saw in the hustlers' eyes. Sometimes I would hang with them when they got high. They would be sniffing away or smoking marijuana or angel dust. And, I would be staring into their eyes watching them transform into someone else. If the person was normally quiet, he became real talkative and would not shut up, the typical blabbermouth. If the person was normally energetic and hyper, they became quiet and laid-back, staring at me, like I was staring at them. If the person was a hustler who was not one of the big moneymakers, the drugs gave him visions of grandeur and he lied about all the big money he was making and all the materialistic things and women he had. One thing I found out from all the years I spent staring at substance abusers was that drugs and alcohol changed people's personalities—lot of times not for the better.

Cisco's actions were a perfect example. He was not the only one that I witnessed bugout on drugs. Even Money Gus, who helped Cisco across the street, fell victim to drugs. Money Gus was already a hyper dude, but when he got high, it did not cause him to become laid-back. Drugs made him even more hyper. But, the crazy thing about it was that he hustled better when he was high. The only drug that bugged Gus out to the next level was angel dust. Dust would mess him up so bad he would have to drink milk to come down off the high. I never liked being around him when he smoked dust.

But like I said, he was not the only one I saw bugging out off of drugs or alcohol. There was a monte player named Roscoe who played three-card monte for more than thirty years. Roscoe reminded me of my cousin Reggie. He was crazy buck wild and loved to drink and fight. Plus, he was as strong as an ox. Roscoe had big fists like George Foreman, the heavyweight boxer. He was from the South and what people would call a big ol' country boy. He had a short afro and Superfly side burns. Roscoe was the nicest guy in the world when he was not drinking, but, if he was, watch out! I saw him knock out a few monte players and hustlers. His boxing style was a cross between 1908 heavyweight boxing champ, Jack Johnson, mixed with a little Sammy Davis Jr. tap dancing, and he had the strength of twenty men. He would have one hand protecting his face and the other stretched all the way out as he tap danced and slid around his opponent. When he fought, everybody watching would be laughing, including his opponent.

He often told me about his experiences working on the chain gangs in the South. He said, "Them white motherfuckers worked me from sun up to sundown." But the work made him stronger. He said, "Mike, the same things that will make you weak, will make you strong."

I guess the vics that I saw him beat down, did not feel that way. A lot of times he would be the lookout in the monte games. Springers liked giving him work because they knew if there was any static with any vics, Roscoe could handle it. All you had to do is make sure you bought him a bottle of wine. Have you ever seen a movie in which the bullies were messing with a skinny guy? And, the guy tells the bullies, "If you don't leave me alone, I'll go get my friend PeeWee." The bullies laugh and say, "Go, get your little friend, PeeWee, so, we can kick both your asses." The skinny guy leaves and then comes back with PeeWee, who is a big Andre-the-Giant-type; the bullies run. Roscoe was the monte players' PeeWee. I saw him whip a vic's ass so bad that the vic would beg for mercy. Or, after he hit them with one punch, they would get up and run for dear life. All the beatings he gave were under the influence of alcohol.

I have even seen vics and other people around Midtown act foolish under the influence of drugs and alcohol. St. Patrick's Day was one of the best money days for playing monte. This is a day when a lot of Irish people show their pride and some show their asses. First they go to their big parade on Fifth Avenue to celebrate their heritage and culture. And, all while they are at the parade, they drink and enjoy the festivities. When it's over, all hell breaks loose. By this time, a lot of them are drunk and still drinking heavily.

You would find them all over Midtown acting wild. On the side blocks, they would start up these drinking parties and the cops would let them do whatever they wanted, because half the police department was Irish. Everywhere you looked, somebody would be fighting. Some guys would be big football player types who would be punching, body-slamming, wrestling and fighting like they damn near wanted to kill each other.

One time I saw two big white boys fighting like they were in a death match. They were taking turns beating the shit out of each other. They had black eyes, swollen faces, and broken jaws and hands. After fighting, they hugged each other and started drinking again.

By the time any made it to Broadway, or any other street where we played monte, we beat them for every dime they had. But, being the nice guys that we were, we let them keep their alcohol. Of course, we got into major battles with some of these guys, but, they never got any of their money back. I made so much money on St. Patrick's Day, I wouldn't have to come downtown the next day. St. Patrick's day was a good day for the pimps and prostitutes, too. After the white boys got drunk, they got horny and went looking for the whores— just like the sailors did when they came to Midtown on leave. Wearing their clean white uniforms and shiny new shoes, they got drunk and went looking for the whores. After the prostitutes finished with them, they were lucky if they had their hats and pants.

One thing I learned about being downtown was that there's always somebody lurking in the shadows hoping to catch some fool who has gotten too high. Sometimes people get this way and don't know when to go home. When they did this in Midtown, it was a recipe for disaster. If your brain was cooked by whatever it was you were taking or drinking, and the criminal element caught you slipping, there was always somebody to pick you up, minus a wallet.

And, if you got too high, you'd better not find yourself on The Deuce because gangs and shady characters would give you the worst beating in your life. Picture this: Some horny drunk guy spots one of those pretty Spanish gang girls looking all sexy and standing alone by a store on The Deuce. But, what he fails to realize is her gang member boyfriend is in watching distance. The drunken guy tries to talk to the girl because he figures this is Midtown and she might be a prostitute. But, this is one night he will not be getting any sex. When he leaves the area he will be weak at the knees, but it will not be because of some good sex. But what he will get is the worst ass-whipping he ever had in his life. He will leave the area with missing teeth, cuts and bruises everywhere and no money. Like Roscoe said: the same things that will make you weak, will make you strong. The lesson the drunken guy learns is never come to The Deuce when your vision is blurry.

On The Deuce there was always some type of violence going on. You could smell trouble in the air. It smells like blood, shit, urine and sweat combined, with a tinge of shish kebab. The Deuce is one area that I did not have to stare in anybody's eyes to find out what was going on inside their heads. I already knew. Danger, so proceed with caution. If someone caught you looking at them a second too long, the first thing they would ask was, "What the fuck are you looking at?" If you did not come up with the right answer, you'd better know how to fight or run like Carl Lewis, the track star. They say New York is the place where stars are born. But, what they do not tell you is, it is also the place where asses get kicked.

8

Crack Attack

News flash: President Reagan declares war on drugs. Nancy says, "Say no to drugs." Well it was news to me, because I didn't see any signs of change in my parts of town. uptown still had cocaine, heroin and marijuana users. In Midtown, you had all of the above, plus the hustlers and players' drug of choice, freebase cocaine, which years later was called crack.

In the mid-'80s, the price of a gram of cocaine dropped drastically, from one hundred dollars a gram to fifty. Before the price change, only people who made good money could afford it, such as entertainers, street hustlers, professional sports players, actors and big wigs. Cocaine used to be considered a rich man's high, but as the price dropped the clientele changed. Suddenly your average Joe Blow could snort his way to the clouds or maybe into the blazing fires headed in the opposite direction.

I first found out about free-basing cocaine when I arrived downtown in 1979. I saw a player stick a tiny white rock in a glass pipe and then light it with a cigarette lighter. It looked like a tiny piece of soap. But, I quickly found out what he was doing had nothing to do with washing. This guy was trying to fly away and not with a plane. When he inhaled the fumes from the piece of rock, his eyes rolled up in his head as he held his breath, taking it all in. After going through the motions, his facial expressions changed like he had just been through the best out of body experience in his life. As I got more involved with three-card monte, my interactions with players who did drugs increased. Not every player in Midtown indulged in this activity, but some used cocaine or any type of drug they could get their hands on. I knew two players whose drug of choice was angel dust. This drug could knock out an elephant, let alone a human being. These two players loved to smoke dust, get high and bug out on the vics downtown. For several years, drugs did not seem to affect their monte skills, but then, the dope affected their minds. They had a zombie look about them even when they were not high, and they talked like punch-drunk fighters. Other players called them dust heads. Then their skills diminished along with the money they made. These were guys who used to make a lot of money and had all the material things and women that any man could want. I watched as drugs took hold of a lot of other players and how it affected their lives. It all added up to the same negative results.

One thing I knew about myself was when I liked something, I was the type of person who would go all out. If I liked money, I went all out to get it. If I liked material things, pretty girls, you name it, I did the same. So, when I arrived downtown, I knew messing with drugs wasn't for me. I knew without a doubt, trying marijuana would turn into trying angel dust, cocaine would turn into crack and then I would lose my mind. I did not know everything about myself, but this was something I knew one hundred percent.

Flaco was another monte player I hung out with from time to time in Midtown and at the Disco Fever Club uptown. When I first met him, he was with his homeboy, Jiggy. Flaco was energetic, smooth, hyper and laid back, all wrapped up into one. I liked him because we had the same personality traits; the difference was that he did drugs.

Flaco always had something to say and loved to crack jokes. He found comedy in everyday life situations. If you hung around him, you would laugh your head off. If he saw an opening for a joke, he jumped dead on it. He once said, "Mike, somebody told me you was thinking about getting into the pimp game. So, when are you going to start selling ass?" We laughed like crazy. One time he grabbed Big-Head Louie's hat off, and all the players laughed at his humongous head, the size of two heads. Flaco was one funny dude when he was not messed up on drugs. But, when he was, it made him get really hyper and crazy as he rambled his words. Drugs turned him into a different person. If he was too high, I would not hang around him. Word was going around Midtown that sometimes when Flaco went uptown, he bugged out after getting high. They said he was getting into all types of trouble with people and drug dealers.

One day while I was playing monte on Broadway, one of the players told me Flaco was dead. Word on the streets was he either jumped off a roof or was pushed. I choose to believe the latter, but you never knew when it comes to drugs. Drugs have made some people do the craziest things imaginable.

I watched drugs slowly deteriorate King. Shooting heroin messed up his life. When I first came downtown, King schooled me on a lot of things to look out for. On our nightly walks around Midtown, we talked about everything under the sun. King had more game in one finger than a lot of players put together. He was a good talker and I was a good listener. But I guess when it came to drugs, he was not listening to his own advice.

I saw drugs not only affect people downtown, they also affected people uptown. Like I said earlier, Flaco, Jiggy, I and a lot of other players used to frequent Disco Fever, a club on 167th Street and Jerome Avenue. This was a notorious place where players, hustlers and hip-hop entertainers came to floss, get high and get their groove on. Disco Fever was known for fast times and fast women who loved cocaine. I heard about Disco Fever for the first time when Spence and I were hanging with Money Gus and Big-Head Louie at a gambling spot called the Bottom Line on 167th Street and Webster Avenue.

The Bottom Line was where I first laid eyes on Criss Boss, who would later get arrested for what the *Daily News* called the "Valentine Massacre." Ten people were found murdered in a Brooklyn house, and he was charged with the crime. He was in his bathrobe and slippers, gambling thousands of dollars. I got a queasy feeling in my stomach, just looking into his piercing eyes.

The Bottom Line is the same place where ruthless, don't-give-a-fuck stick-up men robbed a bunch of big-time drug dealers, hustlers, gangsters, and then raped the pretty bartender. What made it even crazier was that she showed up for work the next day with a smile on her face.

Once, after Spence and I had watched Gus and Big-Head Louie gamble while the smell of danger was in the air, Gus asked us if we wanted to go to Disco Fever. We both yelled yeah like two little kids being asked to go to Disneyland.

When we got out of the cab, I noticed a large illuminated yellow sign with red letters that said DISCO FEVER. Under it was a long line of people waiting to get in a little doorway leading into the nightclub. I thought, *This place doesn't look all that bad from the outside.* Little did I know that one day I would almost get killed at this same club.

When we got to the front, the big security guard looked at Spence and me and told Gus that the little shorties couldn't come in. Gus and Louie tried to tell him we were mature kids and plus we were monte players like them. Even though he knew monte players made a lot of money, the guard still said no. After about a year of the security guy making Spence and me watch our homeboys go in the Fever without us, he let us in, too. I was in ghetto heaven, to say the least.

After we got inside, the security people checked us for weapons. Not everyone was checked, one of the reasons I heard a lot of people were killed in the place. After we were searched, they pointed us towards the pay booth on the left-hand side. This is where we paid our admission of five dollars to a beautiful woman who looked like she did not take any crap from anybody. Then I spotted steps leading upstairs. But, we decided to chill a little while in the small area on the right side, which had a DJ and a dance floor. I saw a few pretty girls, but, I chilled out instead of talking to them.

Upstairs, the first thing I noticed were the mirrors. When I looked up, I spotted a large, round glassy chandelier, like the one John Travolta danced under in *Saturday Night Fever*. Then, I saw a bar where people were standing and ordering drinks from two pretty redbone female bartenders with big asses. On the right side of the bar was a little booth where DJ Sweet Gee was spinning a song called "Ladies Night" by Kool and the Gang.

The sound system was much better than those that Spence and I heard in the parks when the local rap groups jammed. The music was banging and the place was jumping with guys and pretty women everywhere. I looked to my right and Spence was talking to a slim Puerto Rican girl with big breasts. Gus and Louie had already headed to the back, past the dance floor where people were dancing. I already knew from the other players downtown that the girls loved anybody with money to spend. As I walked through the club, I noticed a lot of people seemed to be high from cocaine—I knew the look. Just as I had learned to detect when my mother was drinking alcohol when I was little, I had also learned how to detect cocaine usage downtown.

As I made my way to the back part of the club, I was not surprised when I saw Gus, Big-Head Louie and a bunch of other people drinking champagne and sniffing cocaine. Everywhere you looked some guy had a $100 bill full of cocaine, sniffing away. Next to them there were drop-dead gorgeous women, waiting their turn to get high. I learned a lot in the Disco Fever about what girls will do for money and drugs. If you were a player with money, there was nothing you could not get into there. That's why the monte players loved to go there. We all had money to jerk. We all knew when we went to the Fever we were going to leave with something nice. If our game could not get the girl, our money would. Any monte player who got high, never stepped into that place without a bag full of cocaine. And, by the time he left, all the cocaine would be gone. That is how many drugs were taken at the Fever.

Who knows how much freebasing was going on in the other little rooms. Those rooms were reserved for the owner's friends and the celebrities who frequented the club. Sometimes I smelled freebase flowing through the air. It had an aroma of something stale and something fresh mixed together. I always tried my best to stay in the front, because I did not want to get a contact high from the vapors. I knew if they were freebasing in the Fever, then it had already made its way uptown.

By the time the price of cocaine dropped, people smoked crack all over the city and the ghetto areas did not know what was hitting them and were in for a rude awakening. But as for me, I was well aware of the devastation crack could cause, since I had already witnessed years before of what freebase had done to the players and pimps in Midtown.

9

Spring Time

"Hey, Spence, I think I'm ready to become a springer. I got the lug move down pat. All I have to do now is get behind the box and learn the gift of gab to sell the game to the vics."

"Man, Mike, I've been practicing the lug, but I just can't get it."

"Well, Spence, I can show you better than I can tell you. Let's go across the street to Little Clyde's game and watch him do the lug on a vic. Then, after that, I can show you step-by-step, how to do the damn thing. Understand me?"

We both laughed at my using Honey Combs' saying.

When we got to Little Clyde's monte game he had a big crowd as always. I wanted Spence to see Little Clyde in action because I had learned so much about the game from watching him. Clyde had such a smooth and calm style that vics could not help but get relaxed then fall under his hypnotizing spell. Their money quickly wound up as his money. He made the game look easy. You had the feeling that he had all the time in the world to get at the vics' money. Have you ever been in a store where they had relaxing music playing and then you found yourself buying more stuff than you intended? What you failed to realize was that the music had put you in a relaxed mode. That was like what Clyde's voice and style of play did to the vics. He put them in monte mode. As he beat vic after vic he eventually lugged the card and I showed Spence how Little Clyde quickly took the bend out of the card with his middle finger. After watching his technique a few times, we then headed back across the street and went into Playland so that I could show him how again, but more slowly.

Next to an unoccupied pinball game, I pulled out three cards and I showed him the fast way to take the bend out of the card. He could not get it. I did it over and over again, but he still could not get it. So, I did it slower and he still could not get it. I started to suspect something was not quite right. So, as I threw the cards, I found myself staring at him real hard because something was telling me he was under the influence of something. I started staring at him the way that I used to stare at my mother when she was under the influence of alcohol. As I threw the cards I felt myself becoming Spence as I went into a trancelike state of mind. *I was Spence over at the Grace building smoking skunk weed with some other player whose face I could not recognize. We lit up joint after joint, and I got higher and higher. When the weed was all gone. I asked the guy not to tell Mike I was smoking weed. The guy says, "Fuck, Mike. He ain't your father! You can do whatever the fuck you want." But, I still make him promise not to tell because I do not want Mike to find out that I have fallen victim to the drug epidemic.*

Next thing I knew, I was awakened out of my trancelike state by Spence saying, "Hey, Mike, what the fuck are you staring at? You bugging out?"

I said, "Sorry, man, I was just thinking about something. Let's stop practicing the lug and do it some other time."

Then I put the cards in my pocket and we walked outside. I felt myself getting depressed. Spence asked me what was wrong and I said, "Nothing, I'm all right".

"Well, Mike, you ain't acting like you all right. I'm your best friend. You can talk to me."

When he said that, I yelled, "Spence, you been fucking around with drugs and you wasn't man enough to tell me."

"What you mean, man? I haven't been messing with no drugs. All I did was smoke a little weed," he said, with a stupid expression.

I said, "Oh, you feel weed is not drugs? Next thing you're gonna be telling me is you sniffed a little coke, right?"

"Nah, Mike. It ain't like that. Reefer ain't habit-forming, like drugs."

"Spence, you and I know that you are talking stupid. Out of all the talks me and you had about our parents messing up their lives with alcohol, you still do not know any better. Did you forget that they first started to drink beer, then they moved on to vodka and gin or whatever? Have you forgotten about all the drama we have been through because of our parent's addictions? Still to this day we are going through it and you are going to stand here and make poor excuses about messing with drugs."

He looked dumbfounded because he knew everything I was telling him was true. So, he just shut up and walked off. He knew nothing he said was going to make me change the way I felt, which was good because I was so pissed off, I could have hit him. While all the monte players and hustlers and I stood by the Playland, a few of us watched Little Clyde's game across the street. His girlfriend, Lady Day, who was standing with us, spotted the monte cops, Big Red, and his black partner, Green Eyes, creeping up in the block trying to arrest him. She yelled, "Quick slide," and Clyde took off running, but Green Eyes was too fast for him and he jumped on Clyde's back and they both fell to the ground.

Green Eyes beat the living shit out of him. The way that he was punching and kicking Clyde, you would have thought that he killed ten people. If Big Red had not stopped Green Eyes, he would have killed him. All of this for just playing monte. After they put Clyde in handcuffs, Green Eyes ran across the street and slapped Lady Day so hard that his handprint was on her face.

He yelled, "Mind your fucking business, you stupid bitch!"

Just when he was getting ready to slap her again, Big Red yelled from the police car for him to come on.

Big Red is a Midtown North monte squad cop who had been down with the police force for twenty years. He looked like the western movie star John Wayne. Even though he busted monte players, he was the nicest person you could ever meet. He was a no-nonsense type of guy, but he treated everybody with respect. If he arrested a monte player, he always let them keep the money they won; he did not put it into evidence. And, if they happened to be hungry, he took them to the store before taking them to the precinct. Sometimes he would cut us a break and not even bust us. On the other hand, his partner Green Eyes, was an asshole, who should have been named Blue Eyes because he wanted so badly to be white. He was one of those black cops who despised his own blackness. He treated blacks worse than any racist white cop did. He did it to gain respect from white cops and to show them he did not give leniency to black criminals. If a monte player got busted by them, and Green Eyes processed the arrest, he would voucher all his money into evidence, after beating and slapping him. We knew Green Eyes was jealous because we made more money than he did. When he slapped Lady Day, it was like he had slapped all of us. And we felt bad that we could not defend her honor. Green Eyes knew that Lady Day was just trying to keep her man out of jail. The reason he slapped her was because deep down he was mad at the fact that he could not fuck her. You knew that was what he wanted to do by the way he was always checking her out. In fact, whenever he busted any of the female monte players, he always talked about how good he fucked and how big his penis was. Some people will lash out when they cannot get what they want.

I cannot stand to see a man hit a woman. It gives me flashbacks to when my mother's boyfriends used to hit her and I was too young to help her. Every time I saw a female getting hit, I had the urge to help. But, I know that a lot of times not minding your own business can get you into some serious trouble. But isn't it kind of strange that while I had the urge to play superhero for females, at the same time I saw nothing wrong with running trains on them? One minute I wanted to protect them and the next minute, I was abusing them physically with other guys. Twisted thinking.

Then there was the situation with Spence. I was stressed out about his use of marijuana because I knew all too well what drugs could do to a person's life. I was afraid that he was falling victim to something that was stronger than he was—and a million other people. But, the crazy thing about all of this is, at the same time I was upset about his drug use, I saw nothing wrong with giving drugs and alcohol to a female to fulfill my sick sex fetishes. Something was seriously wrong with my whole thinking process. But, who could I call on to help me sort all of this out? I could not go to any of the players because they would look at me like I was crazy for even trying to figure out all of my hypocritical nonsense. Maybe if people would just take time to figure out what makes them do certain things, it could prevent a lot of problems. Think about it—imagine if a man or woman thought about what they would do if they caught their partner having sex with another person. At least they could go over in their minds some of the scenarios that could play out with this type of situation. Doing this could possibly help save someone's life. Sometimes we act without thinking, which can get us in a whole lot of trouble. Think about all the times we have done something we wish we had not done and paid dearly for it. That is why I sometimes try to go over situations that could possibly happen to me. At least I could stand a chance of making it through some drama.

Everybody has their own way of going about things. I know even the cop, Green Eyes, has his own twisted reasons for doing what he did.

Some of the drug dealers I knew uptown told me stories about a cop named Crazy John who terrorized them. Sometimes when he busted them he gave them an option of either using all the drugs they were selling or going to jail. When I first heard about it, I could not understand why a cop would give them such a strange choice; it did not make sense. They told me some dealers would take him up on his offer and do the drugs. One guy got caught with a bundle of angel dust and decided to smoke it instead of going to jail. The guy bugged out and had to be taken to Bellevue Hospital. They said Crazy John laughed like he was ready for the looney bin. Another guy almost overdosed from fifteen bags of heroin when he took Crazy John up on his offer. When I heard these wild stories, I thought the cop was doing his own form of street justice, which he was, but not because he was a good cop who was trying to rid the ghetto neighborhoods of drug dealers. This was the furthest thing from the truth. He had personal reasons. I was told that he had a secret vendetta against drug dealers for selling dope to his dopefiend daughter who overdosed on drugs and died. He blamed all drug dealers for his daughter's death, which is why he offered the drug dealers he busted a choice of using the drugs they sold or jail. He figured most of them would choose to take the drugs, which could make them sick or wind up killing them. What a sick way of thinking. But, I bet you a lot of law-abiding people thought he was a good cop just trying to rid the neighborhood of drugs. You know like to protect and serve. This brings me back to my own conflicted thoughts.

Sometimes I want to do the right thing, but somewhere along the line, I find myself doing the wrong things. I am caught in the middle. Who will protect the vics who I plan to serve with a smile when I become a springer and beat them all out of their money? Even before I start to play, I already have the notion that a vic's money is *my* money. Who will protect all the women who will fall victim to my cunning ways once I accumulate more money and material things? Who will protect them as I serve them a plate of bullshit? Who will protect me from all the players and hustlers who will continue to fill my brain with even more negative things—things that will be detrimental to my upbringing and transition from a boy to a man? Who will?

* * *

My mother once told me, "Mike, when opportunity knocks, you better be there to open the door."

At the time she said it I was too young to understand what she was talking about. My mother had so many sayings that I could hardly keep up. She would say stuff like, "Mike, you are a man amongst men." Another one was "Mike, I love you just because." Although it took me a while to find out what her sayings meant, I soon caught on. That is why when I went downtown one morning and somebody told me Money Gus had gotten busted for monte last night, the first thought in my mind was my mother's saying about opportunity knocking.

I rationalized that because Gus was busted and I did not want to slide for anybody else, I might as well get a team together. Even before Gus had gotten busted, my thoughts had already been leading in the direction of becoming a springer. Some of the vics I had beaten on the side of three-card monte games could attest to this. One day I beat a guy on Forty-second and Fifth Avenue out of $840 after I tapped him on the shoulder, when he was watching from the back of a monte game. I pulled out my three cards and a wad of twenties and proceeded to get him interested in playing against me. He quickly found out that this little fifteen-year-old kid was good at the game. Cuban Joe, who sometimes schooled me on the tricks of the trade when we ate breakfast at the donut shop, started to stick and we beat the guy out of his $840. And, after that day, I knew it was only a matter of time before I would stop sliding and get my own team. I just needed my shot and that time was now. So, I asked Cuban Joe if he wanted to stick for me and he said yes.

I walked up to Lady Day, who was looking so good in her tight blue and white pants set, I could eat her. I asked her if she wanted to stick and she also said yes. I got Spence and Fronting Cee as my lookouts. I liked Fronting Cee because he made me laugh. He was a guy who took getting fly to another level. You know how when models have a fashion show and they change clothes for the runway. Well, Cee's runway was the streets. Cee changed his clothes three times a day. Plus, he was always flashing his money, just like Spence. That's why they called him Fronting Cee.

The first place we went was Forty-second Street and Fifth Avenue where I had beaten that vic out of the $840. Something was telling me we were going to make a lot of money today. I felt it in my bones. Just Lady Day's presence in my game would be enough to make the vics stop, plus Cuban Joe had more than forty years of experience playing monte. A player once told me that three-card monte, and prostitution were the two oldest professions and now I was about to add my two cents in.

When we arrived on Fifth Avenue, my lookouts set up the game and took their positions on each end of the block. As soon as I got behind the box, I started yelling the same things Money Gus always yelled: "Hey, New York, New York. I'm back. I'm back. Watch that red card, cherry, cherry, red like strawberry."

People gathered around as soon as I started throwing the cards. The next thing I knew, the vics were placing $40 bets left and right.

After about twenty minutes, Spence called a slide because the cops were riding by. During the slide, Cuban Joe pulled me to the side and told me I was doing well, but I had to raise the bets because the vics were ready for the taking. I knew Cuban Joe was right because I had not raised one vic for more money. So, right after Spence told me to spring 'em, I jumped behind the box. "Hey, New York, New York. I'm back, I'm back."

A big crowd had me surrounded in minutes. I raised the bets of every vic. I even won my first one hundred dollar bet. My sticks just smiled as I beat chump after chump. I had total command of the crowd. I felt I was born to do this. Three-card monte was my destiny because I had the voice of a Southern preacher, the hands of a magician and the gift to gab like a pimp. Yes, Midtown Mike is in your town, so gather around as I lay my game down.

After about forty-five minutes of playing on Fifth Avenue, the count was up to $640. I told my team that I wanted to go to Thirty-fourth Street, Money Gus' favorite part of town.

There, we set up shop by the Empire State Building. Little Clyde was playing a half a block away with a big crowd around him. With this crazy adrenaline rush I pulled out my cards and jumped behind the box. I guessed this was the same feeling that all monte springers felt when they stepped behind the box. I felt like heavyweight champion Muhammad Ali when he jumped into a ring, ready for battle. Only I did not want to beat my victims up, I just wanted their money. And, if they fell out after losing, so be it.

As I tossed the cards on the cardboard tray, and started talking the talk, a big crowd just instantly appeared—bigger than the one I had on Fifth Avenue. I was beating vics for forties and hundreds from every angle of the box. I looked in the back of the crowd and I spotted Little Clyde and Pamela smiling, as little old me did my thing. I was getting better and better as I went along.

This is just how I envisioned it all, as I lay down in my mother's apartment all those nights. I knew I wanted to be a monte player from the first time I saw Little Clyde playing across the street from Madison Square Garden. I was a 100 percent right in my element.

Fronting Cee called a slide because some undercover cops were trying to sneak on the block and bust us. I was glad that he called the slide because the money was coming in faster than I could count it. After a few slides we left Thirty-fourth street because it started raining.

So, we headed towards the donut shop, where my eyes lit up when we counted $1,680. Not bad for two hours of work. I was happy and elated until a few players walked into the shop and told me Johnny Ranks was dead.

10

Chain Reaction

Every so often something happened to remind the players in Midtown what a dangerous game we played and a crazy life we lived on these streets of bright lights. It could be somebody getting a beatdown or shot on The Deuce, or somebody dying from a drug overdose right in front of your eyes. Midtown offered many different things to many different people. To some, there was the fun and excitement to be had by going to Playland, movie theaters, Broadway shows and nice restaurants. But, there was a seedy part of Midtown that included drugs, gangs, cops, pimps, prostitutes and con men, who could take you for every dime. These were a few of the things that could lead to violence or even murder, which brings me back to Johnny Ranks.

Johnny was a hustler and a three-card monte player. I first met him when Spence and I used to hold him and Money Gus down while playing monte. Sometimes Johnny would stick, while Gus would spring 'em, then they would switch. Spence and I liked Johnny because he and Gus treated us with respect and never cheated us when it came down to the money. They were just like us, really close. We were like their younger brothers. We loved hanging with them during and after playing monte. Being out with them was a lot of fun, whether we were in Midtown or somewhere uptown. We never knew where we would wind up on any given day. One day we could be in a Dominican drug spot on 107th Street and Columbus where a drug dealer's enforcer might be playing with a 9mm gun on a couch. Or somewhere in Harlem watching Gus get high and act buck wild, while Johnny, the calm, laid-back one, kept him in check.

They brought that same fun and excitement to my life that Reggie did when I was a little kid. They took me to the same type of grown-up places he did—after-hour spots, gambling spots, drug houses, whorehouses, you name it.

Now Johnny was dead. The story goes Johnny loaned his expensive gold chain to a Dominican dude that he was cool with from uptown. They got into an argument about the chain in front of the donut shop and the guy pulled out a big knife and stabbed him. Johnny died from the wounds. He was killed all because of a gold chain.

I found all this out when I came back to the donut shop after I had stopped playing monte on Thirty-fourth Street because of the rain. Why is it when people die, it always seems to rain? Is it because God is crying for the dead? Through the years I have noticed that when my family members died, it always seemed to rain. It rained when I learned that my father died. I guess rain is a way that God calms the living, because watching rain come down can be a peaceful experience.

Memories of Johnny flashed through my mind as the raindrops hid my tears and the monte players continued to talk about his murder. I noticed Spence standing on the side crying. Then I thought, *Damn Gus is in jail and doesn't even know his homeboy is dead.*

Johnny used to love to sing "Ain't No Stopping Us Now" by McFadden and Whitehead. Sometimes I heard him humming the lyrics to it. When we hung out together, he would sing "Ain't no stopping us now, we're on the move. Ain't no stopping us now, we're on the move . . ."

Is a gold chain worth someone's life? Do people have to die because of disagreements? Can't we agree to disagree? Maybe if the guy who killed Johnny had taken a moment to think about the repercussions of taking someone's life, Johnny would still be alive. But, the sad part about it all is, the murderer probably did not care about his own life, so, how could he care about someone else's?

Johnny grew up a few blocks down from 169th Street on Webster Avenue. Like my cousin's block on 169th Street, the Webster Avenue projects were known for their fighters and tough guys. Sometimes either block would get into a little beef, but both blocks shared a mutual respect for one another. If they ever had a beef with some other people from another area, they both would band together to crush the problem. So, when I first met Johnny, and the other players told me he was from Webster projects, I knew from the start that he could not be soft.

I never saw him start trouble with anybody who did not deserve it. I knew Johnny beat a lot of people out of their money by playing monte, but they were trying to beat him, too. No one was an angel in this equation. Johnny was not perfect, but at the same time, he was not the devil.

I guess God only knows why Johnny was taken away from this earth so suddenly. They say, "When it's your time to go, it's your time to go." But, I have discovered that everyone deals differently with death. I have noticed that if a person dies of natural causes you can at least trick yourself into thinking the person died peacefully, as they paid their debt to the rules of nature. But when someone dies violently, you think the grim reaper snatched the person's body and soul without God's consent. Who on this earth has the right to take another person's life? No one except God, the ruler of all things and maker of all things, has that right.

People like to talk about breaking the chains that hold us back. But, it amazes me when I see us pulling each other down, for the minutest things, like money, greed, envy or jealously. People are killed everyday because others want what they have, but are too lazy to do what it takes to get it honestly.

There are even people who are jealous of people they don't even know. Many times one of my friends has told me about a person who doesn't like me, even though that person doesn't know me or has never had a conversation with me. What part of the game is this? Does all of this come about because of the person's low self-esteem? Does it play itself out through jealously and envy of me?

When I first came to Midtown and I saw all the hustlers looking good with their jewelry and material things, I was not jealous of them. I just told myself I had to do what they did in order to get what they had. So, I applied myself and made it happen. Now, Johnny Ranks was dead for something material, which is really immaterial to one's existence on this Earth.

As I watched the players go through different types of emotions— shock, surprise, sympathy, love and tears, deep down in my heart I knew that Johnny died with people loving him. I sing these words up to you Johnny: *"Ain't no stopping us now, we're on the move . . ."* *Rest in peace Johnny. We all will see you when we get there.*

P.S.: Can you please tell my father that I love him?

11

Tax Move

As I headed up the stairs of the Grace Building Park, I noticed a dice game with a bunch of monte players and some other hustlers. Chelsea, Honey Combs and Bones were sitting on park benches. I walked over to say what's up. After exchanging pleasantries, I sat down.

Grace Park was where the players would go after a long day of hustling. Every time I went there, I wanted to laugh because the first thing I'd see was a large glass sculpture with silicone dripping inside. It was supposed to be art. But, what it really looked like was gallons of semen dripping inside a giant glass box. So, as I sat there trying not to laugh, Chelsea asked me where I had just come from and I told him, "I just finished playing monte on Thirty-fourth Street."

Then he said, "Well, Mike, me and my comrades over here are just kicking it around and enjoying this beautiful day. Come holla at some players."

I nodded in agreement, and then looked at Bones and said, "Long time, no see."

Bones replied, "How's it going, brother man? I just came back from New Orleans with about five new hoes, I might add."

Honey Combs yelled, "Man, I better not catch you slipping with them hoes. "

"Shut up, Honey Combs, you know my game's too tight for that," Bones said.

Then Chelsea said, "Yo Bones, you know anybody's hoe can get it. The pimp game is all about cop and blow."

As they went back and forth about stealing another pimp's hoe, I just sat there listening because I knew I was going to learn something else about the pimp game.

Bones said, "Yeah, Chelsea, I know what you're saying, but I'd be damned if I am going to let one of these new jack-wanna-be-pimps fuck with any of my hoes. I'll shoot a motherfucker first."

As Bones was talking, I looked towards the dice game and noticed Eric Mack, who was a monte player and also a good fighter, arguing with a guy about a bet. Next thing you know the guy sucker-punched him. I thought, *Boy is that guy in for a good ass whipping.* The other players and I had watched Eric knock out so many so-called thugs in Midtown. Whenever he fought, I thought that Eric Mack had missed his calling. He should have been a professional boxer, instead of a monte player. He was that good at fighting. Honey Combs echoed my thoughts as he said, "Man, that nigga done fucked up now. Understand me?"

As soon as he said it, Eric Mack stepped back and hit the guy with a two-piece left and a right.

Chelsea and Bones kept talking because somebody fighting in Midtown was almost an everyday occurrence. People on the streets kicked ass and asked questions later. When money was involved, there was always a chance of a disagreement or misunderstanding that could lead to violence. So, as the fight continued, Chelsea and Bones talked.

"Bones, you still got that gorilla shit in you?" Chelsea asked.

"Man, Chelsea, it ain't all about that, but I ain't gon' take no shit from no motherfucker who don't know nothing about pimping. I'll live and die for this shit."

Chelsea said, "Yeah, Bones, I hear what you saying, but you and I both know you don't even fuck with no bum-ass hoes."

"Yeah, Chelsea, a bum bitch will always bring a good nigga down."

Then Honey Combs, who was paying attention to the fight yelled, "That's right Eric. Knock that bum-ass nigga out."

After Eric threw his punches, the guy staggered then threw about five fast punches, which Eric bobbed and weaved. By this time everybody who had been playing dice stopped to watch. I saw Saul and Fronting Cee taking bets on the fight with this guy named Poppa Doc, who sold drugs on The Deuce.

Poppa Doc was a jealous guy who hated monte players because we made more money than he did. Anytime I hung on The Deuce, we said, "What's up?" to one another, but I could see the hate in his eyes. So, I knew he was betting against Eric in the fight. All the while the fight was going on, the two pimps kept on talking.

Bones said, "Chelsea, let me tell you what happened to me right before I left for New Orleans. This new jack-wanna-be-pimp motherfucker, fresh off a bus in the Midtown bus terminal from God knows where, tried to steal one of my bottom hoes. The motherfucker thought because some bum bitches from where he was from, told him that he was handsome and game tight, he thought he could come to New York and lay down his so-called mack game. So, Chelsea, you know the crazy-man game we use to keep our hoes in check sometimes . . ."

Chelsea said, "Yeah, I just used it on Jackie a few days ago. Now the hoe is back on track."

"Well, brother, I pulled out 'old Betsy' my 38-snub-nose and beat that bitch-ass motherfucker, like the hoe he was."

Honey Combs who was still watching the fight said, "Man, did you give him the crazy bulging-eyes look while you kicked his ass?"

Bones said, "Yeah, Honey Combs, but not only did I do that, but I had the motherfucker so scared that he started crying like a bitch. He even told me he was sorry. So, you know what I had to do then."

I jumped into the conversation and said, "What did you do, Bones?"

Then he said, "I made the motherfucker sell ass right there on Forty-fourth Street and Eighth Avenue. The homo-motherfucker turned about two tricks, then he got scared and flagged down a police car, and was looking for me the whole night. My hoes told me that the cops wanted uh brutha for uh pandering charge. I left New York for uh little while and went to New Orleans."

Honey Combs said, "That's what bitch-ass wanna-be- pimps get. Understand me?"

Then I said, "Man, pimpin' really ain't easy." We all could not stop laughing.

"Yeah shorty, pimpin' ain't easy," Chelsea said.

Then Bones said, "You damn right."

While we sat there talking, the fight was still going on. Honey Combs yelled, "That's right, Saul, put your money on my man."

Saul smiled as he held two hundred dollars in his hands. After Eric ducked the other guy's punches, he caught the guy with a punch to the stomach. Next thing you know, the guy buckled over and Eric caught him with a vicious uppercut that put the guy right to sleep while standing up. *Bam!* He hit the floor, lights out. Honey Combs jumped up and ran over to Eric screaming, "That's my motherfucking man! Understand me?"

While Honey Combs pulled Eric's arms up in the air, like they do in prizefights, Poppa Doc, on the side, was paying off Saul and Fronting Cee, who had bet on him.

After the fight, the dice game started back up as the guy lay unconscious on the floor. It made me think about the club Disco Fever. This uptown club was so infamous, that whenever somebody was stabbed or even killed there, people still kept on partying while the owner waited for cops to arrive. Like the saying goes, one monkey doesn't stop the show. And, in Midtown, the same thing applied. The show must go on. A little fight, or even a murder, is not going to stop the players from doing what they do best, hustling. Nothing stopped our quest for that almighty dollar—not even murder.

Two months earlier, a player by the name of Cool Breeze, who I saw in a Harlem barbershop getting his hair, nails and toes done all at the same time, winked his eye at me as I said, "Play baby, play baby." Little did I know that some people play for keeps. He was killed right in this same park, all over a dispute in a dice game. Some guy stabbed him in the throat after arguing about a bet. Afterwards as Cool Breeze was bleeding everywhere, he ran across the crowded Sixth Avenue street and died inside a grocery store. But you know what? The dice game continued. So, like I said, not even murder can stop the wheels from turning in Midtown.

Honey Combs came back over to us and said, "Yo Mike, I know uh nigga seen that devastating knockout?"

I said, "Yeah man, Eric don't take no shit from anybody."

Then Chelsea said, "Eric's big brother, Ruck, taught that boy well. If you think Eric can fight, you should see his brother get down. I did a jail bid upstate with him and he was the jail's middleweight boxing champ.

Then Honey Combs said to Bones, "Did you take a bet on the fight?

Bones said, "Nigga please, I ain't got no time for no stupid fight shit. I'll just put a bullet in a nigga's ass."

Then Honey Combs said, "Yo Chelsea, that mobster nigga still fucking with you about your top broad Jackie?"

Chelsea replied, "Man, Honey Combs, the girl's father is all up in my shit. He told me if I don't leave his daughter alone, he's gonna kill me. But you know what? I ain't scared of no white motherfucker."

Chelsea turned to me and said, "Little shorty, pimpin' ain't easy."

Honey Combs said, "Understand me?"

Then Bones said, "I second that emotion. Understand me?"

And we all laughed as we yelled, "Understand me?"

I stayed chilling with the pimps awhile, then decided to take a walk by the donut shop. I told everybody I would catch up with them later.

On my way out of the park, Poppa Doc came up to me and said with a sly and conniving look on his face, 'Let a nigga hold ten dollars."

I promptly told him, "No, we don't get down like that."

This made him angry, but he kept it moving. The one thing that caught my attention in what had just transpired is, he wasn't asking to borrow the money. It was more like—give me the money. This made me realize it was a tax move.

A tax move is equivalent to a student being tested by the school bully.

"Hey, loan me five dollars!"

The student says, "Nah, man, no I ain't got it."

Then the bully says, "All I find. All I keep." It's a back door robbery.

Asking for five dollars is a test and if the student gives it up, he will have to give the bully money every time they meet. The key to putting an end to a tax move is to stop it before it starts. When I was younger, the way I accomplished this was to tell bullies who tested me that I was broke, while hiding my money in my sock. In order not to lose, I cried the blues. But, I was older and wiser now, and I approached tax moves differently by letting it be known that I would not be taken advantage of. And, if I had to "take it to the streets," so be it. I say, if you let someone rob you once, they will rob you twice. The problem just escalates. On the streets, people take kindness for weakness. I, myself, felt it was better to take an ass-whipping than to let someone take advantage of me. At least you walked away with your dignity and pride intact. Just by the way Poppa Doc looked at me when I did not give him any money, I knew I would have to watch my back because he was a real shady dude and was capable of anything. So, as I walked towards the donut shop, I kept this in mind.

When I got there, a bunch of monte players were standing around. There was Big-Head Louie; Little Glenda, who I heard took $6,000 earlier; Eve and Lady Day, who always gave me a tingly feeling somewhere in my lower extremities; plus, a bunch of other players.

I said, "Yo Louie, did you take a lick today?"

"Nah, Mike, I'm trying to get a team together. You want some work?"

I said, "Nah, I was down earlier. I took $3,700."

Then Louie said, "Mike, where did you just come from?"

I said, "Oh, I was over by the park. There's a big dice game going on. Eric Mack just knocked some nigga out. The dude was still sleeping, when I left. Yo, I know you read that article on the front page of the *Daily News* about your homeboy, Criss Boss."

"Yeah, Mike. They say Criss Boss killed about ten people in that house in Brooklyn."

"Yeah, ain't that some shit. Plus he did it on Valentine's Day. They were calling it the St. Valentine's Day Massacre."

"Man, Louie, I remember when me, you, Gus and Johnny were hanging in the Bottom Line on 167th Street, one night. Y'all was gambling with him. Man, that brother was betting thousands in his pajamas and slippers. I thought something was up with him, then."

"Yeah, Mike, you got a point. Criss was a brother who just didn't give a fuck."

"You know, Louie, didn't Lady Day used to fuck with him?"

"Yeah. They used to kick it around." Then he said, "Mike, let me go and ask Lady Day and Eve if they want some work."

"All right. You take it easy. I'll catch you later."

I thought, *Damn, why do all the pretty girls like the real ill motherfuckers?* You see it all the time—some dime chick messing around with some cold-hearted thug. Maybe it's their need to feel protected. They know if somebody fucks with them, their thug boyfriend will go for the guns. There are a lot of brothers in jail right now because they tried to play the thug role with some new honey they just met. The girl gets into some beef with some guy, then she goes and gets *Captain-Save-A-Hoe,* who's been faking the thug role for way too long. She tells him some motherfucker just slapped me for no reason. So, the so-called thug borrows a gun from his man, because now, he has to live up to the thug role he's been playing. Then he goes and hunts down the guy who slapped his so-called girl. He eventually finds the guy and kills him.

One week later, when he's sitting in a jail cell, he calls his homeboy and his homeboy schools him to the fact that the girl had played him for a fool. She was fucking the guy he killed all along. Ain't that some shit?

I decided I would play my position and not fall for the okey doke. I was a bona fide hustler, not a thug, and what do hustlers do—they rest, dress and progress. Nowadays too many brothers wanted to perpetrate a fraud. I said, play your position. If you were a player, be a player. If you were a gangster, be a gangster. If you were a pimp, be a pimp. But, if you were a pussy, then damn it, be a cold pussy.

While standing by the donut shop, I spotted Little Bit and said, "Yo, Little Bit, what's going on?"

He said, "Man, Mike, me and brother had to beat the living shit out of this vic earlier. The vic lost about $650 and he wanted his money back. We gave him something back, which was a well-deserved ass-whipping, Brooklyn-style.

Peanut said, "Baby pa, you seen how me and my homeboys get down? When we kick a nigga's ass, he knows his ass been kicked."

I said, "Yeah, Peanut, I saw how you and Little Bit, just two deep, beat a vic down that time on Broadway."

Peanut said, "Yeah, we lays it down. Mama ain't raise no chumps."

Little Bit said, "Yo Mike. Let's go get some liquor."

So, Little Bit, his brother, Peanut, and Jiggy, a Puerto Rican guy, and I headed to the liquor store where we bought a gallon of Bacardi. We sat in the little park with a water fountain across the street from the donut shop and got drunk. I guess I decided to drink this time because I really liked Little Bit and his brother, and we did not get to hang out often, due to the bump and grind of chasing the almighty dollar. I was high after the first drink.

I started to get real mellow, which made me bring up the time Little Bit and I got busted for monte and they took us to the family court central booking because we were both under sixteen, and not yet old enough for the criminal courts. All the young prisoners had to stand on a long line before being put into a big cell. Arnold, a correction officer with a big bald head, was running down the rules of central booking before he checked for contraband. While he was talking, I was running my mouth with Little Bit. All of a sudden, CO Arnold came up and slapped the living shit out of me. The slap was so loud it shook the walls. All the prisoners laughed all the way to the cell.

I was not the only one who got laughed at. CO Arnold told one of the inmates it was time to go home, so the inmate proceeded to walk past him. CO Arnold asked, "Where the fuck do you think you're going, asshole?" The prisoner responded, "You said I could go home." CO Arnold replied, "Yeah, get yo dumb ass in that cell." Peanut howled with laughter, which made me tell the story about one New Year's Eve when I and some other hustlers from The Deuce were selling fake cocaine to white boys. There we stood in the middle of Times Square, where thousands of people were waiting for the ball to drop, making a drug transaction with the white boys. As soon as they passed me the money, a white plainclothes cop cold-cocked me. *Boom!* I went down like a sack of potatoes. At the same time the cop punched me, the clock was striking midnight for the New Year 1980. While the big ball's lights were flashing and people were blowing horns and saying Happy New Year, I was on the ground, with a big lump on my eye, seeing stars.

After sitting there for about two hours enjoying the night life and having fun, we all got drunk to the next level. The Bacardi was almost gone, so we went and got another bottle. Then, we headed to Broadway, where we drank and messed with every girl who walked by. I was so drunk by this point, all I could do was mumble as the bright lights of Midtown blurred my vision even more. We ran into Big Burke, Big-Head Louie and Glenda, on Forty-fifth and Seventh Avenue. When they saw how drunk we were, they could not stop laughing. Little Glenda said, "Mike, this is the first time I've seen you high. Boy you're gonna have a hangover tomorrow."

I looked at her and said, "Damn, Glenda, you looking real good tonight."

She said, "Ah, Mike, you know you ain't ready for this."

I said, "Uh-uh. Glen . . .Glen"

"Man, look at you, Mike. You can't even say my name. But, you know what . . . if you was ready for me, I would have you calling my name, 'cause I'd have your ass whipped."

Everybody laughed, but I was so high, I could barely understand the words she was saying. All I heard was laughing and all I smelled was horseshit, as this big cop on a brown and white horse galloped by. Why is it that when you get real high, different senses take over? My sense of smell was ten times more than it normally would be. I guess when you're talking a lot of shit, you're bound to start smelling it.

12

Manhattan, Make It; Brooklyn, Take It

In Midtown there was no Mr. Rogers singing "It's a Beautiful Day in the Neighborhood." No siree. But, what you did have on Broadway were Sunni Muslims preaching about what the so-called white devils were doing to black people. You had Hare Krishnas in their orange robes and sandals, chanting while they gave out rice cakes. You might even see a guy walking by with a sign claiming the world was going to end, or a homeless guy with a sign, which read CURSE ME OUT FOR A DOLLAR. In Midtown you learned rather quickly not to trust anyone. Believe nothing of what you hear and half of what you see. You could not even trust the so-called blind man begging for money with his seeing-eye dog.

I often saw a man I thought was blind and I gave him money every time I saw him on Broadway. One day I spotted him without his dark sunglasses and his dog. He was headed into a movie theatre on Seventh Avenue. I was so mad that I yelled to him, "Hey motherfucker! You tricked me! You're not even blind!" He continued inside the movie theater as he laughed his head off. After that, every time I saw him begging on Broadway with his seeing-eye dog, he gave me a sly wink and a head nod as if to say, "The joke's on you, Jack!"

In Midtown you could not trust a big butt and a smile because you might think it was woman that you were looking at, but sometimes it was a man. And, if you happened to find yourself on Ninth or Tenth Avenue, you would see drag queens, transvestites and male prostitutes looking for a good time. If that's what you call a good time, be my guest.

Ninth Avenue was not the only place that sick stuff happened. Nothing turned my stomach more than the time I saw a woman sucking a dog's dick right on The Deuce, as people stood watching. While she performed this sick act, the owner of the dog stood there smiling with this stupid look on his face. I wanted to do some serious damage to this asshole. But, in Midtown, you learn to mind your business because the person that you are trying to help can turn on you.

How many times have I seen a stranger beating the shit out of his girlfriend and some other guy trying to come to the girl's rescue? Then, the couple turns around and tries to beat *him* up. People have been killed in these types of situations.

On any given day, I did not know what I would encounter on the mean streets. I saw whores being beaten merciless with guns, clothes hangers or anything that the pimp could get his hands on. After leaving his whore's body bruised and bloody, (a pimp never touches his whore's face because he does not want to scare the tricks off), he would then switch his personality to seem like the nicest man in the world. A lot of mind games were played on these streets.

I have even seen people running buck naked through the streets, from God knows where. I have seen beatings, stabbings and shootings in broad daylight. There were even some monte players who fell victim to this. If these things can happen in the daytime, you know what happens at night. The freaks and thugs really do come out at night. I saw a Puerto Rican guy on The Deuce spit a razor blade out of his mouth and slice another guy from ear to ear—all because he felt like doing it. I suspected it was because the guy looked better than he did.

I once saw Roscoe throw a vic through a window. He went to jail and the vic went to the hospital. Yes, if you were looking for some adventure in your life, Midtown was the place to be.

Manhattan was one big cesspool of many races and nationalities. Some came from different cities and states, while others came from the five boroughs—Bronx, Manhattan, Brooklyn, Queens and Staten Island. They came to Midtown for various reasons.

The hustlers I knew came for the many opportunities to make a fast buck from all the illegal activities that Midtown had to offer, like con games, robbery, shoplifting, jostling, prostitution, scalping tickets, just to name a few. These hustlers were looking for the American dream, but with other people's money. A lot of the criminal element was looking for a free ride, so they came to Midtown to make money by any means possible. So, anyone walking around out there with his head in the sky became an automatic target for anybody looking to make a fast buck. If you walked on The Deuce, somebody might take your money and possibly your life.

No area in the city was worse than The Deuce. On any of the streets someone is looking to pick your pocket, snatch your money or rob you for any valuables you might have. The criminal element always keeps a sharp eye out for any tourists carrying cameras or wearing expensive jewelry. At night the stickup kids from Brooklyn run around twenty deep, snatching anything they can get their sticky hands on. Lord help you if you were caught up in their mix. Imagine being robbed and beat down by twenty money-hungry guys. It would be equivalent to jumping into the ocean with a school of hungry piranhas—you would be eaten alive.

Even I, and all the monte players and hustlers, knew to get out of Dodge City when Brooklyn was on the prowl. No one was exempt from getting robbed by them. Sometimes Little Bit and some of the other guys we knew from Brooklyn would let us know beforehand that a lot of their thug homeboys were coming downtown, posse deep, and they were going to rob anybody in sight. "Manhattan make it, Brooklyn take it." On those days we all would make our money early, then get out of town, just like in the westerns. Little Bit was schooling us, which was good looking out!

Spence and I always laughed at a baby-faced guy named Little Infinite who looked about ten-years old but was really fifteen. Little Infinite was a pickpocket from Brooklyn. I guess he chose jostling as a profession because his hands were so small no one could tell if he was going into their pockets. We laughed every time we saw him standing by the donut shop wearing a pair of fake British Walkers and pants with V-flaps on the back pockets. At the time we thought these were funny looking pants, but later, we realized they were some fly tailored pants that all the Brooklyn guys wore. Just like the Bronx and Harlem had their styles, Brooklyn had its, too. But, all the time while we stood there trading snaps with Little Infinite, we never thought about different boroughs having different styles.

Little Infinite never took our snapping to heart. He just snapped back. But, all of our snapping came to an abrupt halt when one day we saw him with about forty of his homeboys from Brooklyn, running buck wild throughout Midtown on a robbing spree.

As time went by we eventually got to meet his thugged-out brother Charlie Rock. I got along well with him and we talked from time to time. But, one look at his wild eyes, and you knew he was a killer. Every time I looked in his eyes, I saw death.

One time I was outside Disco Fever in the Bronx with Dayton from 169th Street, who stole cars for a living. We were standing by his

Lincoln Continental. Let me rephrase that, let me say, not his but owner unknown. All of a sudden Charlie Rock pulled up in a new black Mercedes Benz and got out. I started to talk to him because I had not seen him in a long time. While we stood there, a shiny blue Porsche pulled up and the tinted window came down. Next thing you know a guy with a bald head sitting on the passenger seat, shot at Charlie Rock. This really meant he was shooting at everybody because bullets had no names on them.

Everybody who was standing there ran for cover. Dayton and I ran across the street into a gas station, while Charlie Rock jumped into his car and exchanged gunfire with the guys in the Porsche. For a few minutes it was like the O.K. Corral. Bullets were flying everywhere. After about ten minutes of hiding in the gas station, we went to Dayton's car. A bullet had hit the glass on the passenger's side. The glass was shattered, but the tinted film on the window held it together. Had I been sitting in the car, I would have been dead, because the bullet hole lined up with the exact spot of where my head would have been. Man, I could have been killed by a bullet meant for somebody from Brooklyn.

*   *   *

Some of the best boosters in the city came from Brooklyn. They could get whatever you needed from a store: clothes, shoes, fur coats, jewelry—you name it, they could get it. All you had to do was put in your order and they would come back with it. The Brooklyn boosters always worked with you on the price and they never tried to overcharge anybody. I bought a lot of polo shirts and expensive clothes from them. These boosters were so good they could steal something that was linen and bring it back to you without wrinkles.

A young guy named Jackie, who was a monte player and booster, always sold a lot of nice stuff that he boosted to us. Before he sold to anybody else, the monte players and other hustlers got first dibs on his merchandise.

But Jackie and Spence could not get along. They always argued about one thing or another. One time Jackie was busted for boosting and he went to jail for sixty days. When he came out, he was talking funny and swishing just like a lady. Spence told him, "Ah-hah, just like I suspected. I knew you were taking it up the ass all along."

This made Jackie real mad and he took a swing at Spence. They fought like Ali and Foreman in the *Thriller of Manila,* but without the rope a dope, because Spence was scared to let the newly found-out homosexual touch him. As the Midtown hustlers and bystanders gathered around watching them fight, the two fought the funniest fight I had ever seen in Midtown. And, boy did I see some fights out there.

Spence kicked Jackie's ass real good. Ernie Bowen and Stewart had taught Spence how to fight, so, Spence knew how to use his hands. After the fight, Spence swore that Jackie had tried to touch his ass during the fight. He was so mad, he yelled, "That's why your mother named you Jackie because she knew you were meant to be a girl." Jackie became enraged and he chased Spence all over Midtown with a rusty ice pick.

While I am on the subject of ice picks, one thing you find out really fast is to never start trouble with the drag queens and transvestites. They always carried knives, guns and rusty ice picks. The reason they kept the ice picks rusty was because when they stabbed someone with it, the poison from the rust could kill. The drag queens and transvestites never really bothered anybody, but if you messed with them, out came their equalizers. Some guy was always trying to prove his manhood by messing with them. But in his ignorance and stupidity he failed to realize that it was a man and not a woman he was messing with. Some of the transvestites and drag queens were tall and strong. Just because a man wears a dress does not mean that he has lost his ability to kick somebody's ass. My mother used to say, "Play pussy and get fucked." The drag queens made those guys turn into little pussies.

In Midtown, I witnessed, too many times, a big guy starting trouble with a little guy. The big guy would find out he wrote a check that his ass could not cash. The little guy would jump into some karate stance and commence to kick the big guy's ass. Like they say, "Looks are deceiving." That's why when you fuck with someone who is not fucking with you, you can wind up the person who gets fucked. Bullies always meet their match.

I will not put the posses who come to Midtown from Brooklyn in the bully category or make excuses for them running the streets robbing people, just like I should not make excuses for us beating people in three-card monte. But, the truth is the truth. Those guys are just like me or any other person who comes from bad situations and struggling neighborhoods. If you do not have the proper guidance to help you along in life, you are forced to try to adapt to your dreadful circumstances. Sometimes you can get caught up in negative things as you try to find a way out. We are products of our environment.

You can tell it was rough in Brooklyn just by their sayings such as, "Do or die, Bed Stuy," or "I'm from Brownsville and I never ran and never will," or "I'm from Red Hook, where you get your booty took." Even though Brooklyn had good and bad areas, just hearing any of their sayings would make a person scared to even step in the borough. If you went into some of the rougher neighborhoods of Brooklyn, they could tell immediately if you were not from there. If you were from Manhattan, Queens, Harlem or the Bronx and you went to visit somebody in Brooklyn, you would stick out like a sore thumb—because Brooklyn had its own way of talking, walking and dressing.

Whenever Little Bit or any of the hustlers I knew from Brooklyn asked me to hang with them around their block, I always declined the invitation. I heard many stories about some guy who went there to pick up some girl he met at a club and the story ended with a beating and a robbery. Guys from Brooklyn did not take kindly to a guy from another borough trying to have sex with the girls that they themselves wanted to bone. Picture this: Mr. Smoothe from the Bronx, pulls up to the Pink Houses projects in Brooklyn. He gets out of his shiny new BMW, looking sharp in his fine threads and all his best jewelry. He takes one last look at himself in his car window and says to himself, *I'm looking good and today's my lucky day.* Then, he heads to the building of Mrs. Dimepiece who he met last week in a club. As he walks in the building he notices a few unsavory-looking characters standing in front of the doorway. He tries his best not to make eye contact, but they stare him down, hoping to spot any sign of fear or weakness. When he gets to Mrs. Dimepiece's apartment, he receives an urgent 911 beeper page. Then he immediately asks the lovely lady if he can use her phone. But, she tells him it is not working, but there is a phone on the corner. So, Mr. Smoothe from the Bronx goes downstairs to make his urgent phone call. When he dials the number, a recorded message says the number he has dialed has been changed to an unlisted number. As soon as he hangs up the phone he wonders what all that was about. Next thing he knows, ten thugs are pouncing on him, beating the living shit out of him and taking his money and valuables. What he quickly finds out is, he was set up Brooklyn-style. Mrs. Dimepiece had given the thugs his beeper number before he arrived to pick her up. There's a sucker born every minute.

I was playing monte one day on Thirty-fourth Street when I met a lovely young lady who had become infatuated by my monte skills and the jewelry I had on. In her mind, she must have been thinking this guy's a moneymaking hustler, and I was thinking with my bottom head. This girl had the face of an angel and a body to die for.

After I finished playing monte, the lovely young lady and I went to the movies with Rowan, a Jamaican guy who I had sticking for me that day. Afterwards, the three of us went to his apartment in Brooklyn. The stick kept telling me that the girl looked freaky and he knew she would be down for an orgy. I let him think what he wanted, but something was telling me she was not that type of girl. When you run the streets, you get to learn these types of things.

When we got to his apartment, he tried to run his weak mack game down, but the girl and I could not stop laughing at his feeble attempts. Sometimes even when you want to stop laughing, you can't. So, after he tried and tried without any results the girl and I went to his bedroom to have sex. I had already gone into the bathroom and sprayed my penis with the old reliable Stud 100. As we boned in every position possible on his bed, two big eyeballs stared at us though a crack in the door. This only made me go into porno mode and stroke her like a real man should. After we finished, he came into the room and continued his weak mack game, but to no avail. When he saw his game was not working, he kept asking me in his Jamaican accent, "What do ya tell her, Mike? What do ya tell her? I know ya tell her not ta give me no sex, because ya wanted her all ta yourself."

I howled because what he said was not true. The girl just did not want to fuck two guys. He got so mad that he kicked both of us out of his apartment. When we got outside, she tried to get me to go to her apartment in Queens. I refused and I gave her train fare to get home, while I jumped in a cab and headed to the Bronx. I suspected that she was mad that I put her on the train. But, I had on about $7,000 worth of jewelry and I didn't want to take a chance riding the train and getting robbed.

After that day, I called her a few times and she kept trying to get me to go to Queens where she lived. But I always flipped the conversation and tried to get her to meet me in Midtown. I sensed something was fishy, so I stopped calling her. Two weeks later I was standing on The Deuce with some other hustlers, and who did I see walking down the block hand-in-hand with a tall muscular dude with huge arms and a mean face like the boxer Joe Frazier? None other than the girl I boned in Rowan's apartment. As they walked by me, I thought, *That's why she tried so hard to get me to Queens. She wanted me to meet Mr. Olympia himself, Queens' undisputed weightlifting champ, so he could rob me and use me for strength exercises.* No siree, Midtown Mike was not born yesterday. Before she even asked me to go to Queens, I already knew not to get caught out there.

Some of the hustlers who lived in Queens told me that a lot of guys from Queens often imitated guys from Brooklyn. They tried to walk, talk, dress and act like them. I saw many fights in Midtown over this. The reason I think Queens imitated Brooklyn is because both boroughs were so close that it was only natural that they did some of the same things. Brooklyn did not feel that imitation is the best form of flattery.

When I talk about Brooklyn and Queens it's not like I am trying to paint a broad brush over everybody who lives in these boroughs. I'm just talking about some of the people that lived there, not everybody. You have the good, the bad and the ugly in all five boroughs—just like Midtown has the same things. That's why we all came together to make beautiful music. Can't you just hear the music and the words " . . . *if you can make it there, you'll make it anywhere? New York, New York . . .*"

13

Floss

Ever since my youth, I was always fascinated by fashionable attire, jewelry and, of course, the female persuasion. Anytime I saw someone looking fly in their nice clothes, new sneakers and jewelry, I envisioned myself wearing the same things. I remember when people first started wearing the silver or gold Jesus and Saint Barbara house medallions. If you had one of those you were a bad motherfucker. But, all I had that was worth more than gold was my will and drive to succeed. So I was forced to play the background until I found a way to acquire what I wanted.

When Spence and I started to make money scalping tickets and playing three-card monte, the first things I bought were nice clothes and kicks: Pro-Keds and Clyde Frazier Puma sneakers, especially the blue and white or red and white ones. I also had so many pairs of British Walkers, that I stopped counting. Whatever color or style came out, I had to have it. I had the latest jeans—Lees, Sergio Valente's, Oscar de la Renta's. Boy, did I look fly when I wore my new British Walkers, fly jeans and the sheepskin or Cortifield coats. I had to have the matching hats and gloves. Spence was my hustling partner and we damn near thought alike. We both had Caesar haircuts and wore Mike and Spence name buckles. Man, when we came around the block with those, our homeboys almost lost their minds.

During this period, my fake nylon boxers sets from the Jew man store turned into AJ Lester Paris nylons; my sterling silver house medallions turned into a gold and diamond $3,500 name plate; my pea coats turned into butter-soft leathers; my ten speed bikes turned into motorcycles; and riding around in cabs turned into owning luxury cars.

I remember when I bought the gold house medallion and I met this pretty girl at a DJ Grandmaster Flash jam at Echo Park on Arthur Avenue in the Bronx. These jams used to always be packed with people. There was always gunfire when the music got too good. They used to yell, "Casanova, All Over, Casanova, All Over," and then there would be gunshots and everybody would scatter.

I was in the park with my homeboys from 169th Street, my cousin Bud, Spence, Mitchell, Denny Jackson and a few others when I spotted a pretty brown-skinned girl with a nice ass hanging with a few other girls. I was looking fly in my burgundy suede British Walkers, Oscar de la Renta jeans, burgundy short-sleeve mock neck and my Mike name belt. I had a fresh Caesar haircut and a pocket full of money and was wearing my gold house medallion. I was looking sharp and I knew it. And being that I was not scared to talk to any girls except China (who made me nervous), I walked over to them and I kicked the usual game of, "How are you doing? What's your name? And where are you from?" (Sorry, Biggie Smalls!) Kathy gave the usual answers with a big Kool-Aid smile and I knew she was mine. Then she introduced me to her girlfriends, and they all looked me up and down while smiling.

One of her friends, Tina, was a pretty Puerto Rican girl with long hair and a breathtaking smile. The way she looked at me, I knew I could have her, too. So, I told myself after getting with Kathy, Tina would be my next prospect. After that day at the jam, Kathy and I got together and had sex numerous times.

One time I ran into Tina at the T-Connection Ballroom where DJ Afrika Bambatta was jamming. We talked and I bought her drinks and marijuana to smoke. We danced all night, then I took her to the Bronx Park Motel and had sex with her. Not long afterwards, Kathy found out that I fucked her friend and she got real mad at me. But, it did not stop her from asking to wear my gold house medallion. I saw right through her conniving plan. She wanted to get revenge by borrowing my medallion, and t hen pretending she had been robbed. Fast girls in the 'hood ran this scam on numerous so-called players.

But, she failed to realize I was a monte player and I conned people for a living. So, when she tried her little charade, I had sex with another one of her friends and I cut her off. Boy was I a piece of work!

Not too long after that I bought a gold-and-diamond Mike medallion, which cost me $3,500. If you think a little gold house medallion caused me some trouble, you can only imagine what type of drama this piece caused.

On the day I went to buy it, a strange thing happened. I left my mother's apartment with the $3,500 and a piece of paper with a drawing of the medallion. When I got to the train station the train was pulling in, but I did not have time to buy a token, so I tried to sneak on. As soon as I jumped the turnstile, a police officer arrested me. He took me in a little room and checked my pockets.

He asked me why I was carrying so much money, so I showed him the piece of paper with the drawing of the medallion. I told him I was on my way to a jeweler in Midtown. I explained to him that I never sneak on the train, but I was running late and I did not have time to buy a token. The part about never sneaking on the train was a lie. The cop laughed at my story, wrote me a summons and let me go. So, it was drama from day one, when it came to that medallion.

My medallion was a big, round thick gold plate with 120 little diamonds around it. On the top of the plate was Mike in white-gold Chinese letters with diamonds. In the middle of the piece was a thick, rocky white-gold scale with diamond ten-pointers in it. On both sides of the scale were dollar signs in diamonds. That medallion was so nice that when I wore it, my heart beat fast. I also had my other diamond and gold rings and bracelets. The diamonds in my jewelry sparkled so much they could blind you. When I wore my jewelry, people commented on how nice everything looked. I was only seventeen years old.

The same big Kool-Aid smile that Kathy showed me, I got from females all the time. They knew immediately that this young kid was into something. When I was in floss mode, I wore all of my jewelry on the streets and in the clubs because when I put it on, people noticed me.

What I am about to tell you might be taken as conceit, but it is true. I never had problems meeting women because not only did I have all of the materialistic things, but I also had a baby face and many women found me handsome.

When I started making fast money in Midtown, I could afford anything I wanted. Picture a teenager making between $400 and $1,000 or more a day for himself after splitting up the day's monte winnings with his team. This was a lot of money for a kid to have at his disposal. Then picture a smooth but hyper kid who was very impressionable, hanging with con men, pimps, prostitutes and other characters all day long. This added up to a lot of drama, and misconceptions about life and women. The more money I made, the more women got laid. All while I was making fast money, I did not have the slightest idea of how to treat a woman. I learned everything from my Midtown family. The things they taught me about life, money and women were the things that I used to guide me in my everyday endeavors. At the time, I did not know if what they told me was good or bad. I just went along with everything. The only way I was going to learn was by living and learning.

I often try to understand my mistreatment of women. Did it stem from me not growing up with a positive male role model? Or was it because throughout my childhood, I never witnessed a woman being treated with respect, love and kindness. It wasn't just in our house, I never saw any of my friends' mothers or my female family members treated with respect. My mother's boyfriends, who came after my father died, were full of shit. They verbally and physically abused her. Ma-Ma, finally got to the point where she stabbed them with kitchen knives. I am talking about the sweetest most kindhearted women you could imagine. How is a young boy without the proper guidance going to learn by himself? This is why most of my knowledge on dealing with females came from my Midtown family.

Now that I think about it, before I went to Midtown, I already had problems dealing with females. My sister and I used to fight because I told her what to do. She got tired of this and one day she grabbed a dustpan and whacked me across the face. I learned to give orders from my mother's boyfriends and those same orders got me whacked across the face. I bled everywhere and have a little scar on the side of my nose. But she loved me and I could not stop my sister from joining in my street fights outside.

Another thing I learned from the men that I hung around was how to use women for sexual pleasure. Good old cousin Reggie was the first to teach me this; I watched him have sex in my mother's living room. After observing Reggie's freak shows, I tried to do the same things to any girl who spent the night at our apartment. When one of my sister's friends or our cousins Jenee and Sylvia came over, the biggest Kool-Aid smile would show up on my face. The reason being, I knew by nightfall, I was going to get my hump on. I would jump into bed with both of them, humping on one and feeling on the other one. My sister would get mad and threaten to tell Ma-Ma but she could be bought off with a pack of Now or Later candy.

By the time I made it to P.S. 67 elementary school, I was skilled in the art of humping. In the classroom, I did not use the closet for my coat. I used it for humping. I got caught so many times by my teacher that they eventually called my mother and she promptly whipped my ass in front of my classmates, but that never stopped me from getting my hump on.

One time I happened to be with Ruger, a little gang member who was down with the Black Spades Gang. The Black Spades were around my block, and all the little kids were scared of them, including me. Ruger was in my class, so one day we played hooky from school and we humped on a girl in the basement of a building. This is the same guy who used to try to get his fellow gang members to steal my lunch money. Every time that I hustled in the supermarkets, I had to dodge him and his gang homies, to avoid hearing the ghetto stickup man's anthem of "All I find, all I keep" as they attempted to rob me.

I wound up around some pretty strange characters during my childhood. As I became a teenager, I moved on to new characters—con men, pimps, prostitutes—with names like Jiggy, Bones, Big-Head Louie, Flaco and Honey Combs.

14

Two of a Kind

I first spotted her picking pockets on Forty-seventh Street and Broadway. She was in the process of going in a woman's pocketbook while a Cuban guy played the shield. I had seen the guy many times all over Midtown plying his jostling trade, and he was real good. So, I knew the girl had to be, too.

She was about five feet, six inches, light-skinned with light brown eyes, a nice chest, sleek thighs and a fat ass. She had a look about her that screamed sex, and if you ever had the chance to get with her you'd better be ready for one hell of a ride. Her complexion was as smooth as the caramel-covered cakes that my aunt Mamie made and that I could never get enough of. She looked like a younger version of the porn star, Vanessa Del Rio.

I just knew I had to have this radiant brick house of a woman. Being in the presence of this attractive female kept me from thinking straight. My rational thinking was going out the window and was replaced by things that had more to do with the physical and less to do with the mental. When I should have been wondering if she's was really the right one for me, instead I was stuck on "stupid," thinking. I wondered, *Man, what type of panties does she have on? Or what color bra, or I wonder if she has a tight pussy?*

This was all a bunch of bullshit. What about her character, background, upbringing and her goals in life? That was what I should have been thinking about. But right now I was horny and hot. I didn't have time to be bothered with such deep issues when I had other things that needed my immediate attention, like her body calling me. And, if I did not answer the call, another brother would. A strong vibe sent me signals that she was trouble, but I just had to have her. I

125

was not thinking with my top head. I was thinking with my bottom head, which yielded a lot of power in a lot of my decisions.

Although I loved all different types of complexions, when it came to women, my first preference was light-skinned. I guess I was brain-washed from watching all those black exploitation movies when I was younger. All the beautiful women in those movies were light-skinned. So, as I stared at this girl wearing this nice blue skirt set, with her nice ass pressing against the fabric, I knew one day I had to have her. Little did I know, this would be the woman who would one day break my heart and tear it out of my chest.

I did not get a chance to grace her presence until two months later, when I saw her standing in front of the Playland arcade on Forty-eighth and Broadway. All the monte players met there in the middle of the day before we teamed up. She wore a yellow two-piece skirt set and a pair of beige pumps, with her pedicured toes showing. She looked just as lovely as the first time I saw her. The other players and I watched her without anyone making a move.

I knew I had to act quickly before anyone else tried to talk. So, I walked up to her so nonchalantly and said, "What's your name, lovely?"

She smiled and said, "My name is Misa. What's your name?"

I said, "My name is Michael,"

As I went into kick mode and said, "Misa, Michael, sounds like a match to me."

She smiled with this big ol' Kool-Aid smile and I knew I had her. I then asked her what she was doing standing in front of Playland looking so good. She said she was waiting for someone, but it did not look like they were coming. I told her I was a three-card monte player and today there were too many cops in the area, so I was not going to be able to play. I then asked her if she wanted to go uptown together to hang out. I smiled when she replied, "Yes, let's go." All the monte players and hustlers in front of the arcade looked on in amazement as we walked towards the train station.

We got on the No. 2 train and headed uptown to Harlem. While sitting on the train talking to her, I never mentioned I had seen her before picking pockets on Broadway. My penis was getting harder every time I looked at her face. And I sensed she had the hots for me, too. As we stared at each other, she told me we should get off the train on 116th Street because she wanted to get some skunk. This was all right with me because her wish was my command. The train pulled into the station and we got off.

It was a sunny May day, and a lot of people were enjoying it on the streets of Harlem. There were kids playing and parents watching all the action on the street. You also had the drug dealers selling all types of drugs on some of the street corners.

Misa seemed to know everybody in Harlem. I guess she was popular because she was a dimepiece. The guys standing around were looking like they wanted to kick my ass for being with her. But, I was the lucky guy, or so I thought.

Misa told me to wait outside while she went into a dirty gray building that had a dope fiend sitting on the steps, nodding. When she made her drug purchase, we went to the corner store where she bought rolling paper and two beers. I did not smoke weed, but I did drink a few beers once in a while.

We decided to go sit on the benches in Central Park and found a secluded area where Misa rolled up her smoke and I started to drink my Guinness stout beer. (My motto: Drink a few stouts and figure things out.) As we sat in the park enjoying the weather and the scenery, we talked about Midtown.

Central Park had beautiful green grass, big trees and even small apples. I loved how the park had the smell of grass with a blend of apple Now or Later candy that I used to eat when I was little. When Misa lit up her skunk smoke, I could tell by the smell it was some good shit. As I drank my Guinness stout and she got high off the smoke, we both got a little tipsy. I was catching a contact high off of the skunk. They did not call it skunkweed for nothing.

Misa talked about the players, finally admitting that she was a professional pickpocket. I think she talked so much because the drugs were getting her real high. She asked me about different players downtown. She mentioned that she liked Big Saul's gold and diamond nameplate.

His nameplate was a beautiful piece, which cost him $3,000. It had so many diamonds that it could blind you just by looking at it. When she told me she loved his piece, I could not wait to get her to my mother's apartment, so I could show her all my jewels and my big nameplate that I paid $3,500 for, but it was really worth $4,000. I knew my jewels were better than Saul's, but I would wait until we got to my mother's apartment to let her be the judge. Plus, I had other plans.

As we sat there talking and enjoying each other's company, I asked her when her birthday was. She said, "October 6th. I could not believe it. We shared the same birthday. I thought we were meant to be together. Boy, we had so much in common—con man and pick-pocket.

It was getting dark so I asked her if she wanted to go to my house and get my motorcycle so that we could go riding. She smiled and said, "You have a motorcycle?"

I chuckled and said, "Yes."

Misa said, "Let's go."

We took the No. 2 train to the Bronx and got off on Prospect Avenue. Misa said she wanted something to eat, so, we stopped at a Chinese restaurant down the block from my mother's building.

The restaurant was very dirty. The floors and windows looked like they had not been washed in months. Flies were everywhere, but, she did not seem to mind. So, I did not either. When I approached the counter to place her order, I felt a slight tug at my back pocket. I turned around; it was Misa trying to pick my pocket. I smiled and asked her what she was doing. She laughed and said she was playing. I did not know if she was playing or serious, but I liked her anyway. If she really was serious, it meant that she had heart and she was a money go-getter. There was something different about this girl and something was telling me I would never meet someone else like her in my whole life. Catching her trying to pick my pocket should have been a telltale sign of what was in store. Instead I took it as a blessing in disguise. I thought *Damn I have lucked up and found a girl who is just like me, full of larceny. They say birds of a feather flock together, and she is one fly bird.*

After the Chinese man handed me the food, we headed to my mother's building where everyone sitting on the park benches out-side the projects looked at pretty Misa and her big butt bursting through her yellow skirt. As soon as we got upstairs, I knocked on the door, my mother opened it, looked at us and gave me a funny look, then she went to her room.

Misa sat at the table to eat her Chinese food. I guess all of the weed she smoked gave her the munchies. When she finished, I showed her my Elite red-and-white motorcycle. I bought it because the speed went to 55, and it was an automatic with no gears. I did not like motorcycles with gears because I had crashed one time on my cousin's motorcycle.

I also showed her my jewelry and her light-brown eyes lit up when she saw all the diamonds in my nameplate. She asked me how much I paid for such a nice piece and I said with a smile, "Thirty-five hundred."

She said, "Damn, Mike. Your nameplate and jewels are way better than Saul's!"

She looked like she just realized she was with a boss player. That is when, to her, I turned from plain old Mike into Midtown Money Mike. I knew I could have fucked her right then, but for some reason my ego told me to take it slow. Plus, I had promised her a ride on my motorcycle.

I was concerned that Misa's skirt might pose a problem on the motorcycle. But, she asked me to give her some pants to wear, so we could get this thing on the road. I started to like her even more. As soon as I gave her some jeans, she took her skirt off right in front of me and I got a look at her body. She had nice thighs, a big voluptuous ass, and her lace bikini panties could not hold it all in. Damn, her body was ten times better than what I had imagined! She was a bona fide brick house. She was stacked. As I handed her the pants, I told myself, *Mike, you have got to slow down!* My hormones were raging to a level far more than what I was used to.

Once we started moving, she put her little hands around my waist and I was riding on the clouds of heaven. I rode her all around the Bronx. As her long black hair was blowing in the wind, I was getting hornier and hornier by the minute.

I headed to 169th Street because I wanted to check out my cousins and my homeboys. I hadn't seen them in a while, because I was always in Midtown playing monte.

When we got to 169th Street, I turned off the motorcycle inside the park. Everyone seemed to be hanging out, enjoying the night air. I hugged my cousins Bud and Stan. They both seemed excited to see me as Bud said, "Yo Mike. Who's this lovely lady?"

So, I introduced her to them. Even though my pants were a little big on her, her ass and thighs still managed to bust through them.

She said, "Hi. Are y'all Mike's cousins?"

They both yelled in unison, "Yeah. You got any pretty sisters?"

Misa said, "No, but I have some girlfriends."

Bud said, "Man, hook a brother up!"

She responded, "Well, if I'm ever with Mike again and I see y'all, I'll tell you what my girlfriends said."

I said, "Don't worry about that, girl. You will see me again!"

Everyone laughed.

My cousins were mesmerized by Misa's looks—a combination of cover girl and porn star. People started gathering around us as we stood there by my motorcycle. People who I had not seen in a while came by to say what's up. Even people that I did not know acknowledged my presence on the block. One thing I have learned from years back, when you make a lot of money on the streets, your name travels fast. So, a lot of people knew me, even though I did not know them, because of my street reputation as a moneymaking street hustler as Money Mike. Misa seemed amazed at how many people, old and young, came up to say hi.

Stan pulled me to the side and said, "Mike, you need to take me to wherever it is you find these fly girls."

I said, "Well, they always seem to be where the hustlers be. Fast girls like fast guys. It's as simple as that."

Bud could not keep his eyes off of Misa's ass and thighs. She had a brother fucked up. I let Stan ride my motorcycle as we all walked to the store.

I ran into Denny Jackson and Sticky Hayes on the way there and we hugged and said a few words. Sticky Hayes cracked a joke saying, "Man, Mike you thinking about setting up a three-card monte game around here?"

We busted out laughing.

I loved my 169th Street family and I have pleasant memories about the good times we shared growing up.

After a few minutes talking with my homeboys, we headed to the store where I bought beer and sodas for everyone. The guys admired Misa and winked at me, symbolizing, "You're with the right one brother." I paid the Arab store employee, Zuto, who told me, "Hey, Mike, what brings you around the old neighborhood?"

I replied, "Zuto, I'm just chilling out with my homeboys and this beautiful young lady."

He responded, "I can see that. She's nice, real nice," giving me my props.

After we left the store, we walked back to the park and I let everyone ride my bike. Stan said, "Man, Mike, your bike is nice, but you really should'a gotten that Honda motorcycle with all the gears."

Then Bud said, "Stan you know Mike wasn't going to get that after he busted his ass on our bike and messed up his brown lizard shoes." This had everybody in stitches.

Then I said, "Yeah, that's what I get for showing off riding a motorcycle while looking fly."

We couldn't stop laughing.

After spending about two hours having a good time with everyone, I told them Misa and I had to go because we had some unfinished business to attend to. Everyone laughed because they knew exactly what I was talking about. Misa smiled and her face lit up like she also knew.

We jumped back on the bike and headed to the nearest hotel, the Alps Hotel on West Farms Avenue. When we arrived, Misa continued to smile as I parked the motorcycle in the hotel parking lot and we went in to get a room. The funny thing about it was, I hadn't even asked her if she wanted to go. I was that confident. When anyone came to this type of seedy hotel, sleep was the furthest thing from their minds.

I paid the guy at the counter and he gave me a key to a room on the first floor. As soon as we got in the room, Misa said she wanted to take a shower with me, so we took off our clothes.

I could not help myself as I admired her well-proportioned assets. I knew my eyeballs had to be bulging like frog's eyes. She had round firm tits with little dots going around them. When I looked at her flat stomach, I thought she must do sit-ups. Then my eyes traveled to her shapely thighs and ass and I almost came on myself right there. Her brown, lace bikini panties were on so tight, that I wondered how she even fit her big ass in them. I told myself I had to calm down if I wanted to satisfy this wonderful specimen of a woman. I had forgotten to bring my Stud 100 spray, so, I knew that I would have to use my mind to keep myself under control. A pimp once told me, "Mike, if you are ever with any new pussy, focus your mind on everything but the sex at hand, and you will be all right." So, I kept that in mind, anytime I got with a new girl.

While looking at Misa, I noticed I was not the only person in the room doing some checking out. I caught Misa looking at my big hard penis. My father had passed down some of his strong genetics down to his boy. As I said earlier, I had broad shoulders and a nice slim build with a brown complexion like him. I guess I acquired a few other things from him too. It reminded me of the expression "Shake what your mama gave you." I was about to work what my father gave me on this beautiful woman.

After checking each other out, we headed to the shower. I proceeded to soap her body down giving her a good massage as I went along. Her body was softer than cocoa butter on a hot summer day. I just loved how the warm water ran down it. If you have ever seen the bathtub sex scene in the movie *Superfly*, when he is having sex with his woman, where they were going all out—well this is going to be mine.

After I finished soaping and massaging her, Misa turned around and did the same to me. As the water ran down our bodies, she got on her knees and proceeded to give me the best head that I had ever had. That is a big statement because I have been with some good head specialists in my time, but nothing like this. The head was so good that I almost busted my ass on the slippery floor, and all the while she stayed doing the task at hand. It got so good that my body started to jerk so I tried to pull away, but she just pulled me closer and I busted off.

As soon as that happened, I slipped and hit my ass on the hard tub floor. I screamed like a girl, "Ah, ah . . ." And we both laughed. I was still rock hard. It was time for us to get out of the shower and head to the bed. We had sex like there was no tomorrow. We took that big bed for one long ride, as we tried every position imaginable. The pimp's advice was coming in handy as I performed like a trooper. Maybe I did not need the Stud 100 after all. Mind over matter. Then I heard someone by the open window say, "Ride that ass young buck, ride that ass." Misa and I paid the person no mind as we continued having sex. We put on a helluva show for the stranger that we could hear, but not see. I guess I liked an audience, like good old Cousin Reggie did.

We stayed up most of the night talking about everything. We eventually slept, and when we woke up in the morning, I had a big revelation. I was pussy-whipped. We had sex again in the morning, then we took a shower, got dressed and I dropped off my motorcycle at my mother's apartment. I knew I had to go to Midtown to make some money, so after I dropped off the bike, I put Misa in a cab and headed downtown.

As soon as I got to Midtown, the players who saw me leave with Misa were eager to hear all about what happened. I ran down the whole story. My man Kendall, who had run a few trains with me, told me that he wanted us to run a train on Misa. I told him no, I was saving this one for myself. Kendall got mad and said, "That boy is pussy-whipped!"

Everyone laughed, even the pimps and the prostitutes standing by the donut shop.

I told him, "Get off my dick!"

Then I got my team together and headed to Fifth Avenue. All day while playing monte, I could not get my mind off of Misa. My team laughed whenever they caught me daydreaming because they knew what I was thinking about. But, one thing I never do is let sex come between me and my money. My motto is rest, dress, and progress.

Every vic that stepped in my game got beat for every dime. I had a glow all day. The day's take was $3,200. My team told me at the end of the day to keep having sex with Misa because she brought us lots of luck. Little did I know that she would bring lots of other things into my life besides good luck.

* * *

I found myself spending more and more time with Misa. I was attracted to her because she seemed to be the female version of me. We thought alike, acted alike and we had somewhat the same mentality. We were both street-smart and we both had the love of money. From day one we had a certain chemistry when we were together and everyone sensed it.

My homeboys, Dante, CeeWee, Jaheim and Kendall, got along with Misa. They picked up on the fact that hanging with her was like hanging with a dude. You could talk to her about anything. CeeWee and Jaheim discussed the girls they got with and how they tricked them into having sex. She talked about how guys used to trick money on her, thinking they could fast-talk her into having sex with them. But, she sent them off with blue balls after they spent all of their money. She said some brothers were suckers for a big butt and a smile. I guess I fit into that category because when I saw her pretty face and that fat ass, I was all in.

Kendall even talked about all the girls we ran trains on. I knew exactly what he was trying to do as soon as he brought it up. He was trying to get me in trouble. Deep down he still wanted to fuck Misa even though he knew she was my girl. But, she never seemed to get angry. She understood the rules of dating a player. She knew that sometimes a player is going to step off and have sex with somebody else.

Misa was very calm and laid-back about many things. That's why I liked her so much. When my homeboys and I finished playing monte, we headed to Broadway to look for Misa and we always spotted her going into some lady's pocketbook or man's back pocket. She was one damn good pickpocket! If she made her move, nine times out of ten she came up with something in her hands.

I always liked the fact that she had her own money when we hung out. Let me rephrase that, some *vic's* money. Misa told me she had been pickpocketing since she was thirteen years old. Her father was an old-time hustler and a jack-of-all-trades when it came to hustling. She said he used to take her jostling if his shield did not show up. At the same time I used to run the streets with Cousin Reggie when I was little, she was running them with her father. The only difference between us on this point is, I was in the Bronx and she was in Harlem. We were a perfect street couple.

After CeeWee, Dante, Jaheim, Spence and I found her, we headed to Harlem where we drank, smoked weed and got high.

One time we caught a cab from Midtown to 158th Street in Washington Heights because they wanted to buy some cocaine. When we arrived at the destination in a Yellow Cab, Dante, CeeWee and Jaheim got out to make their purchase while Misa and I stayed inside.

After a few minutes, they came back. As soon as the cab drove a half a block from the drug spot, an unmarked police car pulled us over. Four cops jumped out and ran to the cab. I thought we all were going straight to jail, but Misa who was sitting in the front seat, told Dante to throw the cocaine to her fast.

Dante tossed it to the front and Misa grabbed it and stuffed it in her bra. The cops snatched open the cab's doors and searched everybody except her. When they did not find any drugs, they let everybody go. After the cops left, everybody grabbed Misa and gave her hugs and kisses. After that incident everybody knew she was a down-ass chick with more heart than a lot of brothers.

Misa and I spent so much time together that after spending two nights in the Sheraton Hotel celebrating one year together, her mother had her bags waiting for her at the entrance to her apartment. She told Misa that since she did not like to come home, she should go live with me. It was all right with me because by this time I was pussy-whipped to the fullest. I just could not ever get enough of her good sex.

We had sex everyday and everywhere. We did the nasty on her mother's bed, her brother's bed, in restaurant bathrooms, gas stations, hotels—anywhere was all right with us. Misa would let me do anything sexually that I wanted to do. She was down for everything except a train. She told me that one time this drug dealer that she had liked, set her up and he and his boys raped her. She said when she tried to have them arrested, the cops told her she should not have gone anywhere with the guy. I say if she had been a white woman, it would have been a whole different story.

Sometimes after having sex, Misa would relax and tell me the most intriguing stories. I asked her about her last boyfriend. She became real quiet then looked at me seriously and said, "Mike, I want to tell you about him, but I don't want you to get scared, and I don't want you to think that I am a bad person."

Just by the way she said it, had me a little nervous. I could feel the tension in the hotel room. I said, "What are you talking about, Misa?"

Then she said, "Just let me talk before I lose courage to tell you what's been on my mind since I met you. Before I met you, I had a boyfriend named Keith. Keith was a big drug dealer with a crew of guys who sold drugs for him in Harlem. Keith had big money and all the cars, jewelry and clothes that any eighteen-year-old kid could ever want. His crew did their thing on the streets and inside drug apartments all over Harlem. They had Harlem sold up. I met him one day while me and my girlfriends were walking down 114th Street and Eighth Avenue. Keith and his crew were eyeing my girlfriends and me as we pranced by in our tight tops and jeans. We all were dimepieces with nice bodies, so all the big time drug dealers wanted to get in our pants. Me and Keith made eye contact and he waved me over, but I told him to meet me halfway. He walked up to me and said, 'What's up, shorty? My name is Keith. What's your name?'

"I smiled showing all my white teeth and told him my name. Then Keith asked where we were headed. When I told him that we were going to 125th Street to get something to eat, he asked if he could drive us over there. So, I looked at my girlfriends and they all said yeah. Then we all got in Keith's fly green Mercedes Benz that was parked across the street. From that moment on we knew we were with a moneymaker. Just like when you showed me your motorcycle and all your jewelry—I thought, here I go again, messing with another hustler. Anyway, Keith took us around in his car blasting music. I really liked him. He was dark-skinned, tall with a bald head. Keith wasn't the most handsome guy, but there was something about how he carried himself. He was smooth and suave, plus he had lots of muscles. When I looked at him, I knew before the night was over that I was going to fuck him—and later that day we hooked up and we did. After that day, me and Keith hung together everyday and he would take me sometimes to all his drug houses to count the drug money. He was making so much money, that he couldn't keep track of it. He would always give me stacks of money and tell me to go shopping. I had all the clothes, shoes, mink coats and jewelry that I wanted. The first few months that I was with Keith, he treated me like a queen. But, then I started to catch him with other girls and we would break up. But, he would always beg me to get back with him and I would. Then everything would be good for a while. One day I caught him with one of my girlfriends and he beat me up. So, to pay him back, I went to one of his drug houses, where they all knew I was his woman, and I picked up the day's take. This was not unusual because Keith had sent me many times to pick up money at his spots. I repeated this same scenario in two other spots. I picked up a total of about $48,000. I took the money and disappeared for about a week—spending the money on all my family and friends. Keith and his people were looking for me all over Harlem, but they could not find me. By the time Keith found me, all of the money was gone. He beat the living shit out of me, but he was so in love with me that he could not leave me. His main drug suppliers told him if he couldn't leave me alone, they would not stay down with him. Keith didn't leave me, so they all cut him off. A few weeks later, Keith smoked a bag of dust and blew his brains out on a roof at 112th Street and Lennox—the same building where one of his drug apartments was located."

* * *

The last night's events popped in my mind all the way downtown on the No. 2 train. What was it about Misa that scared me the most? Was it that a man had killed himself because of her, or was it because she told me she stole from him? The stealing part was a telltale sign that maybe she would steal from me. I had been so blinded by her beauty and fat ass that the first day I met her I showed off and let her see all my jewels. I can still remember how her eyes lit up when those diamonds sparkled.

My mind raced back and forth as I got off the train on Forty-second Street. When I arrived in front of the donut shop a funny feeling came over me. Something was telling me that something different was going to happen to me. The crazy feeling got my mind off of Misa for a little while. Someone yelled, "Yo Mike, I heard you took 3,900 yesterday."

I looked and it was my man Fronting Cee. I smiled and said, "Rest, dress and progress, Cee. You know my ceelo and how I get down."

Cee smiled, "Mike, you know you the man."

I got my team together and we headed to Fifth Avenue where vics were everywhere. It was a bright sunny day and I felt like a winner. Saul and Lady Day, my sticks, stood to the side talking shit, while we waited for my lookouts, Spence and Jaheim, to set up shop. Then, Jaheim went to one corner of Forty-third Street and Fifth Avenue and Spence went to the other. I jumped behind the box, screaming, "Hey New York, New York, I'm back letting the cards hit the cardboard."

Saul and Lady Day walked up and after a few minutes a big crowd gathered around and started betting forties and sixties and one hundreds right off the top. Every vic who bet, I raised the bet for more money and they complied with my every demand. Saul smiled when I raised one tourist from $100 to $600 in one shot. Spence called a slide 'em up, which meant cops were in the area. I stepped to the side and let the cops ride by. Then I got back behind the box when all of a sudden Spence yelled out, "Quick slide."

I took off running, with a young plainclothes cop dead on my tail. I ran straight through Midtown traffic with the cop hot in pursuit. I was fast, but this cop was faster. He caught me at Thirty-sixth Street and Fifth Avenue. I was huffing and puffing as he handcuffed me and said, while laughing hysterically, "I don't run in marathons every year for nothing!"

At this point, I noticed that it was Little Willie, the fastest and youngest cop from the Midtown South Precinct. I had seen him and his crew bust many monte players before. But this was my first real arrest. I had been busted a few times before, throughout the years, but now that I was older, this would be the first time I went through the criminal court system, which was quite different.

Little Willie led me to the paddy wagon on Forty-fifth Street and Sixth Avenue. The paddy wagon was loaded down with other monte players and pickpockets. Little Clyde, Little Bit from Brooklyn, White Boy Paulie, Big-Head Louie and some other pickpockets.

Little Bit said, "Yo Mike, this is the second time this week I got knocked."

I said, "Yo Shorty, before I got knocked, I had just took a $600 bet." I told him, "I had a funny feeling as soon as I got to the donut shop this morning that something was going to happen to me today, but I didn't think this in my wildest dreams."

We sat in the hot paddy wagon for about one hour before the cops decided to take us to the precinct. Once there, the cops fingerprinted us, took all of our information and pictures. One cop named Ted from the monte squad went out and bought the other cops beers and pretzels. Little Willie told me they were just waiting for me to turn sixteen so they could put me through the system. All the other cops from the monte squad felt I was getting a free ride. Plus, he told me they were all jealous of the money they heard I was making. My name had been ringing bells all up and down Midtown.

In the precinct, they handcuffed a peddler to me. He had hit a cop on Thirty-fourth Street because the cops arrested him and confiscated all of his merchandise. A few cops kept coming into the room telling the peddler he was going to get an ass-whipping for fighting with cops. And here I was handcuffed right next to a guy who was due a little treat. The cops came in and out of the room a few times then all of a sudden, eight cops just pounced on the peddler, punching and kicking him all over his body.

Another cop was lying in the cut, looking for an opening so he could kick the peddler in the nuts with his hard, steel-toe shoes. I tried my best to move out of the way. I wanted nothing to do with the peddler's beating. The cop saw an opening and kicked the guy in the groin area. The peddler let out a shrieking scream that I had never heard before. The shot to his nuts knocked him out cold and the cop smiled like he had hit a home run. The other monte players who were busted looked on like getting busted was an everyday occurrence.

After a few hours, the cops took us to central booking on 100 Centre Street. Central booking was packed with all the criminals who had been arrested that day. As we waited to be processed, Little Clyde had a hook up with one of the correction officers who went out and got all of the monte players sandwiches and two big bottles of Bacardi rum. We chipped in and gave him $100. I said to myself; *We're already locked up, so why not get drunk?* Meanwhile, the other prisoners in the big cell were wondering how all these monte players wound up drunk when nobody had access to the streets? We, the monte players, lived large on the streets and we lived large in jail.

After a few hours, they took us to a precinct to sleep until the next day's court appearance. At the criminal court building the next day, they put us all in a cell while we waited to see the judge. One loony older guy was talking some crazy stuff about wanting to go to jail. He knew he was going to get three hots and a cot for free at the taxpayers' expense. He said when he got to see the judge, he was going to tell him to suck his big black dick, and that if he let him out, he was going to go fuck the shit out of his wife. When this correction officer told him it was time to see the judge, he went out there and did exactly what he said he would do. The judge gave him a sentence of one year for petty larceny.

I was in the cell about five hours before they started calling the three-card monte players. We all got off with fines and time served. My fine was only fifty dollars, which was nothing because I knew I had won about $960 before I got busted.

Little Clyde, Little Bit, Big-Head Louie and I jumped on the No. 5 train without paying and headed to Forty-second Street. On our arrival, we headed to the donut shop where I waited for my team to show up so I could get my money. I heard someone yell, "Mike, quick slide!" I turned and it was Saul laughing with a funny grin on his face.

"Mike, so tell me how was your first jail experience?"

I laughed and said, "Saul you scared me with that fake quick slide. I guess I'm still a little shaken up."

He responded, "Mike, now you are an officially certified red card player, by way of the court system."

I laughed and said, "Saul, it's all about cop and blow. Now where's my money?"

He said, "Here's your cut from yesterday's take. Lady Day gave me the money to give to you when you got out of jail."

I took the five hundred Saul gave me and told him I was going uptown to take a shower and get some pussy. As soon as I got home, Misa called and I told her I had just gotten out of jail and I wanted her to catch a cab and come to my mom's apartment. About forty-five minutes later, the doorbell rang, and, I let her in.

"So, honey, did you have a rough night?"

I laughed and answered, "You know your man is a trooper. I ain't taking no shorts!"

She asked, "Yeah, but were you scared?"

I said, "I wasn't scared because I know getting busted comes with the territory."

15

Honey Combs (Mr. Understand Me)

In the morning, I dropped Misa off in a cab at the front of her building. I decided on my way to Midtown that I needed a little time away from her—preferably a few weeks. Deep down I wondered if I could accomplish this, being pussy-whipped and all. But, what better way to start than spending more time in the place I love best, Midtown.

After making my money playing monte, I hung out with pimp Honey Combs, cruising Forty-second Street while he picked up his money from his hoes. He was looking sharp with his green silk shirt, gray linen pants and his green 'gator shoes. As we walked towards Eighth Avenue, I noticed Honey Combs was in a talkative mood. He tried to kick it with every girl who passed by. In Honey Combs' mind, every girl was a potential hoe. He didn't care if she was a church girl, working girl, ugly or pretty—he tried to pimp anybody.

"Honey Combs, when did you first decide that you wanted to be a pimp?"

"Well, player, the first time I realized I wanted to pimp was when I was about eleven years old, living in St. Louis. You see, St. Louis had all the major boss pimps that laid the game down hard. They would pimp their mama if she wanted to sell some pussy—understand me? I used to always see the pimps hanging by the bars and barbershops looking sharp in all their fly threads and 'gator kicks. Any type of color 'gators, they had them! Those pimps were real flashy with their pimped out Cadillacs and all their hoes. I was hypnotized by everything I saw them say and do. I never dreamed of being president. I dreamed of being a pimp."

He continued, "I knew I was going to be a pimp if it killed me. I just hung around them all the time until one day they started to send me to the store for cigarettes and chips—understand me? This pimp, Boston Black, took a liking to me and he started to school me on the pimp game. I took it all in like a star pupil in a classroom—understand me? Mike, I been pimping since I was twelve years old. The first girl I ever pimped—understand me—was my fifteen-year-old sister, Pat. The reason I pimped her is she was always giving it away to all the dudes on the block anyway. So, I made her a proposition. I told her if I got some of my friends to pay her for some pussy, she would have to give me half of the money—understand me? She agreed—understand me? So, that's how I pulled my first hoe, my sister."

I said, "You pimped your own sister?"

"You damn right I did. I don't give a fuck about a bitch. Trust them as far as you can see them."

"So, you've never been in love with a girl?" I asked.

"Yeah, I was in love before. The bitch broke my heart by fucking my best friend. I almost killed both of them motherfuckers."

"Well, Honey Combs, I got this girl I've been fucking around with and I know I'm not in love but I think I'm whipped. I think about her all the time. She's like the mirror image of me, and she fucks the shit out of me. But, at the same time I know she's not good for me."

"First of all, Mike, never let a broad know what you are thinking because when they think they got you figured out, they always move on to the next chump—understand me? Second, women think ten steps ahead of most men. So, you got to be twenty steps ahead of them. If that broad suspects that she got you fucked up in the head, she'll take you for everything you've got—understand me?"

I told Honey Combs I understood and we both started laughing. But, deep down I knew dealing with Misa was going to be a hard learning experience. So, for now I just needed to get her off of my mind.

When we got to Eighth Avenue, Honey Combs spotted one of his hoes and said, "Hey, Tina baby, come here and give daddy a kiss."

"Hi, daddy. Who's the kid?"

"Oh, baby, that's my little man, Mike."

"Hi, how you doing, baby."

I replied, "Oh, I'm chill."

"Daddy, your baby done went at these tricks in the worst way."

"That's my baby. She stays on the grind. That's why I never doubt my baby—understand me? You just bring a warm feeling to daddy's heart every time I think about you—understand me?"

"Daddy, Hope been out here, shucking and jiving, all day. That's why she's hiding from daddy now. By the way, here daddy . . . ," and she passed him a knot of money.

"Tina, baby, when was the last time you seen her?"

"Oh, daddy, the last time I saw old girl, she was standing by that Playland on Forty-second Street and Broadway."

"Okay, baby, me and my little man gon' keep it moving," said Honey Combs.

"All right, daddy, you take care of little shorty."

I just nodded as we started to walk.

Honey Combs said, "Yo Mike, pimping ain't easy. That's why I'm never caught slacking—understand me?"

"Yeah, Honey Combs, you put the 'P' in pimp."

"Shorty, you keep talking like that. I'm gonna have to give all my hoes to you, the way you butter a brother up."

"Honey Combs, speaking of butter, you wanna go to the movies?"

"Yeah, but first let me take care of a little business."

As we made our way towards Playland, Honey Combs speeded up, which caught me off guard because he always walked slow. Next thing I knew he made a mad dash to the front of Playland where he slapped the shit out of his hoe, Hope. He was slapping her so hard, I thought he was going to knock her out.

"Bitch, you take me for a motherfucking trick? You want me to get my damn hanger? I do damage, bitch. I do damage—understand me?"

"Daddy, I'm sorry. Please don't kill me. I'm sick, daddy, but I got some money."

A crowd gathered so Honey Combs gave her a push and kicked her straight up the ass.

"Now get your stupid ass back on the stroll."

Then with his eyes bulging, he yelled to the crowd, "What y'all motherfuckers looking at?" He faked like he was going towards them and they all jumped, shook. Then he started to walk off with a pimp swagger and said, "Come on, Mike. Let's get the fuck out of here."

As we headed towards the movie theater on Broadway, I was a little confused about what just went down. One minute he was Mr. Nice Guy with one hoe and the next minute he was beating the living shit out of another one. When I asked him about it, he said Hope was one of his top hoes and today she was setting a bad example for the other ones. He said by her fucking around and bullshitting, she was blowing money on the stroll and a real pimp can't have that.

After the crazy incident, we headed up Broadway to catch a karate flick. Ain't that some shit—a kid and a pimp going to watch a karate flick—so poetic.

16

Whipped

I often ask myself, how did I fall a victim to being pussy-whipped. I have come to the conclusion that there were several factors that played a part, such as physical attraction, sexual compatibility, mind manipulation, obsession and lust. When I really think about it, the stage was set for me to fall victim to something sexually dysfunctional by the time I was seven years old.

I remember going to the beach with my mother, a bunch of kids and a pretty lady from our building. While all the other kids played in the sand and water, I hung around my mother and her friend with the orange string bikini. I could not keep my little beady eyes off the grown women's ass as she lay on her stomach getting a tan.

I had a vivid visualization of us getting our hump on in the hot burning sand. This all happened at the tender age of seven. Now ten years later, I found myself pussy-whipped by a girl with a sinister smile and a fat ass.

17

China (No Nervous, No Nervous)

I was getting a funny feeling in my body telling me I needed a sexual release. I was trying to get it off my mind, but the feeling, and thoughts of sex, kept coming back. I decided that when I finished playing three-card monte, I would go shopping for clothes, and sneakers and then for sex. I got my team together inside the donut shop, then headed to Thirty-fourth Street with my sticks, Lady Day, Saul and my lookouts, Fronting Cee and my main man Spence. Lady Day looked lovely on this bright sunny Saturday with her tight blue jeans, light blue blouse and light blue sandals.

"Yo Mike, stop looking at Lady Day's ass, you horny mother-fucker."

"Shut up, Spence. Look who's talking? You can't keep your eyes off of her chest."

I had to admit Lady Day was looking damn good. You could see her fat nipples just rubbing against the fabric of her blouse. Damn she's a stunner. I wanted to fuck her, but Little Clyde, the top dog, was her man and I was cool with him. Saul laughed as he watched us watch Lady Day. I liked Saul because I always learned something new about selling the game to the vics from him. He was one of the best sticks in the game and I made good money when we played together.

When we got to Thirty-fourth Street we set up shop in front of the Empire State Building. I liked this spot because it was New York's premier tourist attraction. As soon as I got behind the box and started to yell, "Hey New York, New York. I'm back, I'm back. Who saw the red card . . ." a big crowd gathered around and I proceeded to beat vic after vic after vic.

They were coming out of the woodwork with fifties and one hundreds like they were dollar bills. One white chump with a backpack pulled out his wallet and it looked like he had about five thousand dollars in C-notes. The bet started at two hundred and Saul made me raise him all the way to one thousand. The vic lost and started to walk away when Lady Day grabbed him by the hand and told him, "Come on, baby. I'm going to help you get your money back."

She then grabbed one of the cards and threw it to the side. She said, "Play with two cards."

This was my cue to go get the card while she put a small bend in the red card. This move was called the lug. I came back with the card and pretended like I did not see the red card with the bend at the corner. I sprung the cards in one quick move and Lady Day and Saul jumped and bet five hundred apiece before the vic had a chance to get his money ready. I paid them off as they picked the red card. Then I proceeded to spring the cards with one swift move and yelled, "Who saw that red card?"

For one thousand, the vic laid his money down and then tried to lift the card, but I raised him from one thousand to fifteen hundred. I said, "If I can bluff you, I can beat you."

The vic started fumbling in his wallet and laid down the other five hundred. Saul tried to tell me to raise him again on the sly, but I told the vic to turn it up.

"Black you lose."

The vic said, "Damn," and walked away.

Saul tried to bring him back, but the vic kept walking. I continued to beat more vics when Fronting Cee called a slide. The game broke up and we waited for the cops to pass. Saul walked up to me.

"Yo Mike, you should have raised that vic again. He was ready to lose all his money. You did all right but if a vic is that desperate to bet and he is looking for more money, he's ready for the taking. Take him for all you can because you might not get a second chance."

I said, "Thanks, Saul, I know I should have raised him again. I fucked up."

"Don't sweat it, Mike. You're getting better. Just stay focused."

Spence yelled for me to spring 'em. As soon as I got back behind the box, I started to yell, "Hey New York, New York. I'm back, I'm back . . ." As I sprung the cards across the board, another big crowd gathered around as I laid my game down. The vics started back betting as soon as Lady Day and Saul started placing bets. I just loved it how vics always had that followers' mentality. They saw people doing something, so they thought it was all right to do it, too, since everyone else was doing it. Follow the leader; in this case, follow the stick. The vics were betting forties and one hundreds left and right and I was just raising all the bets just like Saul told me to do. Saul and Lady Day smiled as I raised vic after vic. One time I even did this move called the tush.

After the tush move, Spence called a slide, the game broke up and the crowd dispersed. I then told my team we were finished playing and everybody should meet up at Tad's Steakhouse on Forty-second Street to cut up the money. As they walked, I went across the street where Little Bit from Brooklyn, his twin brother, Peanut, White Boy Paulie, and Jody were standing waiting for the slide to go by.

"What's up y'all? What's going on?"

Little Bit and Jody yelled out, "Man, it's sweet out here. The vics are loaded."

"Yeah, I know what y'all saying. I just took about six thousand right across the street. I even tushed it on a vic for eight hundred. He like to lost his mind."

"Yeah, Mike, these vics are ready," commented White Boy Paulie. "We just took forty-seven hundred and we staying down."

I said, "Not me. I just told my team to meet me at Tad's. We finished for today. Plus, I got to go get fresh and then get me some pussy."

Everybody laughed.

After kicking it around for a little while with all the players on Thirty-fourth Street, I headed up to Tad's Steakhouse. My team was already eating steaks and drinking beer. I ordered a steak, then sat down with them to count and split up the money. I noticed Lady Day was looking at me with amazement. I guess she was thinking, *Man this kid is so young and he's making all this money.* She noticed that I caught her looking, so she asked, "Mike, do you have a girlfriend?"

"Nah, Lady Day, I'm free as a bird."

Saul laughed, "So who was that big-booty, light-skinned girl that I've been seeing you with lately?"

I blurted out, "Man, we're just friends." But everybody knew there was more to it just by the way I said it.

"Well, Mike, with the money you've been making, you'll be able to get a lot of friends," Lady Day added in.

"Yeah, some real nice, and I mean real nice, friends," joked Fronting Cee. We all laughed our heads off then we split up the money and ate our steaks.

After we left Tad's, I ran into CeeWee while walking to Modell's to get me some clothes. CeeWee told me Misa was looking for me. So, I hurried up to Modell's, bought a blue-and-white Adidas sweat suit and a pair of white eggshell Adidas sneakers. Then Spence and I got on the No. 2 train because I didn't want to run into Misa. We were headed to my mother's apartment so I could change my clothes. On the train, Spence pulled out cards and practiced. I guess one day he envisioned himself getting behind the box.

"Yo Mike, do you think you're better than Little Clyde, Money Gus or Little Glenda yet?"

When he mentioned Glenda I thought about Johnny Ranks because she used to mess with him before he died. She and another female named Lisa almost came to blows at Johnny Ranks' funeral because they both used to fuck him.

"Nah, Spence, I'm still learning, but I'm getting better. Saul even said so. I guess I'm getting a better feel for the game. I was born to do this."

"Me, too, Mike. That's why I keep on practicing. I'll be ready soon. Then one day me and you can take turns springing them, just like you and Money Gus do sometimes."

"Word is bond, Spence. Word is bond."

As the No. 2 train pulled up to the Prospect station, the doors opened and we got off. We walked down Prospect Avenue, made a left and headed towards my mother's building. When we got to the block, I saw something that I didn't think I was seeing. It was Ma-Ma sitting on the stoop across the street with her drunken friends. She was wearing my new red-and-white Adidas sweat suit that I bought last week, with my new burgundy and grey British Walker shoes. This is stuff that I hadn't even worn yet. She also had on my burgundy Kangol hat. I was pissed and embarrassed all at the same time. But, I wasn't shocked because my mother was known to do some crazy things in her time.

"Yo Mike, is that your mom across the street wearing your clothes?"

"Yeah, Spence, that's her. I can just hear the jokes that's gonna be told up the block at my sister's school. 'Your mama wears Adidas suits and British Walkers!' Ha, ha, ha!"

After laughing with Spence, I didn't feel so bad. I knew he understood what I was going through, because his mother drank, too.

We went up to my mother's apartment and I put on the new stuff I had bought. I decided to put on my Mike nameplate with all the diamonds in it, my diamond-and-gold name bracelet, my diamond name ring, and ME diamond initial ring. I was definitely in floss mode. Then we left my mother's apartment and caught a cab to 169th Street.

It was a beautiful Saturday night and everyone was outside around my cousin's projects. As we got out of the cab and made our way towards the building, the entire spotlight was on us, plus my diamonds were shining.

"What up, Mike? What up, Chilly Spence?"

It was my man, Mitchell, and our other homeboy, Cham.

Cham said, "We know y'all niggas took it today."

Spence screamed, "All day, everyday," as he flashed his money.

"Spence, why you always flashing?" asked Cham.

"Fuck you, Cham, you can suck my dick."

"Ah, Spence, I'm just fucking with you. Buy a nigga a beer." Cham replied.

As they headed to the store, Mitchell and I walked to the park where everybody seemed to be hanging. The older bucks were at the farther end of the park playing dice. I didn't want any parts of that, but I knew when Spence came from the store, he'd head straight in that direction.

I spotted some girls sitting on the bench, so I headed over there.

"Yo Mike, I know you like a book. You came around here because you looking for some hotty," said Mitchell.

I replied, "Nigga, what's my motherfucking name?"

"Money Mike," Mitch yelled, while laughing.

I really liked Mitchell a whole lot because he always laughed at all my jokes. Plus, we have known each other since our Camp Fordham days. Mitchell and I made small talk with the girls on the bench.

"Hi, Mike. Ain't seen you in a long time." It was a light-skinned girl, named Yelena, from the fourteenth floor. Yelena was a big flirt. Besides flirting, she also liked fighting all the other girls on the block.

I said, "Hi, Yelena. What's been going on?"

She said, "Oh, I'm just chilling, catching the night air."

"Oh, so you stopped beating those bitches' asses around here?"

She said with a snicker, "Ah, stop playing, Mike."

"Yeah, Mike, Yelena still throwing down," said Mitchell. We laughed, as I spotted my cousin, Bud, Spence and Cham heading our way. Spence had a bag full of beers and he reached in the bag and handed me a Guinness Stout and Mitch a Heineken. Bud was grinning ear to ear because he was so glad to see me.

He said, "What's up, cuz? Long time no see."

I got up and gave him a hug. "What's up, Bud? How's life treating you?"

"Man, Mike, I'm broke as a dog."

When I heard that, I reached in my pocket and gave him sixty dollars. The eyes of the girls on the bench lit up. I took a long swig of the stout because I was feeling good and I knew in the morning I'd be back downtown busting those chumps out of every dime they had. I couldn't wait. Spence and Cham headed for the dice game as I finished my stout and talked with everybody by the bench. I started feeling a little buzz from the stout so I told Bud and Mitch to give me a walk to the store.

As we were leaving the park, I spotted Chrissy, from the third floor, hanging with this little Chinese-looking Puerto Rican girl. My heart beat rapidly and I got real nervous. I told myself, I know this cannot be who I think it is. My mind instantly went back to the time when I was nine years old and I first spotted her with Chrissy. I had been nervous even though I was not the slightest bit shy. Her good looks had me so mesmerized that I was tongue-tied.

I remember telling Bud that one day I was going to get her. He laughed every time I said it because he knew how nervous she made me. At the time, all the young guys wanted her. She was the prettiest Puerto Rican girl on the block. Now, here she stood right in front of my face, all grown up and as stunning as the day I first laid eyes on her.

"Hi, Mike," Chrissy yelled, as she woke me out of my trancelike state.

I said, "Oh hi, Chrissy." Then she introduced me to her best friend, China. I was so nervous that I was at a loss for words. I tried to speak, but no words would come out.

She said, "Hi, Mike. My name is China."

I said, "Uh, my name is . . .uh, uh, I'm sorry, my name is Mike. Y'all take it easy." They both looked at me funny and kept on walking to the park. Bud looked at me with a smirk.

"Damn, Mike, she still got you fucked up like that?"

Mitchell just could not stop laughing. He said, "Not game tight as Money Mike. Scared of a girl."

Then they both hooted. I was still at a loss for words as we headed towards the store.

I said, "I need a stout so I can figure things out," making everyone roar.

After a couple of hours of drinking with my cousin and all of my other friends, I decided to call Cindy, a pretty Spanish girl who lived on 180th in Tremont. I fuck her from time to time. I met Cindy at the T-Connection hip-hop club on Gun Hill Road, when I was hanging with Light Skin Dev and my other homeboy Bobby. One time Dev took her to the Bronx Park Motel and fucked the shit out of her while I was in the room watching. Cindy was a girl who likes moneymakers. I ran into her at another hip-hop party and, after hanging out together, we went to a hotel and fucked. So, every so often, if I happen to be hanging in the Bronx, I give her a call.

I told Bud and my homeboys that I was going to get me some pussy and I would check them out some other time. As I jumped in a cab, someone yelled out "no nervous, no nervous" and this had us in stitches.

Now, I really needed me some pussy to get my mind off what had transpired earlier between me and the girl—uh-uh, China.

Life is so funny. I left Midtown trying to get my mind off Misa and I went uptown, ran into my childhood sweetheart, China, fumbled and stumbled. Now she was on my mind, so I left 169th Street to get with Cindy, so that I could take my mind off China. Damn! I was so confused.

It was ten o'clock in the morning and I was standing by the donut shop, fresh from having sex with Cindy. I did not fuck the shit out of her like I would normally do. I guess my body was with her, but my mind was somewhere else. Could it be that last night I found out I was pussy-whipped with one girl and maybe in love with another? *Misa, China, Misa, China, Misa, China* . . . I thought my mind was playing tricks on me. Then someone yelled out, "Yo Mike, are you all right?"

It was Money Gus, fresh out of jail.

18

Monte Stalker

My high school, Dewitt Clinton, was a big, six-story brick building on Moshulu Parkway in the Bronx. It was an all-boys high school that went from ninth to twelfth grade. The reason I chose an all-boys school was because I wanted to get my high school diploma without being distracted by the temptations of the female persuasion. When I was in junior high school, some of the students told me not to pick Dewitt Clinton High School because it was known for having a lot of drug dealers, pickpockets, stickup kids and thugs. I took a little bit of what they said into consideration, but it did not deter me from my choice because I had grown up around a lot of bad characters. So, I was not scared of the thug element.

When I arrived at the school, I was already deep into the streets and three-card monte. All I wanted to do was go to school, take my classes and graduate. I had always promised my mother I would get a high school diploma. Like me, I guess some of the other students at the school had some of the same reasons for choosing an all-boys school. But, their thought process played out a little differently than mine.

They threw bottles at any girl who came by the school. There was another high school not too far from ours called Walton High School that had boys and girls. Some of these girls made their way up to our school and were disrespected by the immature students. Even this did not stop the girls from coming.

Every morning on my way to school, I would have to take the No. 12 bus on Fordham Road up to the No. 1 bus or 2 bus headed to Moshulu Parkway. While waiting for the bus on Fordham Road, I would see girls headed to Roosevelt High School. A lot of the Bronx

152

girls were raving beauties, and every single morning I watched them walk to their school, I had to talk myself out of transferring. My hormones were raging and what was going on inside my pants was telling me to make a switch. But, deep down, I knew I had to stay the course and continue my studies at Dewitt Clinton.

After, catching the buses to my school, I would be greeted by a big dice game right in the back of the school. This is where all the drug dealers, pickpockets, stickup kids and thugs hung out. My homeboys, Dante and CeeWee from Midtown also went to Clinton and they loved playing dice before they went to class. One time they told me about an incident that went down at the dice game.

While they were playing dice, a white Cadillac pulled up and a guy got out and robbed everyone playing the game. The funny thing about it is, the guy came back the next day and did it again. Like they say on the streets, there's always somebody crazier than you.

I used to gamble at school, but my odds were better than playing dice. I beat the students with my three-card monte. In the classrooms and in the lunchroom, I brushed up on my monte skills. I beat them for money, watches, jewelry, playboy books and even lunch tickets. Word spread quickly that I was a big time monte player in Midtown. This made me keep my eyes and ears open at all times for the thugs and stickup kids. Even though the thugs knew that Dante and CeeWee were my homeboys, I still had to cover my own ass.

It didn't help any when a few students saw me playing monte in Midtown. I noticed them from time to time in the big crowds of my monte games. One student, who saw me playing and beating all the vics, began stalking me. He stared at me in school like I was a celebrity or something. Then one day he got the nerve to ask me if I could put him down with the monte. He said his girl was pregnant and he needed to make some money. I told him I already had a team, but it didn't stop him from asking. Everywhere I went in the school there he was—the classrooms, the lunchroom and even the library where I sometimes went to read a book or relax.

One day, when I was reading in the library, something told me to look up because I felt a presence near me. Who do you guess was sitting in the seat in front of me? It was the monte stalker, and who knows how long he had been sitting there staring at me. Then he commented on all my nice jewelry.

"Man, that Mike medallion is bad. The diamonds are blinding me. And, man, the diamonds in those bracelets and rings—whoa, all that stuff must have cost you a fortune."

As the stalker babbled on and on about my jewels, I thought I might have to resort to violence, if he tried anything. He asked me how much I paid for this and how much I paid for that. I just replied, "Oh nothing but some short money, not that much." But I was lying.

So, while he continued to ask me questions, I made my answers short. He finally got around to asking me to put him down with monte. I told him the usual answers, that I already had a team. So, he just got up and left as I continued reading.

Even though I had a stalker at my school, I still knew I had made the right decision in choosing Dewitt Clinton High School. Lord, only knows what I would be going through with the girls at Roosevelt High School. A young guy with money and raging hormones in a school with a bunch of dimepieces was sure to find a lot of mischief.

Yes, Clinton was the right choice even though it did have some peculiar things going on, in and around the school. For instance, one time a student brought his sister to school to suck guys off for a dollar apiece. I learned of the incident when the principal got on the intercom making thinly veiled references about some of the students disgracing the school. After class everybody was talking about how long the line was outside the bathroom, and how could a brother pimp his own sister. The first thing that came to my mind was how Honey Combs told me he pimped his sister at twelve years old.

So, hearing about a brother pimping his sister did not blow my mind. He was not the only student caught up in something crazy. I had my own problems while going to Dewitt Clinton.

One day I was in English class doing my work and all of a sudden I developed this burning itch that I had never experienced before in my crotch area. Every few minutes, I would sneak my hands in my pants and scratch like a mad man. One time I scratched real hard and I came out with this little bug with a lot of legs, like a crab. I yelled, "Oh shit!"

This guy who was sitting next to me saw what I was doing and said, "You all right?"

I lied and said real fast, "Nothing, nothing."

I yelled to the teacher in the front of the class, that I had to go to the bathroom and he let me go.

I pulled my pants down and proceeded to scratch my balls in a frenzy. Little bugs were down in my crotch area biting the shit out of me. I tried to kill them with hot water. Every time someone came into the bathroom, I would jump and they would say, "Man, what's wrong with you?"

Then I would respond, "Nothing. Nothing."

When I left school, I went downtown to ask one of the players about the little bugs that were having a party in my pubic area. Pimp Chelsea told me it was crabs and you can get them by having sex. He told me I needed to get some crab ointment, take a shower and that would kill them. I thanked Chelsea for his help, then I went uptown and followed his advice. The crazy thing about it all was, at the time, I did not know about crabs. I guess I got it from someone I had sex with. But, the crab story gets even wilder.

A year later I met a girl at the T-Connection hip-hop spot, where all the hot rap groups used to perform, like Grandmaster Flash and the Furious Five, DJ Bambata, etc. She came up to me with a lame line asking me if I was Tony from 118th Street. Then she told me everything I had on two weeks ago, down to my boxers. She was right about the attire, but I was not Tony from 118th Street. The Tony part was just her attempt at an introduction. So, I went along with the game. While we made small talk, Tina, the Spanish girl I brought to the spot with me, Dante, CeeWee and Raheim, walked up and said, "Who's this bitch trying to get at Mike!"

She and the girl argued until I lied and told Tina the girl was my cousin. Tina did not believe it, but she chilled out.

Later on in the party, I got her number and one day I met her at her mother's apartment. Guess who opened the door? It was the guy who busted me scratching crabs in the classroom. I was shocked, as he laughed and said, "Yo Mike, did you get that little problem taken care of?"

And, I responded, "Yeah, I'm all right," with a snicker and a wink.

His sister said, "Do you two know each other?"

I replied, "Yeah, we both go to Dewitt Clinton".

Then she said, "What's so funny?"

Then he said, "It ain't nothing . . . just a little inside joke."

I wasn't known as little Mr. Innocent at Dewitt Clinton.

19

Gave a Lot of Parties and got Jerked

The shit stacked on my bull, was so thick, a kid could smell it. Take for instance the time I met a pretty young lady sitting at the bar at the Disco Fever. I flashed my sinister smile and proceeded to tell her how I was captivated by her mere presence and her enchanting personality. She fell for it, hook, line, and sinker and after drinking and dancing all night, we wound up at a hotel where we did the nasty all morning. Afterwards we went to pick up her two kids.

When we arrived on 145th Street and Broadway, we went upstairs and she headed to the bedroom to get the kids, while I stayed in the living room exchanging pleasantries with her mother. Her mother was a nice lady, who looked a little like the actress Debbie Allen. I could see where her daughter got her good looks. While I stood there talking to her in the living room, her daughter came out of the bedroom with the kids. They were beautiful little kids, and the son who seemed to be about three years old had adorable chubby cheeks. And, the daughter, about four, was the spitting image of her mother, light-skinned with light blue eyes.

I said, "Hi, you're such a pretty little girl."

She looked at me like she saw through the jive-talking player that I was, who had conned her mother into going to a hotel, and had kept her out all night long away from them. That sweet little girl punched me straight in my Johnson, which caught me off guard and my knees buckled and I dropped to the floor—not in ecstasy, but in pure pain.

Damn, I gave a lot of parties and I got jerked.

20

Gift of Gab

"Man, Mike, what's that rap song playing on Fronting Cee's radio? That song is dope."

I said, "Jaheim, man, it's called 'The Message' by Grandmaster Flash and the Furious Five. Every time it comes on the radio in my car, I blast it."

Then Jaheim said, "As soon as I finish playing monte today, I'm gonna go buy that record. You know Mike, Justin and Talib got a song out now. They play it on the radio all the time."

I said, "Damn, monte players are becoming rappers, too. Ain't that some shit? Man, I hope that don't inspire CeeWee to keep rapping. That boy sucks big time."

Fronting Cee overheard Jaheim and me talking and said, "You know, Mike, if you really think about it, monte players are rappers in their own sort of way. The only difference is we rap the vics right out of their money." Then he rapped, "Red will get you ahead. Black will set you back. Get it."

I said, "Cee, I think you've got a point and being I'm a monte player, slash rapper, let me head over to Broadway, because the vics are waiting for me to put on a show."

We were convulsed with laughter. After shooting the breeze with my homeboys, I got my team together and then headed to Broadway. As I watched all the people walking by, I thought about how Fronting Cee put monte players in the same category as so-called rappers. His rationale made me think, *Who else could be put into the same context of being considered a rapper?* Which, to me, is sort of like someone who is gifted with the gift of gab. You know, people who have a way with words? If you look at it in this context, people like Muhammad

157

Ali, Don King, Rev. Jesse Jackson, ladies men and pimps—these are people who have the unique ability to persuade people into seeing something their way, through the words that they speak. A rapper could have easily said some of the things "The Greatest" used to say before fights to make people believe he would knock someone out in the ring. The things he said like "Float like a butterfly, sting like a bee," "I'm gonna knock this chump out in three." Or, "Liston is still rising and the ref wears a frown, for he can't start counting till Sonny comes down" are prime examples. When Ali said these things there was not a doubt in your mind that someone was going to get knocked out. A lot of pastors, reverends and preachers fill up their churches every Sunday using their charisma and the gift of gab. Some use it in a positive way, and some use it in a negative way. But those who do, usually use it for their own personal gain regardless of who they hurt.

I know of a certain flamboyant reverend who is known for driving Rolls Royces and wearing two thousand dollar suits and diamond and gold jewelry. He had my mother sending him ten dollars a month, even though we were poor. His game was, if you sent him ten dollars, God would give it back to you tenfold. Many people fell for his bullshit. That's why he was able to have all the material things that he acquired. Even though I was a kid, I knew this reverend was using my mother.

The power of persuasion along with the gift of gab can be used to reap tremendous rewards. This gift can work for the people who have it, or it can even work against them, if they use it in the wrong way. I have this gift and I fit right into this whole equation. My gift of gab has also worked against me.

Promoter, Don King, the "only in America" man, was legendary for saying things that made people see things his way. They may not always have understood a lot of the words that he put together—even some of his words seemed like they were not even in the dictionary, like he made them up himself. But, when he finished talking, they all wanted to go see the fight he was promoting.

One day I was walking on Forty-eighth Street between Sixth and Seventh Avenues when I spotted Don King and two white men with trench coats and briefcases heading my way. Don King was in the middle. He wore a long black mink coat with a big floppy mink hat covering his famous spiked afro. He also had a big Don King diamond name medallion with a crown on it, and a pair of 'gator shoes. Don King looked like a million bucks and a man with lots of power.

As soon as I got close enough to him I said, "Play baby, play baby." He smiled a big grin and nodded his head in approval. I knew that his gift of gab was on another level than mine. But, game always recognizes game.

Whenever I played three-card monte and I got behind the box, my gift of gab had to be used in the proper way in order to achieve my main objective, which was to beat all the vics out of every dime. In order to achieve these results, I always started talking slow to the vics. This made them think that my game is slow and easy. But as soon as they started losing, I started talking fast to confuse them. When vics lost their money they could not think straight. So, my fast talking confused them to the next level, sort of like the way Muhammad Ali confused his opponents in the ring by talking to them. Three-card monte is like boxing. It is an art form. Tossing the cards is just one part of the hustle. The other part is the gift of gab and various other techniques.

Now, when I am not playing monte, I use my gift of gab on the beautiful women in the city. I learned some of my gift of gab from some of the older players and hustlers in Midtown. Pimp Honey Combs once told me his ten commandments he used for getting women. 1. Before you attempt to say anything to a woman, smile and act like her mere presence brightens up your day. 2. Always keep the conversation simple, until you find out her likes and dislikes. 3. Always look directly at her when you are talking to her. 4. Let her do most of the talking because women like a good listener. So, act interested even if you are not. 5. Laugh at her jokes, even if they are not funny. Tell your own jokes because women like to laugh. 6. Never talk about how the white man is keeping you down. Women hate excuses. 7. Always come across as confident and strong, even if you are the weakest motherfucker in the world. 8. Never talk about subjects you know nothing about. Women hate a stupid motherfucker. 9. Never stare and by all means do not get caught looking at her chest and/or ass. And, last but not least, 10. Never trust a big butt and a smile.

So, along with Honey Combs' ten commandments, and game from the other people I know, I put it all together and found a happy medium that worked for me. I took the approach when it came to rapping to women, to first make sure I always had a haircut and good hygiene. Plus, I always made it my business to show my pearly whites with my sinister smile. After all this was accomplished, I always made sure not to utter any corny lines like, "Hey, baby, what's your sign?"

Or, "Hey, baby, you are so pretty that you make a blind man see." Or, "Hey, baby, do you have a man? Because if you do, you need to leave that zero and get with this hero." (I once heard that one in a rap song.) What I wanted to know was what type of woman would fall for any of those types of stupid lines? Any girl who would fall for such bull crap would fall for anything. Whenever I rapped to women, I never let this type of nonsense come out of my mouth.

I catered my game according to the type of girl that I was talking to. When it comes to messing with women, your game must be versatile. Some men have the same rap for every woman. That's where they lose. Picture some thug type brother with a white wife-beater T-shirt, baggy jeans hanging off his ass and boots trying to kick it to a college-educated woman with some, "Hey, baby, what it bee's like?' game. She would just look at him like he's crazy and give him the hand. You know how strong women have a way of doing that don't-even-go-there look. So, I already knew if I was going to come into a woman's cipher, I had to be ready and my game had to be tight.

Not everyone has the gift of gab. I have hung out with many so-called ladies' men who supposedly were good rappers when it came to kickin' it with the ladies. But, a lot of times I found out when we would get with some pretty ladies, they would say something stupid that would blow both of our chances of getting into the ladies' pants. Here's a perfect scenario. "Hey, girls, my man Mike told me that y'all was down to go to the hotel with us." This is something that usually would be said after all their weak game was not working. This type of stupid game was coming from so-called Mack daddies. I guess watching *Superfly* and *The Mack* did not pay off.

A lot of my gift-of-gab game was learned through trial and error. I learned from mistakes, then I eliminated the things that did not work for me. The saying goes, practice makes perfect. I learned a lot just from listening to women talk among themselves, when they thought a man was not listening. I learned from these conversations that women could be very analytical and observant. When it comes to dealing with men, some will even let their man think he is smarter and mentally stronger than them, just to soothe his ego. What some men fail to realize is, our mothers are the first ones to give us the tools for the game of life. No one understands men better than their mothers. My mother used to tell me, "Mike, don't believe what people say. Go by what they do, because talk is cheap."

This is coming from my mother who could convince me that getting a beating was good for me. Now that I am older, I beg to differ on the latter. If talk is cheap, why do people pay to hear lectures? If talk is cheap, why do so many people get talked out of giving up their hard earned money through different cons and schemes? If you do not believe me come to Midtown because I've got a little something to show and tell you. How many suckers have been sold the George Washington Bridge by some smooth-talking person? How many women have been talked into having sex even when they really did not want to? Then, after having sex and getting pregnant, the no-good guy leaves them all alone to raise the kid. Now the kids that they have are forced to grow up without a father, to help guide them. I have seen too many times some pretty girl around my neighborhood having kid after kid because the guys with the gift of gab, talked her into having sex. Most of the time it would be some young girl who did not even get a chance to mature yet. So, she did not have the necessary life skills to withstand all the things that were coming at her. Now she is left to raise all of her kids alone. Everything comes at a price.

I grew up without a father because he died when I was young, which made me look for father figures in all the wrong places. This is why you have me, Midtown Mike, to worry about whenever you find yourself walking through the streets of Midtown. How many other fatherless kids like me are getting caught up in negative situations? Have you ever been stabbed, shot or robbed by some young kid? Then, wondered how did this kid turn out to be so violent? Have you ever tried to tell some little kid to stop causing some type of mischief and having him tell you to shut the fuck up before he puts his foot in your ass? This coming from some little nine-year old kid. Well, all of these things started with a little gift of gab.

21

Pimp or Die

Chelsea was killed last night. I found this out as soon as I got off the No. 2 train. Everybody was hanging out in front of the donut shop with sad faces.

"Yo, you heard about Chelsea?"

"Nah, what happened?"

"Well, the police found him in the East River with about sixty bullets in him. They say the mob killed him. The story goes: Chelsea's top hoe, Jackie, had a father who was down with the mob. They say he had given Chelsea ample warnings to leave his daughter alone. Let her go. But he wouldn't listen. So, they killed him."

After being told about Chelsea's murder, I thought about the lifestyles of the pimps that I ran across in Midtown. The way they are portrayed in movies and books is totally different than what I observed. When I first came downtown, my ideas about them were like most people's. Some people had preconceived ideas of what they thought a pimp's lifestyle consisted of. Some thought it was all about being lazy, taking money from gullible women and beating the shit out of them. Others looked at pimps as smooth operators and fancy dressers, who just happened to be a little bit more manipulative than the whores they pimped. We all have seen the portrayals of pimps in movies like *Taxi Driver*, when Harvey Keitel played a Forty-second Street pimp, who pimped a young Jodie Foster in this Robert DeNiro movie, or *Street Smart,* with Morgan Freeman playing a ruthless pimp and Christopher Reeves playing a reporter investigating him.

My first impressions of pimps came from the fiction that I read, which depicted pimps sort of like what I alluded to earlier—smooth operators, fancy dressers and dangerous individuals. But these were just ideas and thoughts that I got from books and movies.

When I first arrived downtown at age fifteen and saw pimp Chelsea standing by the donut shop wearing an expensive suit that everybody told me cost two thousand dollars and a pair of 'gator shoes, I was totally in awe. I looked on in amazement at the tall man with an Indian complexion who seemed to be about six feet, three inches, with long wavy hair. I remember this scene like it was yesterday—him standing there cracking jokes with the other players.

I came into contact with Chelsea many times after that day, and I can tell you in my opinion, pimps are not too different from everyday people. They get up in the morning, eat breakfast and read the morning paper as they carry on conversations about sports and current events. Just like regular people, they go to work. But their work is different. They pimp hoes.

There is an old saying on the streets "Pimpin ain't easy." But if you come from the percentage of people who say, "Bullshit, pimps are just lazy motherfuckers who use women and beat them," all I can tell you is there's always three sides to a story—the pimp's side, the whore's and then yours. I say let the tricks figure it out.

But, if you come from the percentage of people who look at pimps as smooth operators and fancy dressers, who just happen to be a little bit more manipulative than the whores they pimp, all I can tell you from what I have learned while being around them is that when you get to know them personally, some are quite likeable and even have kids who they love and support, just like regular people. Some, I found out, do not even drink or do drugs. Chelsea was one of them. And others, although they were pimps, even had a twisted type of love for some of their hoes.

I say all of this not to make excuses for pimps, or to give my stamp of approval to their lifestyle, but to say, I found them not too much different than the average person with strengths and weaknesses. You have good people, who do bad things and you have bad people who do good things. The only difference about pimps is the fact that nobody cares about a pimp's good side.

Chelsea used to tell me stories about his hoes and the tricks they serviced. He told me about the sick fetishes that tricks loved his hoes to do. Some, he said, liked to be pissed on. This was called a golden shower. They did not want to have sex. All they wanted was the hoes to piss all over them. He said they paid good money for this. Then there were the ones who paid pimps to just watch them fuck one of their hoes. Chelsea said these sickos also liked to be beaten with whips and belts, and they called this sadomasochism. Some even wanted the hoes to dress up in Catholic school uniforms and other types of costumes, so, they could have visions of having sex with someone wholesome and sweet. I had heard about these things in books I read, but this was coming from a real pimp.

I laughed really hard the time he told me about the non-English speaking tourists who would not know one bit of English, but when they wanted sex from a hoe, they would always know the universal language. I can still remember how dumb I sounded when I asked Chelsea what the universal language was.

He said, "Oh, shorty, the universal language is spoken when someone wants to have sex with somebody. But, since they do not know how to say it in English, they just say 'fucki, sucki' to the person they want to fuck. Sort of like a military guy telling a prostitute in a different country, fucki, sucki." Chelsea's and my cackling could have broken one of the big lamp post light bulbs.

I always liked talking to him. He knew something about everything and was a very wise man. I learned many things walking the streets of Midtown late at night with Chelsea or pimp Honey Combs or some of the other hustlers I knew.

One thing about Midtown is, you never knew what was going to happen on any particular day. One day while walking with Chelsea I heard one of the public telephones ringing. I was about to pick it up when Chelsea stopped me.

He said, "Never pick up any ringing phones out here because the person calling could be a pervert trying to make a person-to-person connection."

Then he told me to look across the street. When I looked, he pointed to a real skinny white man wearing a woman's dress, sandals and a blond wig, who was using a public telephone.

Chelsea told me "You see, shorty, that's the person who's calling this phone."

He said the reason that the guy was calling from across the street was, so he could see who answered the phone. When Chelsea told me that, I knew there was a lot I had yet to learn about the streets of Midtown.

Not too long after being schooled about the phone perverts, I happened to be talking to a girl on one of the public phones, when a guy came up to me and asked me for directions.

I replied, "Oh, its about two blocks down . . ."

Then the guy says, "By the way, can I suck your dick?"

I was so shocked that I kicked him in his ass, which I should never have done because the pervert had this look of pure ecstasy, like he loved the feeling of my foot in his ass. Yes, Midtown had some very strange and crazy characters walking around.

On some of my travels I encountered peculiar incidents there. One day while hanging with pimp Honey Combs on The Deuce, we saw a van load of cops smoking marijuana, which did not surprise me one bit because one time when I was arrested for playing monte, the same monte squad that arrested me, had also arrested a Jamaican guy with about five-hundred bags of weed. Some of the cops we knew, showed us some of the weed they stole from the guy. Don't be shocked, cops smoke weed, too.

A lot of times when the monte players got busted, cops stole our money. We all knew it was part of the game. Cops had to find a way to supplement their small salaries. Some cops who did this would sometimes give us a break and let us play monte all day. So, it was like a fair exchange.

Even though Midtown had its secrets, I still loved the place. I saw so many unbelievable things happen on The Deuce that if I didn't witness something bizarre, I would think something was wrong. Take for instance the time I was hanging on The Deuce with Deon.

Deon was a do-it-all type of hustler. He played monte, jostled, boosted and sold drugs. He was down for anything. Plus, he was wild and loony. One day we were hanging on The Deuce with other hustlers while they sold drugs and whatever else to their customers. Deon made eye contact with a girl who was walking by holding hands with her boyfriend. They were like two lovebirds enjoying a beautiful night out on the town. After making eye contact with the girl, he told me to watch what he was going to do. He went up to the couple and started kicking game to the girl, like the guy wasn't even there. Next thing I knew, he told the guy to step off as he gave him his bulging-eyes madman look, which was not far from the truth. The guy stepped off like a little scared puppy dog running from a big rottweiler. The girl took Deon by the hand and they walked off like two lovebirds enjoying a beautiful night on the town. The next day when I saw Deon, he was still with the girl. He told me they fucked all night long. But, that was not the only strange incident that I experienced with him.

Deon was the same guy who almost got me and CeeWee beat down by a whole high school football team on the No. 2 train. He told one of the players who had accidentally bumped into him that all football players were pussies in tights. I do not have to tell you how scared CeeWee and I were when the whole team converged on us. If it were not for their coach stopping them from kicking our asses, those players would have turned us into some pussies in a tight situation.

But that's not all. That same night we went to a hip-hop jam at the Audubon Ballroom and Deon sold fake cocaine to all the rap groups. The stuff he sold them was called coco snow. This stuff tasted like cocaine and it numbed up a person's entire face like real cocaine. If those rappers had found out what he was selling them, we would have been in some big trouble.

After we spent a few hours at the jam, Deon met two attractive girls with really nice asses and tits. It was two of them and three of us—Deon, CeeWee and I. Deon chose the one he wanted to hang out with and CeeWee and I were going to try and run a train on the other one. So off we went to the Bronx, where we bought the girls champagne and weed, then, we all went to the Bronx Park Motel. As soon as we got in the room, Deon and his girl began fucking their brains out. When the other girl found out that CeeWee and I were trying to run a train on her, she refused to get with either of us. So, we were forced to watch Deon fuck his girl all night, and boy did he have stamina. He must have put some of that fake cocaine on his penis because he put on one hell of a show! CeeWee and I sat there like two dickheads watching a movie without popcorn. And, we had blue balls to match.

After watching them fuck all night long, the girl who wouldn't screw said she was hungry and was in the mood for a big breakfast. When Deon heard her, he yelled, "Bitch, you didn't even fuck last night." And, he punched her straight in the stomach.

The girl screamed and cried, then tried to fight back. Next thing you knew, Deon had the girl in a dopefiend yoke, with a wide-eyed Charles Manson look on his face. Everybody yelled, "Let her go, Deon! Please! You're going to kill her!"

The girl's eyes rolled up into her head and Deon yelled, "I'll kill this crazy bitch!" He was the perfect candidate for an insane asylum. Eventually he let her loose. After the girls gained their composure, they shot out of that room like their lives depended on it.

Yes, Midtown had some pretty strange characters; I never knew whom I would wind up hanging with. But I always liked the times I was with the pimps. There was no telling where I would end up when I ran the streets with them, including on Eighth Avenue hanging with their hoes as they sold pussy to the tricks. Some of these prostitutes were the finest women a man would ever have sex with. You had black, Asian, Spanish, white and all different types of nationalities selling their bodies out there. Chelsea's hoe, Jackie, was one fly white broad. She had nice thighs and an ass like a black or Puerto Rican woman. Her titties were big, nice and round. Every time I saw her she smiled and treated me real nice. She told me she was Italian and was born and raised in Brooklyn. I used to kid her about how she sounded blacker than a black girl. That always made her laugh because she said she grew up around a lot of black people.

I heard that the singer, Teena Marie, who sang "Fire and Desire" with Rick James grew up the same way—maybe that accounts for all of her soul. One thing about us black people is we have so much soul that if you hang around us long enough, some of our soul is bound to rub off on you. Maybe that is why some people from different nationalities are scared to hang around us. You know the saying too black too strong.

There were even a lot of transvestites dressed to the nines in expensive women's clothing. You could not even tell if some of them were men or women. I am kind of ashamed to tell this story, but I'll break it down anyway. I once got arrested for playing monte and they took me to the Midtown North Precinct. I was tired when they put me in the cell so I went to sleep. When I woke up, a pretty Puerto Rican lady was in the cell with me. She was drop-dead gorgeous with a small face, Chinese-looking eyes and long black hair. She had on a burgundy silk dress with spaghetti straps. The dress was so tight and it had so little material that you could practically see everything. And, boy did this lady have a body on her. She had nice medium-sized titties with big nipples pressing on the silk fabric. When she got up I could see her little thong panties pressing against her perfect ass. She had little legs and feet, with a pair of burgundy and gray pumps exposing her pedicured toes. Anyone could tell that this woman was pampered. But, what I could not figure out was why she was in the cell with a male. I knew the cops never did that. The cop caught me checking her out real hard and said, "It's not what you think."

I asked him what he was talking about and he said, "That's not a woman. That's a man."

I said, "You have got to be kidding," and he said, "He's been busted numerous times for prostitution."

I was in total shock because there I sat in a cell with the biggest hard-on I had ever had. Looks really are deceiving.

So, the times that I stood on Eighth Avenue with Chelsea I was well aware of the transvestites and drag queens. But, the odd thing about it was, it seemed that a lot of the tricks would always be stepping off with them. I learned anything could be bought for a price on Eighth Avenue. You even had some males selling their asses out there. And, don't let me forget about the runaways and little kids getting picked up by the sickos and perverts. It seemed that the tricks liked the kids real young; the younger the better. I once saw an old man sucking this little thirteen-year-old boy's dick right on one of the side blocks on Eighth Avenue. They picked any spot they could find to perform their devilish acts. Some of them even wanted to be caught. Nothing was sacred in the underbelly of Midtown.

One of the things I noticed while hanging out with Chelsea was any hoe that he came into contact with looked at him in amazement. They seemed captivated by his mere presence. It was like they were his fans and he was a big celebrity. I could tell he could have any hoe out there that he wanted. Their look told me they would do anything he wanted them to do. I guess that's why he had so many hoes.

Chelsea looked a little like the actor Ron O'Neal who played Superfly in the black exploitation movie. But, he was much taller, more handsome and better dressed. He was not one of those corny pimps depicted in some stupid movie wearing gaudy clothes, a big stupid hat with a feather and platform shoes. No, Chelsea was a real bona fide pimp who wore the same type of nice suits that the president or some big entertainer would wear. He had so many different two thousand dollar suits that no one ever saw him wear the same one twice. His double striped 'gator shoes were top of the line, and he always had a nice tie with matching handkerchiefs. His hair and nails were always done and he always carried himself with class. He looked and acted like he was put on this earth to pimp.

Even other pimps looked at him in awe. They told their hoes if they were caught talking to Chelsea, they would be one dead bitch. I say do not hate the player, hate the game. When Chelsea spoke, people paid attention. They knew that this was a man who knew what he was talking about.

Sometimes when he would see me with my book bag, he would ask me about the subjects I was taking in school. He seemed to know more about some of my subjects than the teachers who taught the class. I suspected that maybe he had graduated from college, but I was too scared to ask. I always got the feeling when I was around him that I should stay in a child's place, which was the same feeling

I used to get when I was little hanging around grown folks. So, most of the times that I hung around pimps, I did a lot of listening, and I was not too nosey, so they respected that.

I was like a student being taught by teachers with degrees in streetology. Pimps and hustlers have taught me how to survive on the streets that took no prisoners. So, when I got off the train and heard Chelsea was dead, it hit me like a ton of bricks.

Now there was going to be one more funeral that I would have to attend. I have been to too many funerals where a reverend preached a eulogy that felt like it didn't pertain to the person they were talking about. I sometimes got the feeling the preacher was not telling the real story about the deceased person's life. That's why I felt it was fitting to write what I thought the reverend should say about Chelsea:

"Chelsea was a *pimp's pimp*. He laid the game down hard. There were people who loved him and there were people who hated him. If this were not true he would still be alive today. He was like a sharply dressed smooth preacher with the gift of gab. He schooled and guided his hoes in what he thought was the right direction, which was towards the almighty dollar, just like a smooth preacher who guides his flock to the collection plate, right after a fiery sermon. Chelsea never claimed to be anything but a pimp. If you ever met the man, the one thing you would automatically know was you were in the presence of a bona fide boss pimp, not by the way he dressed, but by the way he carried himself. He was calm, cool and collected. Chelsea died doing what he loved doing—pimping. He did what pimps do—they pimp. The mobsters that killed him did what mobsters do best—they kill. If a mobster feels someone needs to be killed—then that's what they do. Chelsea once told us, he was not scared of any white motherfucking mobster. So, one thing I will always know is, Chelsea did not die scared, even though the mobsters put him to sleep with the fishes."

22

The King is Dying

One night, while standing by the donut shop after a good day of beating the vics on Fifth Avenue, I ran into King and he wasn't looking too good. He appeared to weigh ninety pounds and had the complexion of a dead man.

"Yo King, what's up? Long time no see."

"What's up, Mike? Did you see my brother, Bugsy, today?"

"Yeah, I think he went uptown."

"Man, I was gonna borrow some money from him. Hey man, loan me forty dollars 'til tomorrow."

I looked at King and saw he was sick, then I passed him the money. "Yo Mike, take a walk with me to Thirty-fourth Street."

As we walked, I thought back to how he used to tell me to stay away from drugs and to stay in school because the streets were cruel. As we slowly walked, my thoughts drifted and he asked me if I was all right.

I said, "Yeah."

Then he said, "Man, it seems like your mind is somewhere in the clouds."

"Nah, everything's okay. I just want to tell you thanks for always pushing me to stay in school, 'cause it really helps. I know we don't get to kick it like we used to, 'cause we both always on the move.

"Man, Mike, you know no matter what, we always gon' be cool."

Then he said, "I know everybody told you I got AIDS."

"Nah, I haven't heard that."

"Well, you're hearing it from me. I know it's slowly killing me, but I just can't stay away from dope. I just gotta have it. That's why I'm sick like a dog right now. I feel like snakes are just crawling all over my body and the only way I can get 'em off is with a few bags of dope."

"Man, King, I've always been scared of needles and drugs."

"That's good, Mike, 'cause drugs'll kill you. Get high off money and pussy. By the way, speaking of money, I was watching you a few weeks ago on Seventh Avenue. You're really getting better with selling the game to the vics. I always knew you were going to be a good springer, but now you're learning how to sell the game. When you have those two things combined, you can't be stopped. I saw you raise some vic to six hundred dollars."

"Yeah, King I learned from one of the best—you."

"Thanks, man. I needed that right about now."

"King, I didn't tell you that to gas you up. It's the truth."

"Thanks, Mike. You know everybody in Midtown is talking about how you beat that tennis pro, Jimmy Phillips, out of some money."

"King, I could have broke that chump for every dime he had, but my sticks got scared."

He just laughed as we kept on walking. I felt happy that I was able to bring a smile to his face, knowing what he was going through and all.

We eventually made it to Thirty-fourth Street and Eighth Avenue where he went into the bar while I stayed outside watching the people walk by on this warm Friday night. I felt right at home gazing at the nightlife.

Fifteen minutes later, he came out of the bar as high as a kite, looking like he didn't have a care in the world. All I could think about was, *Damn, my man, King, has AIDS.*

23

The Set-up

Some say you can go but so far up, before you come down.

"Hello, Mrs. McKinley. Can I speak to Misa?"

"Hold on, Michael."

I heard her yell, "Hey Misa, it's Mike on the phone."

"Mike, Misa is coming. By the way, Misa told me you are graduating next week. Congratulations."

"Thanks, Mrs. McKinley."

"You're welcome."

Then Misa got on the phone.

"Hi, Mike, where you been? I've been looking for you all over Midtown. Have you been hiding from me? Or is it you found some other bitch?"

"Misa, what you talking about?"

"Mike, you know what I'm talking about. Don't play stupid."

I started to laugh and then I jumped to another subject. "Misa, I bought you a nice pantsuit from this girl, Melba, who be boosting downtown."

"Oh, so that's the bitch you been fucking?"

"Misa, stop the bullshit. I'm coming to pick you up. I want to take you to the movies, so I'll be at your house in a little while." Then I hung up.

I caught a cab from downtown and headed to her mother's apartment on 103rd Street and Third Avenue. After the cab arrived at her building, I paid the cab driver and took the elevator to the sixteenth floor. As soon as I got off I got a flashback to how Misa and I would sometimes go fuck on the roof when her parents were home. Damn we were a horny couple.

I knocked and Misa answered in skimpy red shorts, a T-shirt and yellow snakeskin pumps. Damn she was looking good and this was just shit she walked around the apartment in!

"Come here, baby, give daddy a kiss," I said to her.

She smiled and I knew I was forgiven.

"Misa, take this brown suit I bought you and put it on. I want to see if it fits you."

She looked at the suit and I could tell she liked it. After checking it out she walked to her room swishing in her skimpy shorts. While she was changing, I thought about going in there to give her some dick. I was horny, but I decided against it since her mom was in the other room. Misa looked stunning in the pantsuit. Her well-proportioned assets combined with the cut of the pantsuit were perfect.

"Come here, baby. You got a nigga fucked up."

She walked up to me and we kissed. Then she put on her shoes, fixed her hair and we headed downtown to the movies.

We went to see *Endless Love* with Brooke Shields. You could tell by the title what it was about. We watched a movie about love, like two lovebirds. Brothers do crazy things when they're whipped.

Later we went to Popeye's to eat. Misa told me she had bumped into my friend, Money Gus, the other day and he was trying to fuck her. She told me that after he tried to kick it and she didn't go for it, he switched the subject and told her she should set me up for my jewelry. He said some other people were already talking about robbing me anyway, so she might as well be the one to do it.

She said, "Mike, I was shocked because I thought Gus was your homeboy and I know how close you and him are. But, I think your man Gus is jealous of you and he got crazy larceny. But to tell you the truth I never trusted him. Gus used to fuck with my homegirl Nikki, and she used to tell me all the time how trifling he was. He tried to kick it with me before I met you, but I would always turn him down. The first time he saw me with you, I could tell he was jealous."

When Misa hit me with all of this at one time, I was shocked. I could not believe what I was hearing. Not Gus, my ace boon coon, my pride and joy. Not the man who grieved with me when our comrade, Johnny Ranks died. Not the Gus who loved me like a son. I thought back to all my dealings with Gus, and what would make him want to set me up. I understand him cracking on Misa because she was pretty and he was a player. That wasn't the first time she told me that one of my so-called friends had cracked on her. But, one of them telling her to set me up for my jewelry was another story.

So, as we sat there in Popeye's one thing suddenly came to mind. Maybe Gus wanted to get me robbed because of that time we fucked that girl together and then she robbed him while we were sleeping. When I think back, Gus found it a little odd that she had taken his money, but spared mine. But, the reason she had taken his money was because she saw where he had put it when he was high. Back then I always used to hide my money in my sock for fear of getting robbed. Maybe all the time he thought I set him up and now he was trying to pay me back.

I didn't tell Misa this. I just kept it to myself as we finished eating. After Popeye's, we got a hotel room and did what we always did—fuck. But, I still couldn't get Gus off my mind.

A few days went by and now it was time for my graduation from Dewitt Clinton High School. My mother and Aunt Mamie came along with her son, Stan, and Misa. They were real proud of me that day. I looked sharp with the clothes I had bought from the expensive store Leighton's on Forty-ninth Street and Broadway. I had on a blue blazer, green silk shirt, blue linen pants and a pair of green lizard shoes. I also had on all my jewelry. The diamonds were sparkling like chandeliers. Damn I looked good! Everybody at the graduation was checking me out. Even the principal, Dr. Feinstein, gave me this big bear hug when he saw me. He just shook all the other students hands as he gave them their diplomas, but, he hugged me. I guess he thought I was some big drug dealer who had somehow managed to graduate. I was happy and my family, and Misa were proud of me.

After graduation, we headed for my uncle Howard's new Lincoln Continental that his son, Stan, was driving. Ma-Ma and Aunt Mamie cried in the car because they were so happy to see me graduate. Stan dropped our parents off, and then drove Misa and me up to Fordham Road because I wanted to have my picture taken in my new clothes and jewelry. When we got to Fordham, nobody was out there taking the Polaroid pictures so I never had a graduation picture.

Three weeks later, Ma-Ma's apartment was robbed. Every piece of jewelry I owned was taken. The only reason they didn't get the $17,000 that I kept in my trench coat was because the previous week my sister had stolen $400 out of my pile of money. So, I whipped her ass and moved my money to another spot. Her theft had become a blessing in disguise.

I found out about my apartment being robbed by Dante and Misa in Midtown. Dante and I were cool. Sometimes he used to slide for me and sometimes we hung out together. Misa ran into Dante and told him she had called my house looking for me when my mother told her that some people came into the apartment and held her hostage while they took my jewelry. I was devastated and heated all at the same time. As Misa, Dante and I headed uptown in a cab, I asked her over and over if my mother was all right. I couldn't think. A million things were going on in my head at the same time. *Who set me up? Was it Gus or was it Misa or was it Dante? Maybe one of the players in Midtown. Maybe somebody I didn't even know?*

As we rode uptown, Dante and I questioned Misa—picking her brains. Misa blurted out, "I think Money Gus had somebody set you up when I refused to do it." Dante was lost. He couldn't keep up with what she was saying, but I could.

When we got to the apartment, I went to check on my mother to see if she was all right. She was drunk, but she wasn't harmed. I asked her if they hurt her and she said no. She said two guys stayed in the room with her at gunpoint and told her if she didn't cause any trouble, she would not be harmed. Meanwhile two other guys went through the house looking for money and jewelry. Once they found what they were looking for, they left.

Yes, all my jewelry was missing. They left my expensive coats, clothes and shoes, but all the jewelry was taken—$9,000 worth. I checked my other hiding place where my money was hidden. The money was still there. Thank God Ma-Ma wasn't hurt. I don't know how I would have been able to live with myself if anything had happened to my mother.

I couldn't think. I just hugged my mother with tears in my eyes and told her how sorry I was for bringing this type of madness into her apartment. All she said was, "It's not your fault, Michael. You got so many people jealous of you and they don't want to see you with anything. You've been nothing but good to me. Baby, I love you."

I thought back to how my mother had told me since I was little that I was a man amongst men. But, right now all I could think was about what man would bring this type of ghetto drama to his mama's apartment and then I cried.

After I knew my mother was okay, we left the apartment because my mind was in a daze and I needed some fresh air. I put Misa in a cab and sent her home. I needed time by myself to think. I asked Dante not to tell anybody downtown what happened because I needed to find out for myself who had set me up. He asked me if I thought Misa was responsible, and all I could say was I didn't know. But, I told him about the incident with Money Gus.

24

Mind Games

They say, when you do dirt, you get dirt. But, why did that dirt have to go into my mother's apartment? I know that I had done some un-scrupulous things in my life. I mistreated women; conned people out of their money, even stole. But, these were things that I did, not my mother. I am responsible for my sins. God has my list and I know there's no getting around it. One day I know I will have to answer to my maker. But, my mother didn't deserve to be violated because of my wrongs. If someone wanted to rob me, rob *me*. If someone wanted to hurt me, hurt me. If someone wanted to kill *me*, kill *me*—not my mother. So, many thoughts flowed in and out of my head as I walked around in a zombie-like state.

I arrived in Midtown late the next day because I just did not feel like playing three-card monte. I had to find Gus, so I could look deep into his eyes. I had to find something in his eyes or something in his conversation that would tell me he was the one who set me up. And if he did, there would be one less con man in the world.

I walked from monte game to monte game looking for him and also to see if any of the other players acted any differently than they would normally act. I searched all around, but I couldn't find Gus. Every player that I ran across acted normal. They all wanted to know why I was not playing on such a good day. Friday was one of our best days because all the vics were always in "Thank-God-it's-Friday mode," which left them open to being conned. But, the only mode I was finding myself in on this Friday, was murder mode.

At the same time that I found myself feeling that way, I also knew I had to stay focused if I was going to weed out the culprit who had violated me to the fullest. And, all while I was trying to do that, I suddenly came to the realization that something else was playing it-self out.

It took me a little while to grasp what it was, but it slowly came to me. I realized that deep down, instead of trying to prove Gus or Misa set me up, I was really trying to prove they didn't, which was alto-gether different. I guess the reason I found myself in this unsettling predicament is because they were two people in my life I genuinely had love for, and I thought they felt the same way about me. I thought they would never do anything to harm me. But, right now I just didn't know. *He set me up; she set me up; he set me up; she set me up; somebody set me up.*

After searching all over Midtown, I finally ran into Gus standing by the OTB betting parlor on Forty-second and Seventh Avenue with his girl, Pinky. I knew I had to act normal if I was going to find anything out. Pinky spotted me first and said, "Hey, little man. Come give your black mama a hug."

She hugged me and gave me a big sloppy kiss on the cheek. I had really liked Pinky ever since the first time Spence and I met her. Be-fore that, Gus would always talk about how pretty she was and how she had his back to the fullest. He would always say, "Pinky this, Pinky that . . . ," which had us curious to see how she really looked. When we finally did get to meet her, she was nothing like what we had pictured. What we saw was this big, black, mean-looking woman who didn't look pretty at all. But, when we finally got to know her, we loved her like a big sister because she was so nice to us. This also made us see why Gus loved her so much. I guess he saw her inner beauty first, then her outer beauty. Pinky loved Gus so much that she would even kill for him. She gave a new meaning to down-ass chick. And she did not take any shit from anybody. Even when she went to jail, she ran things.

I hadn't seen her for a long time, so I hugged her back with genu-ine love. Then I said, "What's up Gus? What's going on?"

"Just chillin', Mike. You know I just got out of jail doing back-to-back skid bids."

I said, "Yeah, I saw you the first time you got out."

Then he said, "I got to take a lick. I'm broke. Did you hit a lick yet?"

"Nah, Gus."

"All right, so lets get a team and go out. We can let Pinky stick. Just get one more."

I really didn't feel like playing, but I knew this would give me a chance to observe Gus. And, so far, he was acting normal.

As I stared into his eyes—nothing. As I stared into Pinky's eyes—nothing. So, I decided to play and I asked White Boy Pauley, who was standing out there, to stick for us. He agreed. We got Chip to slide, then we headed to Thirty-fourth Street.

On our way over there, Gus kissed and hugged Pinky. They were acting like two lovebirds.

"Yo Mike, these vics gon' feel it today. The kid is back. These motherfuckers owe me some money. I know y'all been taking it since a nigga was in jail. Now its my turn."

"Yeah, baby. My baby's a money maker," Pinky added in. Then she said, "Mike, Gus is real proud of you. He told me how good you've gotten."

Gus said, "Yeah, I taught him well. You know that's my son."

Pinky said, "Nah Gus, that's *our* son."

With all the drama I was going through, they still made me smile. And, all the while I'm thinking, *Could this be the man who had thugs come into my place of residence and violate me to the fullest? Not the man who since the first day we met, showed me nothing but love. No, not the man who never once cheated Spence or me for one dime, even though we were just little shorties on the come-up trying to learn the game. Some players took advantage of us, but not Gus.*

All of these things crossed my confused mind as we made our way to Thirty-fourth Street. As soon as we got across the street from the Empire State Building, Chip and I set up shop. Gus decided he wanted to be the first to spring 'em, while we held him down. Then, after he did his thing, I would take over.

When Gus got behind the box, he yelled, "Hey New York, New York. I'm back, I'm back," and a big crowd gathered around. I could tell by the noise coming from the game, Gus was taking it. Vics walked by me after they had lost their money, cursing to holy hell. Every time I looked back, the crowds were getting bigger and bigger. One fat lady mumbled, "That green-eyed motherfucker tricked me good!"

After Chip called a few slides and we had been at the same spot for about two hours, Gus decided to take one more lick by the Empire State Building, which had always been his favorite spot. Gus had taken so much money there throughout the years, the players called him the King of Thirty-fourth Street. Chip and I set up the boxes and then we went to hold him down. While standing on the corner looking out for the cops, I noticed that playing cards was taking my mind off yesterday's events. I still hadn't figured out if Gus had anything to do with me being set up, but, I had my doubts. Then the crazy cycle continued in my mind. *Misa set me up. No, Gus set me up. That bitch set me up; I'll kill her. No, Gus set me up; I'll kill him. No, maybe some haters set me up. Why did somebody choose to rob me?* Never once in all my days of hustling did I ever try to perpetrate being a thug. Was I a baller? No. Was I a gangster? No. I was just a player and a con man who played his position. Nothing more. Nothing less. But, there I stood on a beautiful Friday, thinking about murder.

After about thirty-five minutes, Gus decided to let me spring 'em. I told the team I wanted to play in front of the Sbarros restaurant right across the street from Madison Square Garden. On our way there, I asked Gus and Pinky what our count was, and they said it was eighteen hundred. I thought, not bad for a late lick. But, now it was my turn. When we got to the spot I proceeded to get down to business. As soon as I got behind the box, the big adrenaline rush came over me. Now it was time for the student to show the teacher who's boss.

25

Monte's Revenge

I yelled real loud, "Hey New York, New York. I'm back, I'm back. Cherry, cherry, like in a strawberry. Who saw the red card?"

I noticed Gus at the corner, smiling, because he knew his star pupil had gotten that line from him. The crowd gathered around as I laid my game down. Right off the bat, I started the bets off at one hundred dollars. White Boy Paulie looked at me with disbelief, but placed his bet with a big Kool-Aid smile. As soon as Paulie won the one hundred dollars, I could see some vics getting excited as they went for their wallets.

I sprung the cards with one quick move and let Pinky win for two hundred because I raised her an extra one hundred. Now the vics were ready for the taking. Vic after vic started placing one hundred dollar bets and everyone that pulled out a hundred, I raised. "Turn it up. You lose. I'll do it again."

On one shot, I beat five vics out of seven hundred dollars. The more vics came in the game, the more vics I beat. I was like a man possessed and I spared no one as I took out all of my anger on them. I looked at everyone who tried to beat me out of my money as if they were the thugs who robbed my apartment. I also had something to prove. I wanted to prove to Gus that if he was the one who had set me up, not him, or anybody else, would be able to stop my shine.

I could always make more money and get even better things than what was taken. I had to show him, and anyone else, that my mother was right when she used to say, "My son, Mike, is a man amongst men." And, I believe this one hundred percent.

One thing I know about myself is I turn negatives into positives. So, I continued to bust chump after chump, showing no mercy, because no mercy had been shown to me. This was the very same spot a few years ago that I had watched Little Clyde, in amazement, thinking one day that's gonna be me.

Well, that day was today, and I was in rare form playing the game that I was born to play—yeah, right, three-card motherfucking Mike, taking all comers. So, gather around as I lay my game down.

Pinky couldn't quite gauge what was going on, but she was loving every minute of it. I saw that same look of amazement in her eyes that Lady Day showed that day in a Tad's Steakhouse Restaurant, when we were cutting up the day's winnings. I could tell Pinky was thinking, *I heard he was good, but boy not this good.*

I yelled to anyone who was betting, "Put up or shut up. If I can bluff you, I can beat you. Who saw the red card for five hundred dollars? Black, you lose. Who saw the red card for another five hundred dollars—I saw it. If I can bluff you, I can beat you. Two hundred more. Okay, turn it up. Black, you lose."

Soon after, Chip yelled, "Slide 'em up."

So, I knocked down the boxes. By the time I made it up the block by Gus, I was already depressed again. It seemed like as soon as Chip called the slide, all the adrenaline that had me so hyped was let out of me like a punctured balloon.

Then the negative thought cycle continued. *Gus set me up. Misa set me up. Some hater set me up.*

Gus asked, "Mike, you all right?"

"Yeah, I'm all right."

"So, what'd you take?"

"Oh, I took about twenty-seven hundred."

"So, what's with the sad face?"

I looked him straight in his eyes, as I said, "Just thinking, Gus. Just thinking."

After cutting up the money in Wendy's restaurant, Gus and Pinky asked me if I wanted to go to the movies and then to the Disco Fever to hang out. I told them I wasn't feeling too well and I needed to go home and get some rest. This was somewhat the truth. Yes, it was true that I wasn't feeling well, but no, I wasn't going home.

I jumped in a cab and headed straight to Misa's apartment. I wanted to catch her off guard because there were questions I needed answered. When I got to her mother's apartment, after some small talk, I proceeded to ask her question after question. I interrogated her like I was a mean homicide detective and she was a suspect in a murder investigation.

"When Gus asked you to set me up, why didn't you?

She said, "Because I love you."

"Who were you hanging out with those weeks that we didn't see each other?"

She answered, "Nobody. I was looking for you."

"Why were you looking for me?"

"'Cause I love you."

"Are you jealous of me?"

"No."

"Do you want to see me killed?"

"No."

"Do you want to see my mother killed?"

"No."

I just bombarded her with any question that I could think up. As she answered the questions, tears were falling down her face.

"Mike, I can't believe you think I set you up. Since I've known you, I never once did anything to hurt you. Do you think I'm the devil and that I would do anything to get you or your mother hurt?"

"Misa, I just don't know. There are just so many thoughts going in and out of my mind. I don't know what to think. All I know is someone violated me to the fullest."

"Mike, why would I tell you about Gus trying to get me to set you up and then turn around and do it? You know it doesn't make sense."

As she spoke these words, I was looking her dead in her face and I could not detect any dishonesty. But, the strange thing about it all, at the same time I was looking at her trying to find something that would tell me she set me up, my body started playing tricks on me.

I was getting horny. I told myself this was not supposed to be happening. The next thing I knew, we were headed to the bedroom, kissing and taking off our clothes all at the same time. I wasn't thinking with my top head; I was thinking with my bottom head.

When we fucked, I immediately threw her legs sky high in the air and pounded her harder than I had ever pounded. I wanted to hurt her. I fucked her as if I was a rapist victimizing his victim. No remorse, just physical abuse. When we finished, Misa lay in bed, crying because she knew what had just occurred. She knew it wasn't sex we just had; it was more like a sexual assault. This sick scenario was played out many times.

As the days turned into months, I felt like I was losing my mind. I looked at everyone I ran across with deep suspicion. *Misa set me up. Gus set me up. Some hater set me up.* Eventually word got back to some of the players that I had been set up. I guess Dante went and told someone, and then they told someone else. Some came to me with genuine concern, while others took the approach that I was a fool who had been set up by a conniving bitch who should be killed.

Teddy Pendergrass has a classic song called "The Whole Town's Laughing at Me" and every time I heard that song, it sounded like he was singing it to me, Mike, the pussy-whipped-three-card monte player.

There is a saying: God works in mysterious ways. I had just arrived downtown one day when Dante told me Misa had been busted for picking pockets up on Broadway last night. When I heard this, I knew she was going to do some time because she already had a warrant for pickpocketing. I guess this is where God stepped in, because the week previous to her getting busted, I was feeling real crazy after drinking some beer. I went and picked up Misa with every intention of killing her. The alcohol had given me false courage. So, I picked her up, and got her wasted on marijuana and alcohol. Then, I began the sick ritual of interrogating her about the robbery.

"Did you set me up? Why did you set me up? Did you want to get me killed? Did you want to get my mother killed?"

It went on and on until she finally fell asleep. While she slept in her drunken haze, I put my hands by her throat, thought about what I was about to do, then walked into the other room. This sick scenario played out a few times throughout the course of the night, until I eventually grabbed my coat and left.

Deep in my mind, I knew I had come very close to killing her. I had managed to walk away this time, but what about the next time? Now, here it was a week later and Misa was busted. Ma-Ma's son was not a murderer. God has other plans for me.

* * *

Sometimes love walks in at the strangest times. I spotted her standing on the corner of 169th Street. It was like any other ordinary day. I had just happened to be hanging around 169th Street after a good day of busting chumps out of their money in Midtown. I was feeling good because, finally, I was through with Misa, or so I thought. She had been given six months in jail. And, although this was unfortunate for her, it was giving me much-needed time to think. I concluded that I could not be with a woman who I suspected set me up. So, here on this very day, not even a half a block from me stood China, having a conversation with Chrissy.

My heart fluttered as I got more nervous by the minute. The one time when Chrissy introduced us a few months ago, I was so nervous when she told me her name, that when she asked for mine, I started stuttering like a little nine-year-old boy all over again. As I said, "Uh, uh, uh . . . Mike," then nervously walked off.

But, this was my chance to redeem myself. So, I sent Spence to the corner to tell her I wanted to meet her. I know this was a chump move, but it gave me time to relax. I watched Spence as he talked and laughed with both of them. After a few minutes, Spence returned.

"Yo Mike, I can't believe you still let China get you so nervous."

"Man, shut up Spence and tell me what she said."

"She said if you wanted to meet her, come ask her yourself."

So, I headed to the corner, looking good with my light blue Paris nylon tank top with the boxers to match, my Oscar de la Renta jeans and new light blue suede British Walker shoes. I was sharp and I knew it. I walked right up to them and said, "Hi, Chrissy. Hi, China." Then they both smiled as they looked me up and down, then in unison said, "Hi, Mike."

"So, Mike, you still remember my friend China's name, since the last time I introduced y'all."

"Yeah, I can't lie, I was a little nervous before. I remember what I did 'uh, uh, uh, my name is Mike.'"

They both laughed hysterically as I cracked the joke. At this point, I knew I had her. So, I asked, "Hey would y'all like a beer or something?"

They said yes.

As we walked to the store, making small conversation, I couldn't help but notice how good China looked in her white short set and sneakers. She had a beautiful high-yellow complexion, chinky eyes that made her look part Chinese and hair down to her ass—a fat ass, I might say. I found it hard to stop staring at this gorgeous dimepiece.

After I bought the beer, we headed to the park on this warm August night. While sitting in the park, Spence joked that I had been goo, goo, ga, ga over China since we were kids.

I said, "Shut up, Spence. Mind your business." We all laughed. This was a pleasant change for me, seeing all I had gone through the last few months. "China, I can't lie. I like you a lot."

She responded, "I like you, too, Mike. And it's funny, Mike, my last boyfriend's name was Mike. Do you know Mike Swinton?"

"I don't know him, but I've seen him around."

"Well, he wasn't no good. I hope you're nothing like him."

"Nah, China, I'm one of a kind."

Chrissy spoke up, "Mike is crazy cool. Everybody likes him, even the older people. Even though he's got money, he never acts like he's better than anybody."

I smiled as China took in every word. Chrissy was looking out for a brother, big time. I knew her word carried a lot of weight with her best friend.

"That's good, Mike. You do seem like a nice guy."

"Man, y'all should see him downtown when he's beating them vics," yelled Spence. "I tell you now, they don't think he's nice." We howled so loud that the back of my neck hurt.

"So Mike, Chrissy told me that you play three-card monte," China said.

"Yeah, China," added Chrissy, "Everybody around here knows Mike is the best three-card monte player in the city."

"You're that good, Mike?" China asked.

"I'm all right, but I ain't the best. Would you like to one day come downtown and watch me?"

"Yeah, I'd really like to see you in action."

"Okay, one day y'all could meet me down there, but for now would y'all like some smoke or something?"

"Yeah, Mike. We want some smoke," Spence replied.

"Shut up Spence," I yelled.

"Girls, do y'all want some smoke?"

"Yeah, Mike. Okay, I know where to get some good skunk weed in Harlem," said Chrissy.

"Okay, we can go to Harlem, but first let me go upstairs and ask my cousin Stan to drive us in my uncle's car."

A few minutes later, I came back with Stan and we all got in my uncle's Lincoln Continental. Stan turned on the radio and Grandmaster Flash and the Furious Five's rap song "The Message" was playing. Everybody felt good from all the beer we drank in the park. I was the happiest man on earth, because I was chilling with the woman of my dreams. Things were looking all right.

When we arrived at the weed spot on 144th Street and Bradhurst, I took my money out of my sock and counted about twelve hundred dollars right in front of them. Then I passed Spence forty dollars and told him to get four bags of skunk. I didn't smoke weed, but I wanted to show them all a good time. While all this was going down, my cousin, Stan, who looked like a young Muhammad Ali, smiled because he knew how much I liked China. He also knew his little cousin was trying to win her heart. I liked China even more now because I liked how she carried herself. I could tell she was kind of shy. She didn't act like a fly girl, even though she was the prettiest girl on 169th Street. I knew she didn't have a man because of what she said in the park. So, I had every intention of making her my woman.

Soon after Spence came back with the smoke we headed uptown with the radio blasting. After about a half hour, we were back on 169th Street, sitting in the park. Spence went to the store and bought more beer. As the warm breeze blew, we had a good ol' time. After what seemed to be a few hours, I happened to look at my watch and saw that it was two o'clock in the morning. Chrissy and Spence said good night and went upstairs. I asked China if I could walk her up the block to her building and of course she said yes.

When we arrived there, I asked for her phone number and she wrote it down, smiling the whole time. I walked her upstairs gave her a big hug and kissed her good-bye. I was in ghetto heaven.

As I walked down the block I sang a stupid song I used to sing when I was little: "That girl I seen last night. I knew she was my type. That girl I seen last night. I knew she was my type . . ."

The next day downtown, I could not get my mind off China. I had to have her. I wanted her. I needed her. I wanted her so badly that I decided to put a plan in motion to win her over. The plan was to stay away from her for a few weeks, so she would not think I was desperate.

My team, along with all the hustlers, picked up on my jolly demeanor as I walked around with a big smile on my face. Everyone was happy for me because they all knew that the past couple of months I wasn't acting like my normal self. But, today I was back to feeling good again. When we eventually played monte, our take at the end of the day was twenty-eight hundred dollars. My team had noticed that whenever I was in a good mood, the vics would be in trouble.

Two weeks could not go by fast enough for me. Everyday after I left Midtown, I marked a day off the calendar in my mother's apartment, just like prison inmates do when they are looking forward to their release dates. After about a week, Spence told me he had seen China on 169th Street, and she had asked him where I was. When he told me that, I couldn't stop smiling. I told myself, *Just one more week, one more week.* The last week took the longest as I counted the minutes, hours and seconds. I had already bought a pair of new burgundy British Walkers and new clothes, preparing for the next time I would see China.

* * *

The two-week mark was here and my concentration was a little off. I couldn't seem to stay focused while playing monte on Fifth Avenue. I knew that I should be keeping my mind on the job at hand, which was beating the vics and listening for slides.

One time Spence called a quick slide and I wasn't paying attention. By the time I looked up, a blue coat was right in my face. The cop grabbed me and put me up against the wall. He held me with one hand and tried to grab for the cuffs with the other hand. This was his big mistake because as soon as he reached for the cuffs, I did a quick spin and by the time he realized what was happening, I was already gone and running. That encounter woke a brother up real fast. The rest of the day my mind got off China and on the game of monte. After about three hours of playing, we finished with a count of twenty-eight fifty. My team wanted to take another lick later, but I had other plans, so I divided the money and headed uptown to see China.

I knew I was breaking the one rule that the pimps and players always told me: "Money before bitches." But maybe not, because I did not consider China a bitch. To me, she was a lady.

I jumped on the No. 2 train and headed uptown. When I got to China's block, I called her and told her I was downstairs. Ten minutes later, she came walking out of her building looking fine as ever—with a big Kool-Aid smile.

"Hi, Mike. Long time no see. What brings you to this part of town?"

"Well, China, it's this beautiful girl who lives around here, who I'm nuts about."

Smiling from ear to ear, she said, "Who's that?"

"Well, she's standing right in front of me."

We giggled like two love-struck kids.

"China, would you like to hang out with me today?"

"Sure, Mike. What do you want to do?"

"Well, first I want to go to my cousin's apartment because they haven't seen me in a while."

She said okay, so off we went to 169th Street. On our way down the block, I made conversation, asking her about herself. She said she was eighteen and had worked as a maintenance worker trainee, until she received her GED diploma at Taft High School. I told her I had just graduated from Dewitt Clinton High School. She smiled. She asked me if I had a girlfriend, and I said, "Yeah, you're my girlfriend."

She laughed as she said, "Mike, you're so funny!"

As we got closer to my cousin's building, I noticed everyone watching the new couple in the making. We caught the elevator to the seventh floor and knocked on my cousin's door. When my aunt answered, she looked genuinely surprised, and gave me a big hug.

Then, I introduced China to my cousins, George, Stan, Bryant, Bud and Greg. Everyone was happy to see us. Then Greg said out loud for everyone to hear, "Mom, this is the girl who always used to get Mike all nervous when we were little." They all laughed.

"Shut up, Greg. Don't let me tell her about the time me and Bud caught you smoking reefer at nine years old and we had you doing all our housework for two weeks." Saying that brought down the house. "Or, what about the time when you stole that money from your father and bought Mrs. Jackson a dress. Boy, did you get the worst whipping for that!"

While everybody was having a good time, my cousin George told China I had always had a talent for comedy and maybe I had missed my calling. I guess the reason I was in such a joyful mood was because I loved being around my family, and I didn't get to spend quality time with them like we used to.

Plus, I felt so peaceful and happy being around China. She had an enchanting personality. She was bringing clarity to my crazy world. We all had such a good time that China and I wound up staying with my family for about two hours. Before we left, I mentioned to Stan that in a few weeks I wanted him to take me to buy a car, because I was tired of trains and OJ cabs.

The reason I was tired of the OJ cabs was because there was this one OJ cab driver who would always pick up me and my homeboys, Spence, CeeWee, Jaheim and Dante, in Midtown in a nice Cadillac or Mercedes, but, once we got in his rented cab, he lied about owning them. We all knew the real deal. He was just fronting because he knew we were monte players and made money. So, the last time he fronted, I decided I was going to buy my own car.

Stan was happy to hear that because he knew I didn't know how to drive and he would be doing the driving. I was just content that I still had money to buy a car, knowing that it could have been stolen during the robbery.

After I finished talking to Stan and telling my family good-bye, we went downstairs and I asked China if she wanted to check out a movie, and she said yeah. Then I grabbed her hand and we walked down the block to catch a cab.

When we got into the cab, she scooted right next to me and we held hands all the way to Fordham Road. We caught the eight o'clock movie, *Halloween 2,* at the Valentine Movie Theatre. I bought popcorn, soda and candy, and hugged her all through the scary movie as we ate junk food.

It was turning out to be a good first date. We later had Italian food at Yolanda's Restaurant on 149th Street. All through dinner I continued to crack jokes as we ate and drank a bottle of wine. I think it was Asti Spumante because it tasted like the cheap Thunderbird wine that good ol' Cousin Reggie used to drink. God rest his soul. When we finished eating and drinking, it was late and I asked her to spend the night with me. She looked at me with a serious look and said, "Do you think I'm a fast girl?"

I quickly answered, "No, I don't want to have sex with you. I just don't want you to leave me tonight."

The funny thing about it all was that I really meant what I said. This was a first for me. Never had I ever asked a girl to spend the night with me and not want to have sex—never. I guess she picked up on my sincerity because she grabbed my hand and said, "Let's go."

We caught a cab to the Alps Hotel on West Farms Road. I tell you no lie; we did not have sex. All we did was cuddle and sleep.

After that day I started to hang with her everyday when I finished playing monte. I rode her all over town on my Elite motorcycle. Riding her by the Boys Club on Hoe Avenue, P.S. 67, my old elementary school, my old junior high school, 98 Hermand Ridder, my old high school, Dewitt Clinton, and even by my old neighborhood, 1975 Honeywell Avenue. The building was torn down.

I told her stories about my mother, father and family. I also told her about my Cousin Reggie who taught me how to hustle and make money all at the age of nine. China laughed when I mentioned how Reggie would bring all types of women up to my mother's apartment, have sex and let me, my brother, and sister watch. China loved my Reggie stories.

I eventually brought her to meet Ma-Ma, Carolyn, and Kevin. My family fell in love with her from the very first day.

The day that we finally had sex, I played myself like a chump. We had sex, but I can't really call it sex, because I came so fast. We tried again through the course of the night, but still the same scenario. I was still intimidated by her beauty. The minute I saw her in those red bikini panties, I knew I was in trouble. But, even though I did not please her, she showed no hint of being mad. All she said was

189

everything would be all right after I slowed down. She said she understood that I was anxious, and I believed her. But, in the back of my mind I was saying, *Next time I would have to bring a few Guinness Stouts and the ol' Stud 100 reliable delay spray.*

26

Special Effects

On a cold and brisk February night, while I was standing by the Nathan's restaurant on Forty-second Street and Seventh Avenue with some other monte players, a white guy with glasses and an Actor's Guild cap yelled, "Who wants to be in a movie?"

I was the only one who responded, saying, "Yeah. What movie?"

The guy said, "Well, we're shooting a movie on Broadway and we need a three-card monte street scene."

I said, "How much money does it pay and how long is it going to take?"

"Oh, it pays two hundred dollars and it will take about an hour."

I said, "Okay guy. I guess I'm the one, even though two hundred is a little cheap for my star quality. Let's go."

Everybody laughed, then I told them, "See y'all later," as I walked off with the white guy.

I do not know why I agreed to be in a movie, but maybe it is because all throughout my life I have always had a need to be the center of attention. Could that be a good thing or a bad thing? Who knows? But, one thing I do know is, sometimes it has helped me.

Ever since becoming a springer, I always tried to add a little something different to my style of play, like making the vics laugh while losing their money. Sometimes after beating them I would yell, "Tell Ma I'll be home later!" keeping the vics entertained because they'd think, *Here's a guy who will beat his own family member out of money.*

I remember beating one white guy out of a lot of money and my perceptive powers told me to ask him if he was a college professor because he looked real smart. He answered, "Yes. How did you know that?"

I replied, "Because you look smart."

This made everybody laugh because if he was so smart, why was he losing his money in three-card monte? I guess little things like that, along with my other acquired exceptional monte skills, made me one of the best to play the game.

Now I had movie people looking to put me in pictures. Damn, who knew? Midtown Mike was gonna be a star. I know you're thinking, *Man this guy has got visions of grandeur!* But, weren't a lot of stars discovered in the craziest of ways? Man, let me stop all this bullshit. The real reason I agreed to be in this movie is because it was cold out there and I wanted the money!

The white guy told me the movie might be called *Special Effects*. This had me thinking, if they put some real money in my hands, during the scene I could add my own "special effects," like in *See Johnny run fast!* I was just playing. Remember, I was a con man, not a thief.

27

Doll Syndrome

When is it the right time to come clean? I guess there is no better time than now. Some guys will not admit to what I am about to tell. But, I feel this is a subject that I must speak freely about because it pertains to something I did myself, which is to father a child without knowing anything about being a parent.

A lot of men want kids for all the wrong reasons. Some of us impregnate women because of the need to stake claim to a pretty woman's body, while others just want bragging rights to children, but do not want the responsibility that goes along with it. Then, there are those who have doll syndrome, like some young girls also do. Let me try to break this down in simple terms. It's a need to make a baby because you feel unloved and you want something to love. Your mind gets twisted into thinking that raising a baby will be like playing with dolls—fun. But, what you find out is, there's more to raising and taking care of a baby.

I fell victim to this warped sense of thinking about parenthood. I was just another fatherless child wanting to be a father. I do not blame this on my father. He must have had multiple problems to choose suicide as an option. But, growing up without him affected me deeply.

So, when I met China, these were some of the things I was going through. I guess that is why the first six months of our relationship I made love to her everyday. Yes, you read it right. I made *love*. I just had sex with the other girls. Although, I did have my issues, I was still in love with China. That is why just a few months into our relationship, I started to share my love of reading with her.

I read books, like Donald Goines' fictionalized street tales, *Daddy Cool, Eldorado Red,* and *Ice Berg Slim*, a book about a pimp from

193

Memphis, as well as *Mack and Me*. I read her these books to give her an idea about my lifestyle. These books were about pimps, prostitutes and con men—all the types of people I was growing up around. China was the first woman who I read to and who wanted to really know me.

Once I found out she liked it, I then moved on to autobiographies about Little Richard, Marvin Gaye, The Supremes and *The Life*, a book of toasts with short stories such as, *Signified Monkey* and *Honky Tonk Bud the Hip Cat Stud*. I tried to memorize these toasts then recite them to her. She told me a man had never read to her before.

After being with her a few months and going through the regular dating rituals of going to the movies, concerts and amusement parks, I remember asking her why she stayed with me after finding out I was a street hustler. She looked straight into my eyes and told a story about going through my things at my mother's apartment when I was not there and finding my report cards.

She said looking at my grades of 85s and 90s and perfect attendance for three consecutive years confused her. To her, all of this did not fit her idea of a hustler who ran the streets. She thought, *Why isn't this guy in college?* She was telling me something did not add up. The woman of my dreams was seeing something in me that I had not seen in myself. That's why I give thanks to God for bringing her into my life. Something always told me she was going to make a major impact on me.

So, I tried harder to get her pregnant until one day it happened. I acted shocked and surprised even though all along I knew the real deal, which is, if you have unprotected sex, something is bound to happen. I was the happiest man alive. At eighteen years old, I was going to be a father.

I went to Midtown, telling all the players and pimps my news; everybody was happy for me. I eventually told my mother and the rest of my family. When I told my cousin, Stan, he did not believe me. So, I had to remind him that my father did not shoot blanks and neither did I. Now, his boy was going to be a father.

China was happy, too, even though I had not officially met her family yet. The stupid reason being, every time I came from Midtown to pick her up, I would yell from the window for her to come downstairs, then, we would head to the hotel or my mother's apartment.

All that changed after China's mother, Maria, followed her downstairs when I called her on my loud intercom from the new car I bought. A few minutes later I spotted China, whose stomach was starting to show, with a little lady, who I assumed to be her mother. They walked up to the car and the little lady said, "Hi. My name is Maria. I am China's mother. I know your name is Mike, but what I don't know is why you no come upstairs." I sat there, dumbfounded, and said, "Uh, uh, uh . . ." just like I used to do with China.

She smiled, then said, "You did not ask to do what you did . . . so, you do not have to ask to come upstairs." China and I both laughed as I told her, "Thank you."

One week later, I was living with China's family: her mother, Maria; her father, Julio, who I would soon find out did not speak much English; her little brother, Raphael and her sister, Anna, who were both a few years younger than China. She also had an older sister, Carmen, who did not live with them and another sister, Sandra, who had died. The Rios family took me in and treated me like I was part of the family.

My being black did not make a difference. China's mother became like a second mother to me, as she fed me good Spanish food. To this day I cannot get enough of it.

I could tell China really loved and trusted me because she would let me ride her while pregnant on my Elite motorcycle to her GED courses up at Taft High School. We were two crazy lovebirds riding on a whim and a prayer. People on the street who saw us looked on in shock.

One time when I dropped her off at school she talked to the receptionist at the front desk, someone who had gone to high school with her. Little did China know that I had a crush on the girl when I went to Dewitt Clinton High School. I always saw her on the train on my way to school, which was one stop from Walton High School. This was another girl who I had a crush on, but never spoke to. No, it did not come anywhere near the crush I had on China. My thing with China was more like love at first sight. Later that day when I told China the story, she told me the girl said when she went to Walton, she also had a crazy crush on me. What a small world we live in.

28

A Funny Thing Happened

I know a lot of people have heard someone say, "A funny thing happened to me on the way to work today. . . ." Well, mine goes a little bit differently . . . A funny thing happened to me on my way to jail . . . which brings me to this story.

I started my day playing monte on Fifth Avenue for our first lick. The day was going as usual until a vic in a karate suit lost all of his money. The guy continued to watch the game as the crowd got bigger until he figured out what was going on. All of a sudden he jumped into a Bruce Lee karate stance, then screamed, "Ah, wah!" like Bruce Lee did in his movies before he kicked ass. Then he yelled, "Give me my motherfucking money back. All you niggas are down together."

I immediately stopped the game because our cover was blown and all the vics knew they had been conned. So, the only thing left to do was beat the living shit out of him. My slides, Spence and Winny, and I beat him like he stole something. The vics and tourists who had lost their money laughed as we beat Bruce Lee reincarnated to a pulp.

After giving him his proper ass-whipping, we went to Grand Central where we set up another game. We played about thirty-five minutes when all of a sudden Winny called a quick slide. But, before I could take off, the Grand Central police grabbed me.

Next thing I knew, I was up against a wall and the cop was trying to cuff me. As soon as he grabbed for the cards, I tried to do the spin that had always helped me get away. But, when I did it, an old man just happened to be right there and I knocked him and the cop down. The police grabbed me then put the cuffs on.

A crowd gathered around as the police checked to see if the old man was hurt. Eventually they picked him up and asked him if he wanted to go to the hospital then press charges. He said he was all right, so they let him go. But I was another story. I was going to jail. Even though I knew where I was headed, I still felt a little lucky the old man had not died of a heart attack. That would have added up to some serious jail time. A few misdemeanor charges could have easily turned into a felony murder charge. But with all that said and done I still knew I was in for a royal ass-whipping by New York's finest. And, boy did they know how to give a fine ass-whipping.

So, as the crowd looked on, off we headed to the Grand Central precinct. They handcuffed me to a desk and told me I was charged with resisting arrest, promoting gambling and assault. The assault charge stemmed from the cop falling. While I sat chained to a chair, cops kept coming into the room saying things like, "So, you like to beat up on cops and old men. . . ."

I knew I was in trouble when the sergeant seemed to be pissed off, too. All of a sudden, one of the cops hopped on the desk next to me, then jumped off, right on to one of my cuffed hands. The cuff went to the last latch, which cut off my circulation. My whole hand and arm swelled up to twice the normal size. I screamed as electrical-like shocks went straight to my head. The sergeant yelled, "Loosen the cuffs. His circulation is cut off!" So, a cop came over, loosened them then punched me in the face—all at the same time.

Afterward, they made racist comments about me, my parents, everybody. What these assholes were putting me through could have easily been a scene out of the classic movie *In the Heat of the Night*, when the black actor, Sidney Poitier played a big city homicide detective coming to a redneck stationhouse to help solve a murder. These were one hundred percent prejudiced cops. All night I had to endure police brutality as they beat me then took me to the hospital because I was bleeding everywhere.

The doctors performed an examination, which included X-rays, and pronounced me okay. But, I knew differently; I was hurt real bad. I was dizzy and woozy from the shocks to my head and I had a pounding headache.

Before we left the hospital, the cops let me make one phone call, which is provided by law. I was told not to tell anyone about my being beaten. If I did, they would kill me.

All the while I was making the call, the cops had a nightstick pressed against my ribs. So I could not tell China anything about what was happening to me. I only told her that I had been arrested and to come to court with a paid lawyer tomorrow. I guess this predicament I was finding myself in was all a cruel form of poetic justice. I had beaten up on the Bruce Lee character, and the cops, in turn, beat up on me. Payback is a motherfucker.

After the call to China, we left the hospital and headed to central booking. During the ride, they continued to make racist comments. I was processed, then put in the cell with everyone else. Before the cops left, they called me over to the cell bars. When I slowly made it over there in my dazed condition, one of the cops stuck his hands through the bars and slammed my head into it. Then he said, "Have a nice night. I hope you get fucked."

I lay down on the dirty floor with a big lump on my head. The other prisoners looked on like it was an everyday occurrence.

When I woke up in the morning, it seemed the cell had many more people in it than when I fell asleep. I felt a little better, but I still had a bad headache.

Some of the things I learned from going to central booking during my previous arrests was first, everyone you meet in the cells always says, one they got busted for bank robbery, or two, a big drug deal had gone bad, or, three, they were down with the mob and their father, uncle or cousin, was Mr. Gambino. All lies. So, when I woke up, I was ready for the usual lies and stories.

One guy in the cell talked about how he killed two and injured three. He told a believable story about walking in Greenwich Village with his girlfriend when a few guys messed with them. His story went that someone had slapped his girlfriend, so he pulled out a gun and killed two and injured three. The guy must have told this story to everybody who came into the cell while I was sleeping. Now he was telling it again to me and some other prisoners.

Like I said earlier, the story seemed believable. And, he had a lot of the prisoners scared of him. But, that all changed when we got to the court building.

When you get there, they put everyone in this big cell where you wait for the arrival of the cops who busted you. No one can go in front of the judge until they talk to a lawyer and the cop arrives. Well as everyone waited, the cop who busted the guy who supposedly killed two and injured three, yelled, "Come here you rubber!"

The prisoner yelled, "I ain't no rubber!"

One of the correction officers asked curiously, "What's a rubber?" because he, as well as the rest of us, was confused.

The cop said, "That's one of those perverts who hang in the trains rubbing up against girls' asses."

The prisoner yelled, "That's a lie!"

The cop yelled, "Shut up. You have eight convictions for this bullshit!" This had the jailhouse rocking. Like I said, never believe what a prisoner tells you in a cell.

After the funny episode, the cops who busted me showed up. China had gotten me a paid lawyer, so I saw the judge, who gave me another court date and let me go home. My lawyer was good, which helped me. Plus, the judge saw China was pregnant. So, it all worked in my favor.

29

Mr. Johnson

Let me tell you about my friend, Mr. Johnson, who always leads me astray. Every time I let Mr. Johnson dictate my actions, I always got into trouble. It was as though some tit-for-tat karma game was being played on me. What I found out was, if I listened to Mr. Johnson when he told me to mistreat or use some woman, my payback would be some other woman doing the same to me.

For example, the time I was hanging out in Club 371. My homeboy, Big Denny, told me a girl in the club had a big crush on me. When he pointed her out, I went straight up to her, being the smooth player that I thought I was, and I said, "Hey, do you like me?"

She said, "Who told you that?"

"Nobody, but do you like me?"

"Yeah, something like that."

"Well, do you want to go get a room?"

She said, "What are you talking about?"

I said, "You know exactly what I'm talking about. Yes or no?"

Then, to my surprise, she said, "Okay, but let's chill a little while at the club."

We went to the Bronx Park Hotel where we had sex and I left her there. Not too long after that, I received payback for my nasty deed.

I was hanging at the same club and I met an attractive girl. The girl and I drank and danced all night. Later, she gave me her phone number, and about a week later, I called her and we set up a date.

That night I double-parked in front of her building in the Webster projects. I was looking real sharp in my fine threads and jewelry, which consisted of a nine hundred dollar bracelet and a gold chain. I also had a few hundred dollars in my pockets.

I was feeling real good as I headed upstairs to her apartment. By the time I made it upstairs, five thugs with guns knocked me down and hit me on my head and all over my body with their guns. There were guns pointed everywhere. They beat the living shit out of me and took everything. As they ran off, all I could see was stars because of the hit I took to the head. Once I gathered my composure, I got up and shot out of that building like a bat out of hell.

This was one of the scariest moments I had ever been through. My life flashed right before my eyes. When I got to my car, I sped off like my life depended on it. While driving away, I realized my date had set me up. My other head had got me into trouble again. Mr. Johnson's karma had come back to haunt me.

Another time while following Mr. Johnson's advice, I talked to a girl I met while hanging in an after-hours spot. I told the girl a bunch of crap about being ready to settle down and I wanted her to be my girlfriend. This was all lies because I already had a girlfriend. She fell for my crap, at least I thought, and after persuading her that my intentions were honorable, we went to a hotel where we had sex. I then told her I was going to the store to get some beer and food. I jumped in my car and never came back. I laughed all the way home to my girlfriend's apartment. I was even laughing when I got home and my girlfriend thought I was crazy.

Two days later I found out the girl had given me something to walk with—gonorrhea. Every time I took a piss it burned like I had a thousand cuts inside my penis. All I could think of when I pissed was, *Damn, Mike, maybe you do need to settle down and be happy with your woman!*

These stories may sound funny, but it was not funny when it was happening to me, although I bet Mr. Johnson was laughing the whole time. Mr. Johnson can show his head in so many different ways in a man's life. He will help you to make choices when you need advice on what cars, clothes and jewelry to buy, all because of his insatiable need to please. I, myself, let him guide me when I bought all my expensive jewelry. Check this out, I even bought a customized car so that I could be seen by everyone, then I let Mr. Johnson tell me to put tinted windows on it, so as not to be seen, which was thinking ass-backwards. His influence was even guiding me when I missed my firstborn son's arrival in this world and that's deep. While my son, Curtis, was being born, I was cheating on my woman. That little gem from Mr. Johnson cost me something I can never get back. A father is supposed to be there when his son is being born—no excuses.

I know of one smooth player, whom I will not name because what happened to him has happened to a lot of other brothers. This guy took a woman he had just met to a hotel to have sex. When they got into the room, she told him to take a good warm shower because she was going to lick him all over. Well, good ol' boy took off his clothes and valuables and headed for his much-needed shower. When he came out, ready for some good head, *boom*, she was gone with all of his clothes and valuables. Picture him calling his mother . . . "Hey, Mom, I just got robbed. Can you please bring me some clothes?" He was just another brother taking the advice of Mr. Johnson.

So, if I was asked right now, when is the right time to come clean? Is it right after you do something that you know is wrong or is it before you even act on it. I would say from what I have learned from dealing with my own problems, the answer would be it is better to talk to someone besides Mr. Johnson before you decide to do something wrong. That way you might get some positive feedback with your situation and maybe not have to suffer any unwanted repercussions. But, please, by all means, do not listen to Mr. Johnson's advice, because karma will come back to haunt you.

If anybody is still confused about who Mr. Johnson is, you will find him hiding inside a man's pants.

* * *

I used to love conversing and at the same time getting advice about women from some of the pimps' whores I knew downtown. Honey Combs had two hoes named Minnie and Cookie whom I used to kick it with from time to time. Whenever I needed advice about women, I went to them, especially Cookie, because she was good as a cookie, when it came to knowing about women. I found out from her that, like men, some women had their own Mrs. Johnson offering advice and guiding their actions. Their pimp, Honey Combs, once told me he would pimp "Mona Lisa" if she would just get out of her picture frame. From Cookie and Minnie's point of view, Mona Lisa was not going to do that unless he bought her and the picture frame first. In other words, you have to pay to play.

Cookie told me, "Mike, if you want to get in a woman's pants, their Mrs. Kitty Kat is telling them, 'Do not have sex with any man unless he provides for your every need.'"

A woman's need can consist of a lot of things—money, material things, food and maybe even love. Whatever it is the woman wants, we, the men, must provide it, if we want sex. Women know most men think with their Johnson, so they set their rules accordingly. For example, women know if they show up at a club looking good, with their hair and nails done up, and are wearing something nice and tight, some brother out there who's thinking with his Johnson, will spend every dime to get a chance to have sex with her, even if it takes perpetrating something he's not. This brother could be a messenger, making six dollars an hour, but he will spend every last dime of his hard earned money, if he thinks he has a shot at Miss Tight-Ass.

He can even be a college professor with book smarts, but when it comes to a pretty woman, he will forget everything if he thinks he has a chance at her crown jewels (even if it takes spending his whole check). Women know the math—no romance without finance.

If Mrs. Kitty Kat, who is closely related to Mr. Johnson, offers her advice to a woman, most of the time they listen. Women know from their prior dealings with Mrs. Kitty Kat, her advice is on the money 99 percent of the time. So, as I stood there taking in all of this information from Minnie and Cookie, I tried to keep an open mind to the things they were schooling me on about women. But deep down in the middle of my crotch area, I was getting the feeling that sometimes Mr. Johnson would win, even though some of the things they expressed had turned out to be true in the past. I still had a problem heeding their advice because how could I listen to everything they said, when I already had Mr. Johnson guiding my actions. He was all right when he was not hot and heated, but if he was, watch out! He could bust off at any time!

Mrs. Kitty Kat, she could be real vicious if a woman did not listen to her advice. She could make a girl set up a man for all of his valuables, or even talk him into stealing from his job or his family. Some will get pregnant so they can get child support. But, if that does not work, some go to another crazy level and claim rape so they can sue for some serious money. This extreme measure normally is taken when a brother is known to have a lot of legal money, like celebrities or professional sports figures. These are just some of the things Mrs. Kitty Kat will advise women to do. She has an uncontrollable addiction to getting what she wants at a stupid man's expense.

We men need to start thinking more with our top heads and less with our bottom heads. A man's self-worth is not determined by how much Kitty Kat he can get.

The moral is, from a whore's point of view, Mr. Johnson's wrath does not stand a chance against the wrath of Mrs. Kitty Kat. This is why they might as well get together and create some beautiful karma. In the words of a certain someone, "Can't we all just get along?"

30

Men and Women Drama

"Yo Mike, you won't believe what happened to me last night."

"What happened, Dante?"

"Man, I caught my woman getting out this nigga's car last night. And, I beat the living shit out of both of them."

I said, "Dante, why did you beat them without finding out who the guy was? Maybe it was a friend of hers that you don't know."

"Yo Mike, stop playing with me. I ain't got no time for no bullshit."

When Dante said that, it made me think that here was a brother that I knew for myself had cheated too many times to count. But when he suspected that his woman had cheated, he went ballistic and kicked her ass and the guy's. This was without even finding out what was really going on between them. What really made this situation so ludicrous was that Dante would think nothing of fucking his girlfriend's best friend, or even fucking some girl in her apartment. But, here he was telling his story and damn near wanting to kick my ass because I told him, just maybe, the guy was a friend of hers.

I often wonder why some men cheat on their girlfriend with a thousand women, but if their girlfriend even thinks about cheating, they go ballistic. You can imagine what they would do if they actually caught their girl cheating. I know exactly what would happen. They would either give their girlfriend the worst beating she ever had, or kill both of the cheaters.

On the other hand, when a woman catches her man cheating, she at least gives him the benefit of the doubt. She does not just go flying off the deep end without getting the facts and finding out the reasons for his betrayal. A woman will sometimes take this approach even after having previously caught her man cheating. I think women go through so much drama with men that they naturally get stronger, mentally and emotionally when it comes to dealing with problems of the heart. This is the reason I was getting mad at Dante for snapping at me. Deep down Dante knew I was not trying to make fun of him. I was just trying to rationalize the situation, from a woman's point of view. We brothers are not so stupid as to think that we are perfect creatures, even though we as men sometimes act like little immature boys. I choose to think that females mature much faster than males.

While all of these thoughts were going on in my head, Honey Combs and a few other players that were standing with us in front of the OTB betting parlor decided to join in the conversation.

"Man, when I was a lame dealing with that relationship bullshit . . ."

Dante interrupted, "Stop. So Honey Combs, now we're lames?"

'My mellow, my man. You take it how you want to take it. Understand me? But like I was starting to say, in my own dealings with women, I found out they always think ten steps ahead of us brothers. Before we even think about some shit, the woman done already went over the same shit ten times. Understand me? So, when you dealing with a woman, you'd better be on top of your bullshit. Understand me? For example, if you and your woman was walking down the street and a beautiful woman was headed your way, you may have just noticed her, but your woman saw her ten blocks away. Understand me? So, why does the brother get so surprised when she gives him a sharp elbow to the ribs right before the discovery? Understand me?"

Pamela and Jody jumped into the conversation saying, "You know that's right," as they gave each other a pound.

Then Jody added, "Y'all brothers think y'all be putting some bullshit over on us women, but we ain't having none of your bullshit. Tricks are for kids."

Then Pamela said, "We are much smarter than you think. Just because we let brothers get over every now and then, y'all think you're smart, so, y'all go overboard and take the bullshit to another level. Then, y'all force us to cut y'all brothers down to size."

All of us standing there nodded our heads in agreement at the deep shit the girls just stated. But, at the same time the girls were breaking it down, we were looking at their breasts and asses. Ain't that some shit!

"Boy, ain't it crazy how some brothers can get deep with women and still be thinking with their penis at the same time? We have all witnessed from time to time, some brother sitting at a table some-where in deep conversation with a woman, but at the same time his eyes are focused dead on her breasts. I guess it is what you might call a brother's physical Freudian slip, talking with his mouth, but his eyes giving him away. While I was thinking, Honey Combs jumped back into the conversation after the girls had expressed their thoughts on the subject at hand.

Honey Combs said, "You see that's what I'm talking about—that's why I trust women as far as I can see them, and they should do the same. See, when a woman fucks with me, she already knows from the jump, I'm a pimp. So, she knows exactly what she's getting. Understand me? She knows she's getting a pimp that's going to guide all her thoughts and actions. The hoe knows she's a reflection of me and I'm a reflection of her. So, if she gets out of line, I got to check her. Understand me? So, if I'm all right, she's gonna be all right. Understand me?"

Then Pamela said with a big smile, "Yeah, Honey Combs, I understand what you're saying. But, you are talking from a pimp's perspective. What the players here are saying, is a little bit different than your situation because they are talking about their girlfriends."

"Yeah, Honey Combs," said Jody, "we know you don't care about your hoe's having sex because that's what hoes do. But a guy doesn't want his woman having sex with anybody, especially for money."

Honey Combs said, "Man y'all can believe that if you want to, but to me, men and women in general are not too much different from pimps and hoes. The only difference is we get paid for sex, while the average Joe Blow fucks for free, and don't tell me nothing about love, because love ain't free. Understand me? After y'all get through that love-at-first-sight bullshit, then the brother's got to wine and dine. No romance without finance. Understand me?"

All the girls yelled, "And you know that!"

Bringing the house down, I yelled, "Man, Honey Combs are you trying to turn these ladies out?" This made him grin.

All this analyzing of men and women's issues, had me thinking about how we as men sometimes internalize our problems. We normally try to figure out our problems by ourselves rather than go to another person and tell them what we really are going through. We think it is a sign of weakness to talk about some deep issue. That's why Dante got mad when I tried to rationalize his situation. He just wanted me to listen and not to offer any advice on what he went through. It was his problem and he thought he solved it the right way.

206

Now, women are another story. If they are going through any problems, they always have some girlfriends they can talk with to help them find a reasonable resolution. Women don't mind heeding the advice of friends they respect. Two heads are better than one. Brothers sometimes get things twisted. What I mean is two *minds* are better than one. I was talking about our top heads and not our bottom heads. We brothers should know by now that thinking with our bottom heads always gets us into trouble. Some men have been doing women dirty since day one, so women have become accustomed to dealing with infidelity. They try to handle their problems in a positive way, and then try their best to move on.

On the other hand, some men cannot handle knowing that their woman has stepped out on them. We men are mentally inferior to women when it comes to dealing with problems of the heart. We bug out to the next level just thinking about another man infiltrating our woman's vagina. We vividly visualize some slimy brother with a bigger penis than ours ejaculating some shit into our women. This thought alone has made many brothers lose their minds. That's why it always gets ugly when Larry Lump Lump from Lenox Avenue, with a Napoleon complex, catches Johnny Packawood stroking his woman. We take this as a direct assault on our manhood, even though we may have caused our women to cheat. Our egos wonder how our women can stoop to the same level. Ain't that some bullshit.

Pimp Bones had walked up while all of us players were standing there talking and he overheard Honey Combs expressing his thoughts so he joined our conversation.

He said, "Honey Combs's got a point in some of the things he was kickin'. If a pimp treats his hoes right, then he gets to keep them and he even gets more in return. Now if the brothers treat their women right, then they will act right. The problem with the brothers is they don't keep it real with the sisters. They lie about all types of shit, so in return the woman goes them one better and beats them at their own game without detection, if they chose to go that route. But, if everybody could just be straight up and down, then they could expect the same. We pimps give it to our whores straight with no chaser. Another problem I find with some brothers is they try to make whores into housewives, which can't be done 'cause a hoe gon' be a hoe, any way you flip it. And, what the sisters also have to understand is, if they want to keep their man, they can play a church girl in the front room all they want, but they better be a whore in the bedroom."

I thought, after Bones finished, *Damn, the pimps have got a point.*

31

Cheating Hearts

I once heard a woman ask a man, why do you keep cheating on your woman? And the man replied, "Because I got more fucking to do." When I heard him say it, I thought, *Man, does this brother feel that he has some unfinished business that he has to attend to before he can be faithful?*

I think one of man's greatest challenges in life is dealing with the temptations of sexual lust. Sometimes, whenever I am asked by a woman why some men cheat? Sometimes I say lust and excuses, and then they give me a funny look. The reason I give them that answer is because when you really think about it, some men make too many damn excuses for their sexual lust and cheating ways. "Oh, my woman wasn't catering to my needs," or "Oh my woman kept on accusing me of cheating so I proved her right," or the thug brothers' favorite, "It takes more than one woman to satisfy me." All excuses that still don't answer the question of why some men cheat.

This brings me back to what I said about the temptations of sexual lust being one of man's greatest challenges. Some men damn near want to fuck most of the women that they run across, because they see it as a challenge and are looking to validate their manhood through their sexual conquests. In reality, they still wind up with low self-esteem and the insecurities that had them cheating in the first place.

Women are not exempt from cheating, although they do it for different reasons. Some cheat because they want a little nookie on the side or, like some men, use the excuse that something is lacking in their relationships. But that's more the exception than the rule. Try this one—some women cheat to get caught. I know what you are thinking, *Man, what is this brother talking about?* But hear me out.

The reason I say some women cheat to get caught is, because they want their cheating boyfriends to catch them, and feel the pain they made them feel. This could be the case if Dante's woman was actually cheating in the first place. Maybe she wanted to pay Dante back for his cheating on her, and not because she was looking for a little nookie on the side. In my dealings with a lot of women I have found out that most of them want to be mentally stimulated before they choose to get physical with a man where some men on the other hand can just look at a woman's physical attributes and be ready to do "the nasty."

Yes, women like good-looking men, but looks are not always their deciding factor in getting with them. If a woman meets an unattractive guy and he treats her like a queen, is a good listener, plus provides her with good conversation and laughter, he has a pretty good shot at winning her heart. In my opinion, this is one of the reasons you tend to see more pretty women with ugly guys as opposed to more handsome guys with ugly women.

I remember when I was a little kid, my penis would get hard for no reason, nothing. I could be in bed watching television and all of a sudden I would get horny and hard. Other times if I just heard somebody just mention anything about sex I would immediately start to rise for the occasion. Even just the wind blowing was enough to get me aroused. I eventually learned to channel all my sexual energy into humping on any girl I could find. But now that I am an adult I know I should not let lust rule my life, instead I should let my conscience be my guide. Because for every action there's a reaction, and I am the one who will have to deal with the consequences.

If I cheat on my woman, how can I be mad if she does the same? Instead of being unfaithful I should be content with the love my woman has to offer. But the sad part is when it comes to cheating my conscious mind tells me not to do it, but my body tells me yes.

When I think about it, maybe I'm just another stupid brother "who's got more fucking to do."

* * *

Why is it when everything is going good, some people get a weird impulse to sabotage themselves? Well, you can put me in that category. I cheated on China with Misa.

It all started with Misa calling my mother's apartment from time to time when she was in jail. I accepted her collect calls and talked to her, but I told her I had moved on with my life and I was in love with my new girlfriend. Every time I spoke to her, I never got the chance to ask her more about the robbery, due to the fact that China was in the other room and I had never told her about the set up, which was a big mistake on my part. The first time I told Misa about my new girlfriend, she became really mad, but then she acted like she understood. So, I talked to her from time to time when she called. China even knew that sometimes we talked, and even heard me tell Misa that I had moved on. I told China that the only reason I accepted Misa's calls was because I felt a little sorry for leaving her while she was in jail. When I told Misa this, I really believed it. But I also felt I could not be with a woman who might have set me up, so I had gone on with my life.

After serving six months, Misa got out of jail, and by this time China was pregnant, because I was having sex with her every day without protection. Little did I know that while I was gearing up to be a father, Misa was putting her plans in motion to get back together with me. She started to come around all the places she knew I would be in Midtown. She would hang around looking good with her hair done nice and wearing these tight designer outfits. I stayed strong about two months thinking I was over being pussy-whipped, plus I still was not sure if she had set me up. But, one day after playing monte, I ran into her when I was tipsy from beer. The next thing I knew, I started thinking with my bottom head. You know the rest of the story. Afterwards we started having sex every so often. When we did, I went into a deep depression because I knew what I was doing to China was wrong. Plus I felt like the worst type of fool. I was having sex with a girl who had possibly set me up. What a fool! This was after coming to the realization that Gus might have put the thought in her head, but she was the one that probably went through with it. As I was coming to this conclusion, I found something else out.

One day after playing monte I was walking on Forty-second Street and saw Gus playing monte so I stopped to watch while he beat all the vics in his game. A drag queen, who was wearing a long purple gaudy dress, had lost all of his money and eventually discovered that he had been conned. So, while Gus was beating other vics, I saw the drag queen reach inside his big orange bag, fumbling with a big 45 gun. I yelled "quick slide" and Gus took off running. The drag queen was confused about what had just transpired. So, he walked off. I thought maybe I had just saved Gus's life. That incident alone told me I still had love for him, even after thinking he might have set me up. But, deep down I could not believe he would do something to harm my mother or me. This is the same reason I had a hard time coming to grips with the fact that Misa had carried it out. I did not think a woman could be that devilish and deceptive. But, I still felt like pure shit all the same.

The last straw came when I found myself with Misa, the day my son was born. I made the stupid mistake of letting my penis lead me in the wrong direction and I did not go home. China went into labor that night and I missed the birth of Curtis, who was named after my father. China never let me live it down, and I deserved every bit of her wrath.

Is it true when they say, "what you do not know cannot hurt you?" A player once told me if he ever got caught cheating by his woman, he would not confess, even if she caught him in bed with the girl. He told me all he would say, is it was not him, it was his twin brother, even though he did not have one. I guess in some ways I was just like this guy. I never admitted to China that I had betrayed her trust. In some sick way I thought I was protecting her from my demons. I just continued to lie whenever she would ask me where I was the night of our son's birth. I would say, "Oh, China, I already told you a thousand times, I got busted." All lies. So many times I would sit there lying to her with a straight face.

How could I betray the trust of such a loving, kindhearted woman who loved me and brought our son into this world? I was going through the best times of my life with China. Then Misa got out of jail and I start thinking with my penis. I was a stupid asshole. We men sometimes pick the most critical times in our lives to act the fool. Why is it we choose to run around like dogs, when our women are pregnant? We, as men, have got to change this madness or else our sons will do the same negative things that we do. Over the years, the turmoil I had put China through has weighed heavily on my heart. And if I had another chance to come clean, this is what I would tell her about where I was the day our son was born: *China, I know I never told you the real story and I do not know if you will ever forgive me for my dishonesty, but I am truly very sorry for all of the pain, sorrow and suffering that I have caused you. No woman on this earth deserves to be deceived in such a way. How could I be such a fool?*

I guess it is true what they say about what is done in the dark will always come to light.

32

The Vacation

There's something about being in the presence of a newborn baby that makes a young couple understand that their number one priority is the child's well-being.

Although China was still angry and did not believe all my stupid lies about getting busted, we still tried to enjoy the precious times with our new arrival.

Curtis was a healthy seven-pound boy who bore a strong resemblance to my deceased father and me, which is why when he was born China suggested we name him after my father. I guess her other reason is she knew how much I loved and missed my father. Even after all my bullshit she still put my needs over hers.

While we sat there playing with the baby, the possibility loomed that I would have to do some jail time because of my latest arrest. Even though I knew the court case was coming up soon, all I could do at the moment was to try to get it off my mind.

When China got out of the hospital I decided to stay away from Midtown for about two weeks to enjoy those precious times with my family. Curtis had a healthy appetite and a smile that could light up a room. We laughed hard when he mimicked my facial expressions. People say laughter cures stress and I believe it. I had put my son's mother through some major drama but, beyond a shadow of a doubt, we both still loved each other.

After the two weeks came and went, I headed back downtown, and the players congratulated me on the arrival of my son. Everywhere I went in Midtown some of the players tried to offer me advice on raising him. This made me laugh as I pictured a funny scenario with Honey Combs saying, "Hey Mike, don't let no bitch trick your boy, understand me." As I stood there chuckling, one of the players said, "Mike, are you all right? That baby ain't making you crazy is it."

I said, "Nah, man, I was just thinking about something." Then I gave him and everybody cigars, got a team together and I did what Monte players do, I went to play monte.

My court date eventually came around and my paid lawyer got the judge to drop the bogus assault charge, but he gave me thirty days for resisting arrest and promoting gambling

When the judge announced my sentence, I turned around and spotted China crying while holding our baby. I yelled telling her that I would call later and the court officer told me to shut up.

The bullshit was starting already. My lawyer looked at me and said I had gotten a raw deal. But I did not say anything else as the court officer escorted me upstairs.

Upon our arrival he put me in a big holding cell with about twenty other prisoners who were waiting to go to Rikers Island.

While sitting in the cell, I noticed a big muscle-bound Cuban guy with his shirt off, flexing his muscles. Everybody in the cell was watching him as he made funny noises every time he touched a muscle. He sounded like a pig snorting, combined with some *um, uh, um, uh*, sounds. After repeating the same routine numerous times he walked to the other side of the cell and yoked up a guy, taking his money and jewelry. Then he nonchalantly walked back to the other side and started the same flexing routine. *Um, uh, um, uh* as he breathed in, *um, uh, um, uh* as he breathed out.

After fifteen minutes he walked back to the other side of the cell and snatched another guy with braids in his hair and robbed him, too.

Every time a new prisoner came into the cell it immediately got quiet because we all knew what was going to happen. We all thought the Cuban guy was finished robbing people, but he robbed this old Spanish man we thought he liked. I thought they knew each other from the streets because they got along so well.

This guy was ruthless and he did not care about anybody. If his own brother had come into the cell, he would have robbed him, too. What we later found out was, the guy had just gotten out of jail doing fifteen years for raping a twelve-year-old boy. He had only been out for a week before he got busted again.

I guess this robbing spree was just a little practice until he got to prison. All I could think about was *if this is going on in the court building, it will only get worse at Rikers Island.*

So as I sat there my mind drifted back to when I was a little kid.

My mother had friends who always used to hang at our apartment. Every so often one of them would disappear for short periods. My sister and I, being curious kids, inquired about them. My mother answered nonchalantly, "Oh they went on vacation to an island." I remember telling my sister, "Boy I can't wait to go on a vacation." When we were older we learned that the island her friends vacationed at was Rikers Island Jail. Well, I finally got my wish for a vacation; it's ten years late but it is an all-expense-paid trip to Rikers Island. They say you get what you ask for, and it may not come when you want it, but it's always on time. So there I sat, waiting for the jail bus to take us over to Rikers Island, and wondering what the fuck had I gotten myself into?

After we watched new prisoners come into the cell for about four hours, a correction officer yelled for us to get ready because the bus had arrived. Then he escorted us downstairs to the bus and we all got on.

I decided to take a nap soon after taking a seat by a window. An hour later, I was awakened by a correction officer yelling, "Everybody stand up and be counted." We were finally there. After he had counted everybody, he escorted us off the bus and into the jail.

They put us in a big cell called the receiving room. This is where all new inmates get processed before going upstairs. While everybody waited his turn, I sat on a dirty wooden bench with some of the other inmates and observed the surroundings. I wanted to see who else besides the Cuban guy was going to be a problem. As I canvassed the place, I noticed a Puerto Rican guy with a big head and cockeyes acting nervous. He told anybody who would listen about all the people he knew and hung out with. I guess he wanted to let all the thugs know, he was not to be fucked with. I myself already knew he was just telling the usual lies that always get told at central booking.

When we all were processed, they let us take a shower. I caught one guy staring at another guy's ass. Immediately visions of being offered candy bars by "Mother Dear" flashed through my mind

Mother Dear is a large muscular six-foot-four effeminate thug on Rikers Island who was known to take what he wanted. He was what I call a serial buttocks predator.

I told myself if anybody tried to rape me, he would be one dead motherfucker. So I was not worried about that. But I was worried about getting jumped without the chance to fight one-on-one. I had already heard a lot of stories about how they jumped people on Rikers Island. One of the guys would slice you across the face with a razor; leaving you with this nasty scar requiring one hundred and fifty stitches. They call it a "buck fifty."

I knew a lot of my homeboys from Midtown and uptown were on Rikers Island, so at least I would get a one-on-one. But, one of the first things you learn on the streets is that no one will help you unless you are willing to help yourself. During my life on the streets I have been in fights. Some I won and some I lost, but I always fought back.

I remember one time when I was in fifth grade and this fourth-grader kicked my ass real good. This was after all through the school year I spent beating up other students. I had even beaten the crap out of this sixth-grader who wouldn't let me play with his basketball. But in the fight I had with the fourth-grader my punches didn't faze him one bit. He jumped into a karate stance like Bruce Lee and proceeded to kick the living shit out of me. He beat me so bad that I wanted to get up and run for dear life. But I stayed and took my ass-whipping like a man. So I knew as I sat there that I was not scared to fight.

After about five hours in the receiving room a correction officer told us to get ready to go upstairs. Then we heard a loud siren-type of alarm go off. Somebody told us it meant a riot was going on some place in the jail, which proved to be correct, because we still had to wait. After the loud alarm sounded, about thirty cock-diesel correction officers came marching military-style into the receiving area. These officers had humongous arms plus mean and serious demeanors. Just looking at them told me they were capable of doing serious damage to anybody on the receiving end. While standing near us, they did not look in our direction once. They stood there a few minutes in riot gear, and then they marched upstairs to squash the riot.

All I kept thinking was, *I have gotten myself into some serious shit, winding up in jail. Daddy if you hear me—can you put a word in for me to God, tell him your boy done went and got himself into a whole mess of trouble, and he needs some help, pronto.*

When the riot squad handled its business, we got escorted to a long corridor with a bunch of other correction officers and inmates. As they passed by, some gave us the once over with these funny screw faces. I guess the inmates wanted to see who looked soft, so that they could try to rob or rape us later. If any of us were scared to make eye contact with them we would have trouble later in the dorms.

The nervous guy who had been in the receiving room talking all that junk about who he knew tried to start up a conversation with one of the inmates mopping the floor. He said, "Yo bruh, do you know crazy Lou up on 118th Street?" The guy answered, "I'm not your bruh, you bitch-ass nigger." The nervous guy just looked down, like he was cold pussy. I told myself he was definitely going to get robbed, maybe even fucked. I did not feel sorry for any of us because I already knew, "Don't do the crime, if you can't do the time."

A correction officer yelled at the inmate mopping the floor, "Hey, you stupid motherfucker, don't you got a job to do?" He answered with a sly look, "Yeah, CO." Then the correction officer said, "Well get your ass away from all these new jack motherfuckers and go mop that fuckin' floor."

The correction officer, who was escorting us, was the one cursing out the inmate. Then he said to all of us, "Now y'all punk motherfuckers keep it moving." So we continued to walk down the long corridor. When we made it to the end, I spotted jealous Poppa Doc who sold smoke on The Deuce. He was kicking it with these other inmates. The last time I saw him was when he tried to tax me at Grace Park. So I knew immediately there was going to be some trouble. But I still tried to make a little small talk anyway. I said, yo Poppa Doc, what's up? He looked at me with this dumb look then yelled for everybody to hear, "That boy's a snitch. Tax that boy, tax that boy."

I said, "What the fuck you talking about?" He just walked away laughing. The moment he mouthed those words I knew I was headed for some serious jail drama. I knew exactly what he was trying to do. He figured if he labeled me a snitch. The worst thing you could be in jail, I would surely get robbed or beat down. This is why everybody was looking at me funny as we stood there in the corridor.

When the correction officer took us to a dorm called 9U we had to wait inside a fenced area to be let in. While we waited about twenty inmates looked at us through this glass window in the bathroom. Some were pointing down at our sneakers, screaming, "Those is mine, those is mine." While others yelled, "New Jacks, new Jacks."

The correction officer opened the gated door and we all walked into an area that looked like a hospital dorm with bunk beds everywhere, carrying our jail issued sheets and pillowcases. When the correction officer walked off, the prisoners in the dorm converged on us. "Yo baby. Pa, come here and let me holla at you," said one inmate to the nervous guy from the receiving room. Like a stupid ass he walked over there. The next thing we saw was the little guy slapping him up and taking his sneakers and little gold chain.

Some black bald-headed guy standing with his boys yelled at me to play the back. I yelled back, "No let's play it right here." Because I already know the back is where you get beat down." He said, "Oh, it's like that." I said, "Yeah, it's like that."

A correction officer heard the commotion and said "Break it up y'all, break it up." I walked to a bed, made it up and lay down. A few minutes later I heard somebody say, "Yo Mike, what the fuck you doing in here? I looked up and it was this guy named Andre who lived around my homeboy Cee Wee's block in the Bronx.

I said, "What up Dre, what's going on?"

"Yo Mike, you get too much money to be fucking around in here."

I said, "Man, it be's like that sometimes."

He said, "You know I got your back if anybody fuck with you."

"I'll be all right, Dre. I just want to take a little nap, then I'll kick it with you later."

"All right, Mike, just remember what I said." I lay down for about twenty minutes, then I heard a correction officer yell for everybody to line up and be counted because it was chow time. We did what he said then headed to the cafeteria. I noticed while standing on the line that some of the new guys I came in with had gotten robbed. I could tell because they had on different pairs of cheap sneakers, plus some had black eyes and bruises. While walking to the cafeteria I ran into a lot of my homeboys. Some of them asked me the same questions that Dre asked me.

When we got in the cafeteria there were inmates everywhere. I spotted my man Ness who used to slide for me sometimes; he was big as a house. He said with this big grin, "Not my mother fucking man Money Mike. I must be seeing things, what the fuck you doing in here?"

I said, "Well, Ness, it's a long story."

He said, "I know Mike they got us in here for some little skid bids. But is anybody fucking with you?"

"Nah, Ness I'm chilling."

Then he looked at the other inmates standing on line with me, and with this crazy look on his face said, "'Cause I'll break these niggas off something proper."

Then he walked off. All the inmates from my dorm had these shocked looks on their faces, while I stood there smiling, lapping it up.

One of them said, "Damn you know a lot of motherfuckers." I just continued to smile as we made our way down the line. Along the way I spotted Light Skin Tony, Jeff Red, a monte player, my man

217

Bishop and Kendall. They all wanted to know what was going on in the streets since they've been in jail, and I told them. Monte players were in full effect. When I got to the front, who did I spot? My main man Fronting Cee, who was working with the house gang. He yelled for everybody to hear, "We got a real player in this motherfucker. Money motherfuckin' Midtown Mike, so back the fuck up."

I laughed, then I said, "Chill, Cee, chill," as a lot of the other inmates took notice. Cee started laughing too, as he put his hands in about ten inmates faces and said, "If any of you motherfuckers fuck with my homeboy I got twenty days left and I'll lose them for him, I'll lose 'em for him. Then he walked off bopping. I felt so good when he said it.

Afterwards they served us food, and we sat down and ate. When we finished we headed to the corridor and lined up. While waiting to be counted and escorted back to our dorm, all of a sudden Poppa Doc walked up to me with a stupid smirk on his face and looked down to see if I still had my sneakers on. Then he said, "Yo Mike, you know I was joking when I did that, right?"

I lied and said, "Yeah, Doc but you shouldn't play like that."

Then he said, "Nah, I just wanted to see if you could hold your own, no hard feelings right?"

I said, "Nah, it ain't nothing man." He said, "All right, Mike I'll check you out later. Let a nigga know if you got any problems, I got this whole shit on lock." Then he walked off.

When we got back to the dorm the guys who told me to play the back said they were sorry for fucking with me. They said when Poppa Doc had yelled that I was a snitch, it left them no choice. But now that they knew he was just joking, they wanted to squash our little beef. I said, all right, and we all shook hands. All night long inmates started coming up to me asking questions like, "Are you that nigga Mike from Midtown?" Or, "Can you put me down?" Or, "Can you teach me how to play three-card monte?" It went on and on.

* * *

After the first night everything became quite routine. Get up in the morning, take a shower, get ready for the count, go eat breakfast, come back to the dorm. Chill a little while, another count, then go to your assigned work detail in the jail, come back take a shower and a little nap, then count, lunch, dorm, chill out, count, dinner, dorm, chill out, then go to bed and the next day start all over.

Then there was your everyday jail drama that consisted of beatings, robberies and soft inmates getting fucked in the ass. In my dorm we had a few homosexuals who fucked the inmates who were down with that. I could not believe how these young guys, most of them with skid bids, could be in the dayroom where the television was, hugged up with another guy.

I say if you fuck a homo, you a homo. If your dick gets hard for a man, you a homo. I didn't want any of that bullshit around me. So when I saw this one tall skinny homosexual who thought he was a ballerina, doing twirls around the dorm, it made me want to puke.

One night I saw him crawl into a bunk with this guy. They had a sheet covering the bunk bed at the bottom. All of a sudden I started hearing them fucking, as "the ballerina" made noises like a girl. He said, "Ooh fuck me baby, fuck me baby, ooh, ooh, fuck me."

I could not believe two men were having sex behind a sheet. Then he started to yell, "Please, daddy, don't come in me, please. Then somebody yelled from the back section of the dorm, "Let the mother-fucker come, you ain't a bitch, you can't get pregnant." Everybody started laughing, even me.

After that incident the days started to go by fast as I passed the time kicking it with my homeboys and working in the laundry room folding clothes, instead of being on the streets folding money.

I also started looking at and reading porno magazines that the other inmates lent me. Every magazine seemed to be talking about the pleasures of eating a woman's pussy. This was something I had not tried yet, I was still stuck in don't-eat-pussy mode. I was like a lot of young guys who think going down on a woman meant you could not handle your business with your tool. So when they got asked by another guy, "Hey you ever ate any pussy?" They would say, "Hell, no." Well, China was in for a little treat when I get out.

It is crazy how things work out. Here I was lying up in a jail dorm reading porno magazines when I should be with my woman and our son sharing quality time together. I guess I was just another stupid hustler thinking ass-backwards. But the odd thing was, a lot of in-mates looked up to me because of the money they heard I made, and the lifestyle they envisioned of a Midtown three-card monte player. One thing I learned from being on the streets and in jail was that people always thought you made more than you actually did. They also envisioned the life of a hustler to be flamboyant without any pitfalls. It is like looking in from the outside. The grass always looks greener on the other side.

There is a statistic that says half of the young men are either in jail, on drugs or dead. Maybe if some of those young men had had positive male role models in their lives to guide and direct them in the right direction, they might have been saved. Without positive male figures, this negative cycle will continue to spin. How could I guide my son in the ways he should go, if I was the one in need of guidance? It's like a student trying to teach the teacher. No matter how you flip it around, it's just not going to work. *Please, can somebody save me because I am falling and I can't get up? But please do not call 911 because all they will do is send the cops. And the cops are the ones who beat the living shit out of me and helped me with my sorry predicament, which is sitting in jail reading porno magazines.*

"Hey Mike, what are you doing over there, you horny motherfucker?" It was Andre.

I said, "Man I'm just killing time."

Then he said, "Yo Mike, I was thinking could you bring me downtown to make some of that big money, y'all be making?" All I could think as I heard the words is, *where does it all end.*

* * *

Just when you think it is all blue skies and sunshine, a storm comes out of nowhere raging with thunder. It started to go down a week before my jail release date. The inmates in my dorm were complaining about the food, work details and the cruel treatment they were receiving from the correction officers. It all manifested itself one day when this correction officer hit an inmate with this big black metal flashlight that he carried. The inmate's head and face got busted up pretty bad.

All of us in the dorm bore witness to this horrendous act. Inmates yelled, "We ain't going for it, we can't have that." It was total chaos. One of the correction officers yelled for everybody to shut up and get on the count. The inmates refused because it was not count time. The correction officers sometimes made us line up and get on the count because they knew it was an inconvenience. But this time everybody refused to do it. So the correction officer got on the phone and called the riot squad. A lot of the inmates ran to their lockers and started putting on extra clothes to use as padding. I lay down on my bed scared like a motherfucker. I knew we were in some deep shit because of what I had witnessed on my first day in jail in the receiving room. I knew the riot squad included some big motherfuckers and they looked like they knew how to whip some ass. It was going to go down and there was nothing I could do to stop it.

As I lay there waiting, all I could think about was that movie I saw a while back about the Attica riots. Visions of inmates being hit with buckshot from shotguns and clobbered with billy clubs entered my mind. I whispered, *Daddy, if you hear me, please talk to God or even to one of his angels, your boy needs some help.*

About twenty minutes later about eight correction officers rushed into our dorm and beat all the vocal instigators to a pulp. They even rammed some from one end of the dorm to the other into metal lockers head first. Then they asked if there was anybody else who was big and bad and wanted an ass-whipping. Nobody said a word, it was quieter than a church mouse. I was glad it was over, so I thanked God and my dead father that I did not get hurt.

* * *

The final week went by and it was time to go home. I packed my stuff, giving things that I did not need to the other inmates. I made a little small talk, said my good-byes and headed downstairs with the correction officer who had hit the inmate with the flashlight.

Let me tell you how sick the mind-set of a hustler can get. When I was released from Rikers Island with a few other inmates, the first thing I did with the three measly dollars they gave me for transportation home was to buy two Guiness Stouts. Then I snuck on the train. It gets crazier. Instead of taking the train home to my family, I headed straight to Midtown to show all the players I had not gotten robbed in jail. I had to show them I still had my shit. It gets even crazier. After I got off the train and made it to the donut shop, I said, "What's up?" to everybody, told a few jail stories, then got a monte team together. I took my team straight to Broadway where I set up shop. I yelled, "Hey New York, New York I'm back, I'm back" and my team started to laugh because they knew I had just gotten out of jail. Now that I think about it, what I should have yelled was, "Look at the clown and his three-ring circus."

After playing monte for about three hours our count was $2,200, so I decided to quit and go uptown. Then I split up the money and caught the train.

When I got to China's mother's apartment, China showered me with hugs and kisses. Then I went into her bedroom where my little son was sleeping. He looked a little bigger than the last time I had seen him. While looking at the baby, China and I made a little small talk, then I went to take a shower.

When I got out of the shower I looked at China and sensed that somehow she knew that I had left the jail and gone to play monte. I thought maybe she had searched my pockets when I was taking a shower and had seen the $900 that I made playing. How stupid could

I be? Shouldn't I have known that the average person does not come out of jail with nine hundred dollars in his pockets? There I go again thinking ass-backwards.

When I walked into the bedroom my son was up, so I picked him up to play with him. While I held him in my arms, I whispered softly, "Curtis it's gonna take a minute for your father to get his act together. Can you nod if you hear me?" I could swear I saw him nod. China asked me, what I was whispering to him? I laughed and said, "Nothing, just a father talking to his firstborn son."

33

Twin Parks

After Curtis was born, we moved to an apartment complex called Twin Parks on Southern Boulevard in the Bronx. It consisted of four, large reddish-brown buildings of different dimensions in a three-block radius. The biggest had sixteen floors. My homeboy, Kendall, from Midtown had gotten an apartment there through a shady under-the-table money deal with a guy he knew. The guy managed the same buildings that Kendall and his brother CeeWee grew up in. After Kendall got an apartment, he helped China and me get ours.

I knew about Twin Parks from hanging out with CeeWee and Dante. Late at night, they would bring me to their block after a long day in Midtown making money playing monte. Something was always going on there.

The first time I arrived on their block, all the people wanted to know who the new guy was. I quickly let my presence be known by meeting and having sex with one of the prettiest girls there.

Wherever I went—be it, Midtown, 169th Street or Harlem—I always brought myself with me, meaning I was a hustler and a player wherever I went. A pimp downtown once told me, "Use what you got." Sometimes that was not good, because you can use what you've got in the wrong way. I used my handsome looks, along with my acquired street skills, money and material things to manipulate women. I may have had the face of an angel, but when I arrived at Twin Parks, I already had the mind-set of the devil. By the time my family and I moved there, I had already used a lot of the women for my own devilish pleasures.

For example, there was Tammy, who lived around there. I had run into her while hanging in one of the Twin Parks buildings with

Dante and CeeWee in the past. We were playing dice when a light-skinned girl walked by, who used to be in my class in elementary school P.S. 67 on Southern Boulevard.

I yelled, "Hey, Tammy!"

She looked at me like she did not know me from anywhere.

She said, "How do you know my name?"

I told her. She lied and said she didn't remember. I could tell she was lying. So, there I stood looking like an ass in front of my Midtown homeboys. She walked off, grinning, while their laughter filled the hallway that seemed to have better acoustics than Carnegie Hall.

Not more than a week later, I was hanging with them in a gambling spot on 183rd Street and Garden Avenue, not too far from the Twin Parks complex, who walks in? Tammy. I was standing in the back of the dingy little hole in the wall listening to the jukebox and drinking a Guinness Stout, while my homeboys played dice. She admired my jewelry and nice red and white Adidas suit and said, "Mike, I am sorry about not remembering you the last time I saw you. But, the funny thing about it all is, later, when I got upstairs, I remembered you did use to be in my fifth-grade class."

I knew this was a lie because CeeWee had already told me downtown a few days ago that Tammy had been asking him about my street status. When he told me that, I knew she was going to have to pay for embarrassing me in front of my friends. So, I played along with her little game, but she failed to realize that I had been taught my gift of gab by pimps—the best bullshit artists in the business. So, I got into Mack Daddy mode, flashed my pearly whites and sinister smile, then bought her drinks at a bar the size of a dinette table. Then I faked like I was listening to her tell me her life story.

She was a pretty, light-skinned girl with a nice petite body and a big chest. I was getting hornier by the minute. After we had a few drinks, she asked me to dance. I played a slow jam called "So into You" by Ray Parker Junior. As we slow danced, she held me close like I was her man. When the song finished, I came straight out and told her I wanted to take her to a hotel. She said yes before I could even finish my next sentence.

While we danced like two lovebirds, CeeWee, Dante and everybody watched. After we finished, I told my homeboys I would see them later because I had some important business to attend to. They all knew what time it was, including Tammy. Then we left the hole in the wall and jumped in my new customized burgundy and white Oldsmobile with the vogue tires and powerful stereo system.

This was the same car I always pulled up in when I went to pick up China at her mother's apartment, waking up the whole block with my loud stereo and intercom system. This time I was headed to the hotel with Mrs. Tammy I-forgot.

I took Tammy to the Alps Hotel on West Farms Avenue—the same hotel where I had impregnated China. Before we went in, we stopped at the store and I bought beer although we were already tipsy from drinking in the gambling spot. When we got in the hotel room, I went to the bathroom and sprayed my old reliable Stud 100 on my penis. When I came out with just my boxers on, she was already buck naked, messing with the television. She turned the channel to some porno. I knew I was not going to need an x-rated movie because I was already harder than ten men.

Tammy had a curvy body with a caramel complexion. I was ready to do some serious fucking and while looking at her, I told myself it was my duty to please this booty. We started having sex like two dogs in heat. She was a big noisemaker and I knew we were waking up the whole hotel. She could not stop her loud yelling and moaning. After putting her in every position imaginable, I put her legs up and went into slam mode, like a mad man. She started to moan and scream louder than before. This went on most of the night. I had Stud 100 staying power.

In the morning when we left the hotel, she was walking like she was bowlegged, and I was right beside her with my sinister smile. When I dropped her off at Twin Parks everybody who was outside made her the butt of all their jokes. They knew she had just come from the hotel by the way she was walking. The funny thing about it was every time she saw me, she wanted to have sex. Some women like rough sex and Tammy is one of them. My whole reason for having sex with her was so that I could brutalize her sexually for making me look like an ass and it backfired on me. Sometimes things don't go as planned.

34

Gut Check

One beautiful summer day China and I decided to go to the movies on Fordham Road. On our way, we stopped at a grocery store to buy a Guinness Stout. After making my purchase, I walked outside and next thing I knew, Alonzo, a stickup kid, tried to rob me.

He stuck a gun in my stomach area and asked, "You Mike?"

As soon as he said it, I knocked his hand to the side and ran off. Foolishly, I thought he only wanted to rob me, not China. When she came out of the store, he grabbed her, took my high school ring off her finger and told her he was going to kill me the next time he saw me. China walked up the hill to where I was and told me what Alonzo had said. I was furious and I had murder on my mind.

At this point, we were in no mood to watch a movie. So, we hailed a cab and I went to get my homeboy, Kendall, who at this time was my ride-or die-homey, and was always down for anything. Whenever I had any street drama, all I had to do was knock on his door, tell him I had static and he would grab his gun and say, "Let's go."

One time, after my sister's boyfriend, Toby, had taken her jewelry, she called me. I went and got Kendall and we headed to the 169th Street projects where Toby lived. We went to his mother's apartment and he wasn't there, but his mother and his brothers were.

We got into an argument and Kendall pulled out a gun on the whole family, ready to shoot everybody. I told him to put away the gun and then told them if my sister did not get her jewelry back, there would be trouble. The next day Toby dropped off all of her jewelry.

I'm telling you this to let you know that Kendall is a guy who has always had my back. So, when I told him about what had happened to me, all he did was grab his gun and say, "Let's go."

We looked all over the Bronx all night long, but could not find the stickup kid, which was good for both of us because if we had found him, he would have been a dead man, and I would have gone to jail.

About a year later, Kendall and I spotted him hanging with Mickey Hart on 169th Street. I called Mickey over and told him that guy had robbed me once and we were going to shoot him. Mickey asked us not to do it while he was with him. Mickey was one of the older guys that Spence and I looked up to when we were younger, and I respected him to the fullest. I listened to him and decided to get the guy some other time. Not too long after that, the stickup kid was shot nine times for some other street drama. Karma has a way of providing its own street justice.

35

Shaky Mike

My monte team had been jokingly calling me "Shaky Mike" because of my jumpiness behind the box. Any little sound I heard while playing monte made me ready to take off running. It had a lot to do with my being robbed when China and I were going to the movies.

When the stickup man put the gun to my gut, I chose to run away rather than staying there and being robbed or killed. This was really like choosing the better of two evils because sometimes during robberies they still shoot you even though you give up your valuables.

Taking all of this into consideration did not help me come to grips with the action I took. Maybe it was because I had heard many stories in which a person decided he was not going to let the stickup man take his gold chain worth three hundred dollars, then wound up being killed.

Is a person's life not worth more than that? I think no material thing is worth dying for. But the crazy thing about all of this is, even though I knew these things before the robbery, I still chose to run and risk being shot in the back, and possibly getting China and myself killed, all because my misguided instincts told me that all the stickup kid wanted to do was to rob me. What I should have done was give up the money and jewelry, hoping he wouldn't harm us. This was why I found myself on pins and needles now. I had started to doubt myself because now I did not know what my judgement would be in certain situations. What if some guy lost his money playing monte then pulled a knife on me, what was I going to do? Was I going to give him the money back or choose to go up against a knife?

A wrong decision could cost me my life. This is why I wondered, *Does "Shaky Mike" have a reason to be shaky?*

36

Mistaken Identity

Somebody killed Little Bit's twin brother, Peanut. The day started out like any other normal day. I arrived downtown fresh and early on what I thought was going to be a beautiful summer day. It was Friday and the weatherman on the radio in the donut shop predicted that the temperature was headed into the nineties.

The donut shop was already packed with monte players and other hustlers when I walked in. I was feeling good, because the night before, China and I had gone to a Luther Vandross concert at Madison Square Garden and had had a great time.

I never knew that women went so crazy over male singers at concerts. They were yelling, screaming, crying and even throwing panties on the stage. China was screaming so hard she could have broken a glass. After we left the concert we went out to eat. Then we went home and did the nasty.

So, when I arrived downtown in the morning I was totally relaxed and ready to make the vics pay for last night's entertainment. I stopped to talk to everybody in the shop, telling them about the concert and how China and I had such a great time. Little Clyde and his team were sitting in the front eating breakfast and talking about where they were going to play monte. Black Jack, a monte player and a pimp who looked like the singer Barry White, bragged about hitting the number last night. Little Glenda and Big Burke were sitting in the back talking about taking turns springing them. Little Bit and his brother, Peanut, were cracking jokes about a springer named Tee's clothes and shoes.

Tee had on a red-white-and blue sweat suit with blue pointy shoes. Little Bit asked him if he was going to play basketball with the Harlem

229

Globetrotters or going tap dancing with his ugly shoes, making him the laughing stock of the shop.

Sometimes Little Bit could be as funny as the comedian Richard Pryor. Saul and his two sisters, Eve and Jody, asked me where I was going to play. I told them, "Broadway."

"You'd better watch it over there," Jody replied.

"Little Petey and the monte squad were all over Broadway yesterday arresting monte players," said Saul.

"Yeah, Mike, my whole team got busted and I was the only one to get away," said Jody.

When they told me all that, I told them maybe it would be all right to play monte today since the monte squad had already gotten their arrest quotas. They all said maybe I was right and I asked Jody and Saul if they wanted to play with me. They both said okay. So, I sat down, ate a hearty breakfast of bacon, eggs and pancakes, then I got my homeboys, Spence and Fronting Cee to lookout for me. We all headed to Broadway and Forty-third Street to play.

When we arrived, there were teams already playing. I saw Little Clyde and his team on Forty-second and Broadway, by the Carvel's ice cream shop. He already had a big crowd around him and Little Glenda and Big Burke's team was playing on the same block. Black Beauty's team was on Forty-fourth Street and Seventh Avenue, and Little Bit and Peanut's team was across the street on Forty-fourth and Broadway.

The temperature was already about 85 degrees. It was not even noon yet and I already had sweat on my forehead. I told my lookouts to go get the game set up before anybody tried to steal our spot.

While standing waiting for my slides to come, I asked Jody if she ever cried at a concert. She said, "Mike, I'm not gonna lie. One time I went to see The Temptations and I liked to lost my mind, trying to get on stage! Security had to damn near arrest me, I was going so crazy!"

I said, "Well, China was yelling so loud, she made me nervous."

Saul said, "Man, Mike, once I took my girlfriend to a Blue Magic concert and I thought she was going to take her clothes off. I told her, 'Calm down girl, calm down.'" That made us chuckle.

After the lookouts brought the setup, we got down to business. As soon as I jumped behind the box, I yelled, "Hey New York, New York, I'm back, I'm back. Find my red, get my bread. Find my black, get nothing back. Midtown Mike's the name; three-card monte's my game. Twenty will get you forty back; forty will get you eighty. Anybody can win, even if they are blind, crippled or crazy. Who saw that red card?"

In about five minutes, I had a crowd bigger than the ones across the street.

A Japanese guy was itching so bad to bet that he could hardly stand still. I thought I had spotted him in another game, just before we set up. Now he was in my game pulling out his brown wallet and all I saw was fifties and hundreds. I started my bets off at one hundred dollars. I threw the cards across the board in one quick move. I said, "Who saw it for one hundred?"

Saul said, "I saw it."

He and Jody placed one hundred dollar bets real quick, before the vic had a chance to get his money ready. I paid them off and I started throwing the cards real fast. As I yelled, "Cherry, cherry like a strawberry, who saw that red card?"

The vic yelled, "I did."

So I said, "The bet is one hundred dollars," and he placed the bet and I raised him all the way up to six hundred dollars.

I yelled, "Turn it up. *Bam*, black you lose!"

The vic looked shocked, but he still stood there. I started back tossing the cards and yelling, "Red, gets you the bread, black sets you back."

Even though the Japanese guy lost, that did not stop the other vics in the crowd from betting. I was taking forty, eighty, and one hundred dollar bets left and right. The Japanese guy started fumbling for his wallet again and came up with a different little black pouch. Jody whispered to me, "C-notes, C- notes," which meant the vic had even more hundreds. She placed a $400 bet real fast, and I raised her a hundred dollars. *Bam.* You win, and I paid her off.

After that everybody was ready for the taking. So, I came ready shuffling the cards in slow motion, as I said. "Red card, you win. Black card, you lose. Which card do you choose?" and I laid the cards down on the cardboard.

The Japanese guy counted out five hundred dollars and I raised him all the way up to eight hundred. The other vics that wanted to bet lay low.

I yelled, "Turn it up. *Bam*. Black. You lose."

The vic's eyes started popping out of his head like a clown in a circus, where I was the magician, the star attraction.

Saul whispered to the guy, "We're gonna get your money back" and he threw my black card out of the game yelling, "Play with two cards."

231

So, as I ran and got the card, I yelled to my slides, "Hold me down. Hold me down."

Fronting Cee and Spence just smiled as I winked at them. While doing this, I looked across the street and noticed some type of commotion going on, but I could not really tell what was happening, because of all the people clustered around. So, I ran back in the game, telling Saul, "Hey, don't you mess with my cards. I play with three cards."

Then I came back faking like I did not know that Saul bent the red card. I shuffled the cards real fast across the board. I laid them down and Jody bet five hundred dollars before Saul or the vic had a chance to bet. I paid her off real fast and threw the cards in one quick move and came ready for the vics. Saul and the vic placed five hundred dollar bets and some other vics came up with fifties and one hundreds. I raised Saul and the Japanese guy up to nine hundred dollars apiece, and all the other vics that had money I raised whatever their first bet was.

I yelled, "Turn it up. *Bam.* Black. You lose."

All the vics and onlookers yelled, "Damn" or "Ah, fuck." I just smiled as I stuffed the money in my pocket.

Fronting Cee yelled, "Slide 'em up!"

I got from behind the box and the crowd dispersed. I knew the count had to be about three thousand or better. As I stood on the side waiting for the blue and white police car to go by, Jody came by me and said, "Man, Mike, these vics are greedy today. Our count is already $3,740."

I said, "Jody, they owe me for all that money I spent yesterday."

She said, "That's right, Mike, make all them motherfuckers pay, make them pay. And I yelled, "Show ya right."

While we stood on the corner shooting the breeze, Saul and my slides came up and told us that they think Little Bit was across the street arguing with some vic he beat out of all his money. This was nothing new to us because we, monte players, always had problems with vics from time to time. It was just a part of the game. So, we did not pay it too much mind, even though it seemed like something was going on. Plus, I thought since there were no police cars over there, it could not be all that bad. Spence told me to spring 'em, so I got back behind the box.

I yelled, "Hey, New York, New York. So nice they named it twice. Cherry, cherry like a strawberry . . . " as another big crowd gathered around to watch me lay my game down.

I thought, *the weatherman was right; it's turning out to be a beautiful day.*

I was like a man possessed as I beat vic after vic. Whenever I played monte, I took on a whole different personality. I was like Christopher Reeve turning into Superman or like a big entertainer right before he hit the stage—Luther Vandross comes to mind. I had a crazy adrenaline rush whenever I played monte. I felt unstoppable; no one could penetrate my force field. As the crowd watched, I put on the Midtown Mike show. I would provide entertainment, but for a hefty price. My admission was more than the price of a concert ticket. And this they would find out rather quickly.

I yelled, "Red, get you the bread. Black will set you back" as I beat all comers, for forty, sixty, eighty and hundreds. They bet it, I won it. After about two hours of playing and a few slides here and there we decided to go split up the money. My count was $4,560, which was a good day's work and I knew if I wanted to, I could take another lick later. This was wishful thinking on my part because as soon as Fronting Cee walked up to the rest of the team, he hit us with a bombshell.

He said, "Remember that commotion that we saw earlier across the street?"

We all said yeah.

Fronting Cee continued, "Well, Little Bit had beat this vic out of some money and the vic wanted his money back, but Little Bit paid him no mind. Later Little Bit and his team went down a few blocks to set up another monte game. They had totally forgotten about the vic that wanted his money back. The first person the vic saw when he finally found out where they were, was Little Bit's twin brother, Peanut. The vic thought Peanut was Little Bit and he stabbed him in his heart. Peanut is dead."

As soon as Cee said it, Jody's knees buckled and she fell to the hard concrete street. As we all helped her up, I could not believe what I had just heard. I felt nauseous and dizzy. Jody cried hysterically and Saul and Spence had looks of disbelief as they comforted her. My mind was a total blank. After we gained composure, I told the team we should go to the donut shop. In a daze, we all headed in that direction. Jody could not stop crying.

When we got by the Popeye's Chicken on Forty-second between Sixth and Seventh Avenue, we ran into Little Clyde and other players who confirmed that Peanut was dead. Little Glenda, Pamela, and Eve were crying and comforting each other. All the other monte players and hustlers we ran into on the block of the donut shop also looked stunned. Everybody up and down the block was discussing what happened and how dangerous the game was getting.

A million memories flew through my brain as I thought about Peanut and Little Bit . I thought, *Damn they were just cracking jokes, just this morning and making everybody laugh.* I started to think about all the close calls that I had had throughout the years of playing monte.

I thought about the time I beat a guy out of all of his money and he flipped out something awful. He waited until my lookouts called a slide, then he pulled out a .38 black, snub-nose gun and demanded his money back. I could tell by his look that he was dead serious so I gave him back every dime, plus an extra forty dollars.

Another time a guy pulled a knife on us, but we managed to take it from him and beat the living shit out of him. We had beat so many vics who wanted their money back, that I lost count of the ass-whippings we gave out. It was like, "You, want your money back? Okay, take this ass-whipping first."

Not all the vics who lost wanted their money back. I once beat a white guy from Sweden out of $3,000. He didn't seem to be mad, though. He waited around and told me how good my team and I were, even though he had been conned. He was a big-time dance choreographer looking for work on Broadway. I took such a liking to the guy that I taught him how to stick and I put him down with me, until he could find work on Broadway. I made so much money with Fred (I called him that because I could not pronounce his Swedish name.), that he made all his money back plus tenfold. He stayed in New York about six months playing and being a part of my monte family. All the monte players loved him and his funny accent. The day he left to return to Sweden, I almost cried.

As these thoughts flashed through my mind, all I could think about was the time Peanut, Little Bit and I got drunk, and how we had had so much fun. I though about how Peanut schooled me about the game, and told me when I first came downtown to concentrate on holding my springer down, and, one day I would get my own chance to spring 'em. Now another player had been murdered by someone with a knife. Johnny Ranks was killed with a knife and not too long ago Springer Tee, who Little Bit was snapping on in the donut shop, was cut with a knife by a vic who lost his money. The vic cut Tee from ear to ear and he almost died. Now every time he looks in the mirror he has a nasty scar to remind him about the awful price we pay for living the lifestyle we do.

As I thought about all of this, I knew that no one was exempt from getting caught up in some Midtown street drama, not even me. The vic who killed Peanut thought he was his brother, Little Bit, who had beaten him out of his money. What a crazy case of mistaken identity. How was Little Bit going to be able to live for the rest of his life knowing his brother died because of him? As I watched everyone grieve, an odd revelation ran through my mind. I thought about how the weatherman had actually lied. It was not such a beautiful day; Peanut was dead.

37

Ma-Ma's Baby Boy

Damn, my brother, Kevin, was messing around with drugs. I found this out from the crackhead daughter of one of my mother's friends. She just came up to me and said, "Mike, you better talk to your brother because he's smoking crack and he's keeping your mother up all night begging for money and worrying her."

I was totally caught off guard, because for years I had told my brother never to mess with drugs. I told him all the things I saw drugs do to a lot of the hustlers in Midtown, and that if he messed with them, he would get addicted just like the millions of other people who thought they could handle it.

Every time I talked to him about it, he would "yes" me to death, nodding his head and saying, "Yeah, you're right. I'll never mess around with drugs."

Ever since we were little kids, I noticed that he was very easily influenced. He has always been more of a follower than a leader. I think the fact that his father was not in his life, played a major part in all of this. My brother always had a sad, faraway look in his eyes. You could see he was going through inner turmoil, while at the same time not knowing how to seek out help or express it in words.

A lot of young kids who have grown up in the ghetto without fathers to guide them, fall victim to the streets and all its negativity, myself included. Even though I had never fallen victim to drugs, I still found myself looking up to the criminal element. Then eventually I became a con man myself. I do not know what is worse, being easily influenced or impressionable.

I still tried my best to guide and help my brother. I, myself, knew the pain I felt, living with the fact that my father committed suicide, leaving me fatherless. But, what about the kid who has to grow up knowing his father lives right down the block and chooses not to be in his life? Imagine the rejection that kid must feel. Then he grows up hating his father, and hates himself, too. What a nasty pill to swallow.

One thing I knew was that when drugs take control of a person's life, they could turn them into a different person. As soon as the crackhead told me about my brother, I started to second-guess everything I told him throughout the years about drugs. I thought that maybe I hadn't told him enough or maybe I hadn't spent enough time with him. In the streets they have a saying "money over bitches." Could it be that I chose money over my brother? Chasing the almighty dollar might have taken priority over a lot of things in my life, including spending more time with my family.

When my sister stole four hundred dollars from me, I told myself she did it thinking that I didn't know how much I had. Was she crying out for her big brother to recognize that she still existed? People sometimes do things just to get attention. Finding out about my brother caught mine. The thought of him with a crack pipe in his mouth just tore me up.

Somebody once told me there are drug addicts and homosexuals in every family. Mine was no exception. They even say some people are born homosexual. I do not know too much about that, but I do know people are not born with crack pipes in their mouths.

38

Redbone

I was lying down in bed with a pretty redbone after some good sex when she said something that really got my attention. The girl said, "Mike, I like black guys, but I want to have a baby by a white man."

Normally after having sex, I do not feel like talking and I had mastered the art of pretending like I was listening by mumbling things like, "Uh-hm, yeah, exactly, that's deep." But, what she said woke me out of my stupor and I asked, "What did you say?"

"You heard me. I said I want to have a baby by a white man so that my kid could look fly and have light-blue eyes."

I said, "Girl, you buggin' out. What you think? White people look better than black people?"

"Nah, it's just that I like light-blue eyes and that's what a lot of white people have."

At this point I was real mad and I felt like cursing her out, but I kept my composure.

I said, "You know your thinking is real superficial and you need to get a grip. Light-blue eyes, green eyes or whatever, don't make a person fly. What makes a person fly is what is on the inside. If you are a fucked-up person on the inside, your outward appearance starts to look ugly. Have you ever met a guy who was all stuck up and conceited and always talked about how good he looks? If so, didn't it make him look ugly?"

She said, "Yeah."

Then, I continued, "Take for example the statement you made. Even though you're an attractive young lady, what you said about wanting to have a baby by a white person makes you ugly to me. You should be proud that you are a pretty black woman and not get caught up in such nonsense. The sad thing about it is there are a lot of other people out there who think being light-skinned, like you, is better than being black or brown-skinned, thinking the closer you are to a white complexion, the better you are. Take for instance the stupid brother who bends over backwards to get to an average-looking light-skinned woman. He could be hanging at a club and spot her sitting at a table in deep conversation with her attractive darker-skinned female friends. He will interrupt their conversation just so he can try to rap to her. The number-one factor being he thinks her light-skinned complexion makes her prettier.

"I, myself, have been accused of only liking light-skinned women, which is not true. I have been with black, brown and even Chinese women. My last girlfriend was Spanish. (I was lying because China was still my girlfriend.) I may have a preference for one or the other, but I attribute that from getting confused by all the mixed messages told to me as a kid. This is why I am trying to school you on your warped sense of thinking. Black is beautiful, so don't let anyone tell you different."

After telling her how I felt and talking her to sleep, instead of sexing her to sleep, I was thinking about everything I told her. A lot of it was true, but I wondered why I was too ashamed to tell her that my own preference was light-skinned women, which made me think, *Am I also one of those people who was caught up in thinking the closer your complexion is to a white person, the better?*

It would be real simple for me to take the easy way out and say there's no particular reason why my first preference was light-skinned women. It's just what I like. But, for me deep down, I knew this reasoning was not sufficient. Had I been brainwashed into thinking white is better because of the negative portrayals of black people on television and in the media? Was it easier for me to make excuses, but harder to admit to myself, that I was guilty of having some of the same distorted views as the female who was lying next to me? Maybe I was scared to face the reality of my stupid way of thinking. If so, it still didn't stop me from asking, *Why do I always end up with light-skinned women?*

39

Walking Dead

I did something I haven't done in a long time. I looked into my brother's eyes, and what I saw almost brought tears to mine. I did not have to stare like I used to do when I was trying to detect if my mother was drunk or if some of the hustlers I knew were doing drugs. All it took was one good look and I found out all I needed to know.

My brother was a drug addict. Even if I was blind like Stevie Wonder, I could see it. And, the way he looked told me he had been doing drugs for a long time. His eyes had a watery, glassy look to them. His lips were black, chapped and cracking. His face was that of a dead man lying in a casket without makeup. The nickname, Spooky, that they used to call him when he was little, fit him more now than ever. He looked like the walking dead.

"Kevin, talk to me. What's going on?"

Not really looking at me he said, "I'm all right."

I said, "No, you're not all right. Didn't I always tell you never to mess with drugs?"

He didn't say anything.

I yelled, "Look at me when I'm talking to you. Do you know a crackhead is the lowest of the low? Even dopefiends think they are better. Do you know crackheads will even suck somebody's dick for some crack? They're the walking dead. And, if you are going to continue to smoke that shit, then you're dead to me. But, if you are willing to get some help, I'm with you one hundred percent."

"Mike, I know you care about me, but I'll be all right."

"Man, how the hell you gon' be all right when you fucking with crack?"

He said, "Yeah, you're right, you're right."

I said, "Don't even go there with that yessing me to death shit. Just go look in the mirror. You're all fucked up. And you're keeping Ma-Ma up all night begging her for money for your habit. I'm telling you right now, if you do something to her, I'll kill you myself."

"Mike, you know I would never do nothing to Ma-Ma."

"Man, I don't know shit. Crackheads are capable of anything. You just better remember what I said. If you keep smoking that shit, to me you are dead to the world."

Then I walked off.

40

Pillow Talking

Sometimes we men do things in our relationships with our women that sabotage all the love they have to offer. Instead of giving them flowers, candy and the little things that make relationships grow, we back off and only do just enough to sustain the relationship.

Maybe it's the fear of not being able to handle all the love our women are capable of giving. Instead of accepting something that is in our best interest, we run away from it, while at the same time, wanting and needing the love we run from. Is it a fear of being perceived as soft and sensitive that makes us not let the love shine in? I, myself, have heard some men say they hate it when their women get all lovey-dovey and mushy with them, especially when their women say things like, "Come here, sweetie pie, and give your lady a kiss." Or, "Honey, you know I love you." This, by itself, has made some men cringe. You even have men who will never tell their women "I love you" around other men. They don't want to leave themselves open to some guy saying, "Man, isn't that sweet, ol' sugar puss is in love!" Maybe if we didn't care what other people thought and just took time to listen to what our women were saying, we might just learn something.

One day I noticed that my girlfriend had taken to calling me sugar plum and I was offended. I felt there was nothing masculine about being called that. So, I said what's up with this sugar plum stuff? She told me she called me that because sometimes I would say, "I plum forgot. . . . " when she asked me to do something I was supposed to do. To my surprise, one day I caught myself saying it. And, all the while I had thought she was getting mushy with me. Silly me. So what if she was adding some sugar to my plum! After all, why can't we let a little tenderness flow into our hearts, instead of being bitter? What is wrong with being sweet? And, I don't mean anything derogatory. What does all of this have to do with love? I say, love has a lot to do with it because if you can't let the little things touch your heart, how are you going to let the power of love penetrate your soul?

41

Tough Love

Rule 101: If you are having sex without protection, don't be shocked when somebody turns up pregnant. One day China and I were lying down kissing and hugging and about to get into some serious lovemaking, when all of a sudden she tells me, "Mike, I'm pregnant."

I blurted out, "How did that happen?" I said it to give me some time to think.

But, my stupid question made her mad, and she yelled "What do you mean, how did that happen?

I said, "Oh, China, I was just playing."

And she replied, "Well, Mike, this is the wrong time to be playing. How are we going to bring another kid into this world when you are still caught up in the streets?"

Her statement made me mad. I yelled, "Here we go again with you talking that same old, same old."

"Well, Mike, when a person becomes an adult, and they have kids, they have to put away childish things."

I yelled, "Oh, so what I'm doing is childish? Okay, you go find me a job that pays the money that I make, then I will stop doing what you call childish."

"You see, Mike, I do not want to argue with you, but you and I know that you cannot spend your whole life playing three-card monte. We need more stability. There is no future on the streets."

After saying what she had to say, China got up and left the room, slamming the door as she headed to Curtis' room. While she stayed there, all I could think about was, are we really ready for another baby, and why was she always telling me to leave the streets? Even though I took an occasional bust, I still made more money than the average guy my age did. China knew when she met me that I was a bona fide street hustler. Maybe that was what attracted her to me in the first place. The first time she questioned me about how long I planned to play monte was not too long after Curtis was born.

At the time she asked, I just thought maybe she was an inquisitive type of person, who was just being curious. But, after the topic kept popping up, I knew she was serious. She always told me that she felt there were two sides to me. One side was the one who ran the streets with enough hyper adrenaline for ten men, hustling, gambling and getting involved in all types of street drama. The other side was calm, laid-back, and smart, with an obsessive love of reading, who managed to graduate from high school, with a near-perfect attendance record, while maintaining an 83 average and running the streets. I must admit, China was always seeing things in me that I was not seeing in myself. Just the fact that she cared about me graduating was more than I got from the other girls I messed with before her. They only cared about how much money I made, and how much money I was going to spend on them. They all would say, "Get money, Mike, get money. You the man!" Never once did they tell me to leave the streets, but China did. She never asked me for a dime and she always showed genuine interest in the things that I cared about. That is why I always used to come home and read books to her, and she loved when we held each other as I flicked through the pages.

I could tell after being with her a few months, that money did not rule her world. All she wanted was to be treated with respect. China showed me she loved me, not by talk, but by actions. How many times has a person gotten involved with someone and after a few weeks, they tell them they are in love? But, after the first little disagreement they have with the person, they split. That is not love. It is not even infatuation. It's pure stupidity. I told China all the time that I had been pussy-whipped by others, but what I felt for her was love. They are two different things.

My family loved China from day one. They immediately picked up on her beautiful personality. People always say that if your mother does not like the girl, the relationship is doomed. A lot of mothers are good judges of character. One thing about my mother is you cannot be around her and try to perpetrate a fraud. She would see right through it. There is no putting one over on her. God help the person if Ma-Ma has been drinking and didn't like them. She would curse anybody out like a sailor, especially if she thought it was a girl who was after her son's money. When she first met China, she said, "Mike that's the best girlfriend you've had yet. And, I never really liked that big-butt girl, Misa. She had sneaky eyes."

Even before my family fell in love with her, I knew she was a rare find. That's why, deep down, I knew she had our best interest at heart, but I also knew that leaving the streets was not going to be easy. I could easily say, "China, being that you are pregnant, I am finished with the streets." But, that would be easier said than done. Actions speak louder than words. My seed was planted in her, and her mental seeds were being planted in my brain. But, they were going to take some time to grow.

42

Mikey and Curtis

When China gave birth to our second son, Mikey, it was one of the most profound experiences I had ever gone through. I was very nervous the day she went into labor. While we rushed to the hospital, China was in a lot of pain. After she was admitted, we waited for her water to break. She was in labor for hours and her pain became so unbearable that I had to run to the nurses' station every five minutes. As her pain worsened she cursed me out like a sailor. Another guy, who was waiting in the hospital for his wife to give birth, told me this was not unusual.

Not too long after, little Michael was born. I cried as I thought about my whole life and what I stood for. All of China's indispensable advice that she used to try to get me off the streets ran through my mind. I knew it had taken some time for me to make it to the streets of Midtown and it was going to take some time to get street life out of my system. But, as I looked into our newborn son's eyes, everything she ever told me was taking hold in my brain. I was questioning my values and lifestyle. I had been living a regressive existence for such a long time. But, looking at God's precious gift to us, I knew I did not want my sons to go through the same trials and tribulations that I had been going through since day one. So, if I was going to prevent it from happening, I had to work hard at changing my life around.

But, all I could do for now was cherish this beautiful moment with my family.

* * *

I liked to watch my two boys, Mikey and Curtis, interact together. My kids had so much natural energy. They got up bright and early, ate cereal, watched cartoons and messed up the whole place before China and I were up. Imagine waking up to an apartment that looks like a bomb exploded in it. China and I yelled to the high heavens, telling the boys to clean it all up. Even though they tried, it often looked even worse. But we could not stay mad for long because kids do not always cause mischief on purpose. They just do whatever their little minds tell them to do.

I loved to see kids of different nationalities and races playing together in the parks without regard for the skin color of their playmates. The drama only comes if parents plant negativity in their little brains, such as racism, hate, jealousy, insecurity and stereotyping.

Kids ask questions and if they are not given the proper answers, life can become confusing and complicated for them. My sons always asked us the darnedest questions such as, "Why do you and Mommy make funny noises when your door is closed?" Or, "Where do we come from?" Or, "Why can't we eat candy all day?" Or, "Why do we have to go to school?"

Not only did they ask the darnedest questions, they also knew how to give answers to unasked questions. For example, every so often their mother and I would get into a big argument and she would refuse to have sex with me until she got over her anger. During this period, she would walk around the house wearing sexy nightgowns and lingerie, bending down in front of me while I read newspapers or watched television. Sometimes while watching television I would be at the top of the bed and she would make sure, she went to the bottom, so that her sexy undergarments would be facing me. It was pure torture for a man who was not reaping the fringe benefits of all this visual foreplay and had no chance of having sex. She used these tactics to pay me back.

Before, when she did this, I would have sex with someone else. But, now I was trying to be faithful. So, I had a dilemma: Either cheat or find another way to satisfy my cravings for sex. After two weeks of her refusing to have sex, her tactics would have me at my wit's end. I had already experienced waking up in the morning with splattered underwear, due to a wet dream.

Then I had a brainstorm. I decided to go to the video store, get a porno video, and satisfy myself with some Vaseline and my five little friends. I was already skilled in the art of moving my hands real fast from my years as a monte player. So, why not use them for something else. China was at work, so it was the perfect opportunity for me to do what I had in mind, without her finding out.

I got the porno movie and told my little sons to go into their room to play with the door closed. Then I went to my bedroom, closed my door, and I put the tape in the VCR. I watched the porno tape and did my duty. When I finished, I thought, *Job well done.* Now China would not be able to torture me with her cruel and unusual tactics.

As soon as China came home, she resorted to bending down and walking around with her sexy lingerie. But, what she could not understand was, why her tricks were not working anymore. I just smiled as I read the newspaper in total relax mode. I was satisfied and my hormones were not raging due to my previous activities. Every time she tried her cruel tactics after arguments and disagreement, that's when I rented a video.

One time after a big argument, the scenario played out differently. When China came home the kids ran out the room and said, "Mommy, Mommy, Daddy's been watching nasty movies all day." I was shocked beyond belief. How did they know what I had done? China was heated to another level as she asked our kids, "Was your father watching these movies in front of any of you?" They yelled, "No, Ma. We could tell by all the *uhs* and *ahs*." Boy did I feel stupid. It just goes to show you, whatever is done in the dark, always comes to light.

Even though I was a little mad at them, I could not stay mad for long. These were our little mini me's and I loved them more than words could express.

43

Unspeakable Things

A lot of unspeakable things go on in our society that most people refuse to talk about. This also applies to the neighborhoods in which I grew up. I learned that some things are not always what they seem. My girlfriend's sister, Anna, had a two-year-old daughter named Little Maddy, whose father was a piece of shit. He was what you would call a deadbeat dad; the only thing he cared about was himself, nothing else. He never came to see his daughter even though he lived in the same building. Every time I saw him, I looked at him with pure disgust. I know what it feels like to grow up without a father, so I have no respect for any man who helps bring a kid into this world, then fails to act like a responsible parent. I really despised this poor excuse of a father.

But, when I saw Little Maddy's paternal grandfather coming to visit her and giving Anna money every week to help out, I was happy for the child. Here was a caring grandfather taking up the slack for his piece-of-shit son. *Man, such a beautiful thing*, I thought.

Everyday he came to the apartment to play with his granddaughter and also drink alcohol, sing Spanish songs and have a jolly good time with the other grandparents. It got to the point that he was trusted to be left alone with Little Maddy.

One day Maria, Little Maddy's maternal grandmother, woke up early after leaving the old man with Little Maddy. She went into the living room—no Little Maddy, and no grandfather. Then she checked the kitchen and then Little Maddy's bedroom, but still no sign of them. Something told her to check the bathroom. So, she opened the door and what she saw blew her mind. The pervert had two-year-old Little Maddy sucking his dick as he sat on the toilet seat. Maria screamed, "Oh my God," and snatched her little granddaughter out of the bathroom. She cursed the pervert out and then kicked him out of the apartment. When I heard about what had happened I immediately wanted to kick his ass, but Maria and Anna told me not to. They said he would never be able to see his granddaughter ever again. Their rationale was, making a big deal out of it would not be good for Little Maddy. They felt if the cops got involved in the situation, it would do more harm than good. I, myself, thought totally differently. My thinking was, first he needs a good ass-whipping and then he needed to be arrested. I felt if he did not go to jail for what he did, he would prey on other little kids.

Not only was I mad at the grandfather, I was even madder at his son for letting a pervert around his daughter. We found out later that the pervert's family already knew about his attraction to little kids, way before they even moved into Anna's building. The older brother told us their family had been run out of their old neighborhood for the exact same reason—their father messing with little kids. How could a father of a little daughter let a known pedophile hang around his kid? The sad thing about all of this madness was that good ol' grandpa was not the only pervert living around Little Maddy. We all found this out not too long after this incident.

China's parents had a thirty-two-year-old nephew from Puerto Rico, who came to New York to live. He was a real street dude, who was always getting into trouble and going to jail. China's family were his only relatives in New York, so every time he got out of jail, he came to stay with them. This guy's last jail bid was ten years and he called them just before he got out and told them he was a changed man and that he needed a place to stay until he got on his feet. They felt sorry for him and let him stay at their apartment. The first time I met the guy we talked for a long time and he seemed very sincere about changing his life around. I identified with him because I was a street guy and I knew a little about what he was going through. He talked a lot about God and how his girlfriend had stuck by him throughout his ten-year jail bid. He seemed to be a little rough around the edges but I knew jail could do that to a person. The whole time he lived at Maria's apartment, I never had a problem with him until one day my two little sons told me that he always yelled at them and their cousin Little Maddy. I had a man-to-man talk with him and told him not to yell at the kids. If he had a problem with them, he could tell me about it and I would do the disciplining. He agreed and the yelling stopped.

After a few months of living at Maria's apartment, he moved in with his white girlfriend and her two little kids. She had a seven-year-old son and a five-year-old daughter.

One day while she was at work and the boyfriend was at her apartment baby-sitting, she received an urgent phone call from the police telling her that something had happened to her son. She left work and frantically rushed to the hospital where the cops told her that her son was dead. Maria's nephew had molested the kid, and then kicked the kid's testicles into his stomach, causing the kid to hemorrhage and die. This was the same man who had been in the same apartment with my two little boys and Little Maddy. A lot of unspeakable things go down in the 'hood.

44

The Ying and the Yang

Even though I was a conflicted and complex individual, when it came to dealing with life and women, I tried to have a somewhat normal home life. Everyday of my life was not drama and chaos. Although I could quickly flip into a Midtown Mike mind-set, I also had a side to me that could be pleasant to be around. I do not know if it had anything to do with my zodiac sign of Libra or because of my genetic make-up, but I do know I could be very balanced at times. That's why some people saw me as the nicest person in the world, who could do no harm to anyone. Other people saw me as this "Slick Willie" type, who was a fast-talking, money-making, unpredictable street hustler. Sometimes one person can be different things to different people.

In my mother and Aunt Mamie's eyes, I was a smart, calm, laid-back individual with a captivating smile. They thought I could do no harm to anyone. Of course, they never saw me in my Midtown Mike street mode. They knew I was a good student like my father was, and I went to school everyday, never disrespected my elders and always seemed to have a pleasant demeanor. They saw the side of me that loved to read books and crack jokes. I was always the one to make everybody laugh. I had the knack to think up long, comedic stories at the drop of a dime. They also knew that ever since I was a little kid, I was a go-getter who liked to hustle in the supermarkets, sell newspapers, free lunches or run errands for adults. If there was a dollar to be made, Mike would find a way to get it.

When I got into scalping tickets in my teen years, my mother saw no harm in my doing that to make an honest dollar. She did not find out about my three-card monte playing until later on. And even then, I still went to school and got good grades. So, she overlooked my playing three-card monte because she did not know too much about it. To her, it was just some form of gambling. My mother already knew that when I was little I pinched pennies and played blackjack with my other friends. So, she took my gambling as harmless and kid stuff. Maybe she put three-card monte in that same context. Boy, was she wrong!

It did not hurt any that I always helped my mother out when she was struggling with bills. What son wants to see his mother struggling? In a lot of ghetto areas, families were at their wits' end to keep their heads above water. So, if some extra money came from another source, it was widely appreciated.

I remember when I was seventeen years old and my mother told me she needed a new bed. I took a day off from playing monte and we went to the 149th Street shopping area in the Bronx.

Once we got to the furniture store, my mother looked at everything they had. She spotted an expensive, shiny wooden bedroom set and commented on how nice it was. Then she made the saddest face I had ever seen and said, "I never had a new bedroom set before." Well, you know the rest of the story. I walked out of that store with a $1,500 sales receipt and my mother had a smile that lit up the whole 149th Street shopping area. Now, I knew where I learned to make those sad faces at Fordham Camp when I needed it to con the parents for their extra tickets. I loved my mother and there was nothing in this world I wouldn't give her.

But this loving and sensitive side of me was one the vics I beat in three-card monte would never get to see. Whenever they encountered Midtown Mike, they saw a fast-talking, cunning, and deceptive person, with a lot of energy and a sinister smile. Who could recognize any good from a person who beat them out of their money? I say all this to stress I was many different things to many different people.

When it came to China, she sort of accepted me for the person I was. At least at first she did. She knew I was a complex and conflicted individual with issues that had to be worked out—the ying and the yang. I just loved it when we were not going through any problems and everything was going well, such as when we went to movies, concerts, amusement parks, out to eat or just spent quality time together. Those were the times that let us know we really did love each other, even if we did have problems like any other couple. We still managed to make it through.

One time we went on a vacation to Florida and experienced everything that Walt Disney theme park had to offer. We rode all the rides, ate at all the nice Disney-inspired restaurants. We even got on all the water rides. My adventurous side revealed itself when I jumped from a twenty-foot cliff into twenty feet of water. China could not believe I did it.

I loved making China and my family members happy whenever I could. The Christmas season has always been my favorite time of the year. Even since a little kid, Ma-Ma, could not afford everything we wanted for Christmas. But, she bought what she could and I will always love her for that. When I was little, every kid on the block wanted a ten-speed bike, but their parents barely had rent money. Oh, there were maybe one or two who could, which was a rarity in the 'hood, but most of us were in the same boat. We were all *po*-without the *-or*. So, when I got older, if I could afford something my family wanted for Christmas, I bought it.

One year I bought China a fur coat because I knew how much she liked them. I went to Midtown and hustled all day in order to have enough to pay for it. When I showed up with it, she almost lost her mind. While China was trying it on, unbeknownst to us, our two little boys were in their room destroying their new toys. When I finally went back there and opened the door those two bad boys were in the process of dissecting a boxing robot and ring set that cost us one hundred dollars. Santa Claus did not buy that toy, we did. Even though that would call for a beating with most families, I could not beat them because, first it was Christmas, and second I was never a strict disciplinarian.

My father never beat me and I did not like spanking my boys. So, if I ever gave them a few taps, it was a rarity. My cousins used to always tell me to beat my boys when they were bad. But, I could not bring myself to do it.

When I was little, people always told me, "Boy, you look just like your father." When I look at Curtis, I see my father and myself. I remember when China and I gave him a birthday party when he was two. He could not stop dancing in his little blue-and-white birthday pantsuit. I can still picture his little chubby hands and legs just moving in sync with the music. I knew our downstairs neighbors in Twin Parks could hear the little pitter-patter of his feet just tapping away as he danced. I always used to pick him up and sing my favorite song I wrote for him. It went something like this:

He's my little smooch'em and I love him so.
He's my little smooch'em and I told him so.
I really love him.

Yes, I really, really love him.
Plus he knows how to dance a lot.
I really love him, I really, really love him.

Although I knew more about being a con man and hustler, and less about being a father, it still did not stop me from trying. Even though I wasn't the best person in the world, I knew I wasn't the worst.

That's part of the reason I wanted a kid so much when I met China. I wanted to be a father and to give a kid the love that I missed growing up. When Curtis was born, it was like my father had been reincarnated by way of my own son.

45

Switching Trains

Sometimes I bought the morning paper to read on the train on my way to play monte. I read my daily horoscope that supposedly was going to tell me about how my day was going to go. I am not saying that I really believed what I read, but I was curious. The horoscopes told me whether I was going to have a good day, a bad day or something in-between.

It might say, "The stars say today's your lucky day and many things will be revealed." Then when I went downtown, that would be the day I got busted. Some days my horoscope said, "You should stay home because bad things can happen to you today." Then I would go downtown and make a lot of money. So, on these train rides, I knew not to take the horror-scopes too seriously. People say that my sign of Libra is like a scale, up and down, which somewhat applies to my everyday life. Sometimes everything is good, other times, not so good and then there are the times when everything is balanced.

I can remember the first time Spence and I headed downtown to play monte. My thoughts were moving a mile a minute as the long silver train stopped at every station. I was so hyped up thinking about what we were about to get into downtown that the veins on the side of my head began to pulsate. I could not believe that we were on our way to Midtown, the place of bright lights, to partake in one of the oldest professions—three-card monte. Spence and I had heard many interesting stories about it from monte-player Bugsy. He eventually took Spence downtown, and then Spence took me.

That day the train could not move fast enough. Little did I know that there would be many more trips dealing with my newfound hustle. What I quickly found out was that not every ride would be the same, as my days turned into years as an official certified three-card monte player. The reason I say certified is because I eventually got busted for promoting gambling.

Sometimes during my commute, I would either be the happiest person on the train or the saddest, depending on what transpired that day. Sometimes my thoughts would be very deep as I thought about problems. I always loved the days when I got on the train with a pocket full of money after playing monte. Let me rephrase that, I mean with two socks full of money; protection against the stickup kids everywhere. I would be happy as I thought, *Damn, I just snuck on the train with enough money to pay the fare for every person on this whole train.*

I was content to be a bona fide, moneymaking street hustler, doing what I thought I was born to do. But, then there were the days that I rode the trains after not making money playing monte, due to the fact that cops were everywhere, busting some of the monte players who managed to get caught in their mix. My thoughts flipped from being grateful that I had not gotten busted, to being mad that I had not made any money. Even though I knew it was all part of the game, I still found myself caught in the middle.

I loved the times when subway entertainers performed comedy, danced, sang or just plain acted crazy. When you took a seat on public transportation anything could happen.

One time a crazy guy got on in the back car where I was sitting. The back car is always the wildest car on public transportation. He wore a fake conductor's hat backwards and he had the big black bag they carry, but with stupid artwork on it. As soon as I looked at him, I knew he was not playing with a full deck, just by his crazy wide-eyed look. It was that Jack Nicholson's *One-Flew-Over-the-Cuckoo's-Nest* look. Everybody watched as he headed to the rear of the car. There he put down the bag and acted like he was the conductor. He made crazy sounds as he moved his hands on his imaginary train controls, which were really the door handles. The guy was animated as he played his game of Mr. Train Conductor. Everybody laughed, even though he was dead serious as he yelled, "Next stop, 125th Street."

Another time I was headed uptown with my homeboys, CeeWee and Dante. CeeWee always went into an empty train conductor's booths to flex his so-called rap skills. He really thought that he was Mr. Super Rhymes. Whenever he tried to rap in front of the donut shop downtown, all of the players would walk away, his rapping was that bad! But, on this day he got a rude awakening.

As soon as we got on the train, CeeWee headed towards the empty booth and rapped on the intercom. Everybody was forced to listen to the horrible rhymes of Mr. Super Rhymes. "I'm CeeWee. Don't call me PeeWee, 'cause I'm the baddest MC and Y'all can't see me." But, he was 100 percent wrong about the "see me" part because a plain-clothes cop happened to be watching the whole rapping scene. The cop quickly arrested Mr. Super Rhymes for trespassing and possibly rapping without a record contract.

Years ago, I used to think I was a rapper when I rapped with Spence and my homeboys in the projects. We weren't good, so we kept our efforts confined to the hallways of our project building. While chilling out there, I would bust all the rhymes that I bought in my school lunchroom for a dollar. Boy, did I laugh when they finally found out my rhymes were bought. One day they heard a rapper on the radio saying my same rhymes and they thought, *Hey that's Mike's rhymes*. But, then one of them said, "Man, Mike's been using other people's rhymes." We could not stop laughing. After that I ended my so-called rap career. LL Cool J had nothing to worry about! So, when I rode the trains with my homeboys, I knew better than to make an ass of myself.

Once we were riding the train uptown, tired from a hard day. On this ride we drifted in and out of sleep. While Dante slept with his three hundred dollar designer glasses on, another guy snatched them off his face right before the doors closed. Dante jumped up out of his deep sleep, yelling to the guy, now on the platform, "Hey, give me back my glasses," but the guy paid no attention as he admired Dante's glasses on the subway platform. These were the train trips that had me laughing so hard that the back of my head would start hurting.

But then there were the depressing rides. I call them the murder rides—the critical times when a monte player or hustler that I knew got stabbed or killed because of the same street lifestyle I was living. On the days that Johnny Ranks, Pimp Chelsea, Peanut, or some other hustler had been killed—those were the rides that filled my mind with gloom and doom. My eyes would swell up with tears as I thought about the good times we all shared as Midtown street hustlers. I would remember all the memories I had with the person who had died that day, and it would really tear me up inside. When Johnny Ranks died, I thought about how he would always sing that song, "Ain't No Stop-ping Us Now." I thought about the times Spence and I hung out with him and Money Gus, as we ran the streets of Midtown and Harlem. While I sat on that train, I just could not believe he was dead.

When Peanut died, I thought about all the times he schooled me about the game and the time he, Little Bit and I got drunk and laughed at everything. The day he died, I lost a good friend and Little Bit lost a twin brother. Little Bit was never the same afterwards. The big smile that used to grace his face was now gone for good. And, I can't forget the days King and Pimp Chelsea died. I had so many memories with both of them, too.

What happened to all of these hustlers could easily have happened to me. Anytime one of the hustlers died, it was like losing a family member. We did what we had to survive. Every time I had to deal with another one of them dying, I hoped that I would not have to go through those feelings of despair again. But, I was sadly mistaken because I quickly found out that there was another kind of train that I never should have taken.

These are train rides that I am not proud to discuss, but I feel that I have to tell the whole truth about my life. The good, the bad and the ugly. These train rides are sort of like me getting off of one train and switching to a totally different type of train. I am talking about running trains on women. What I mean by this is two or more guys having sex with the same girl.

At the time that I indulged in these negative activities, my mind had already been poisoned and polluted by all the players' and pimps' crazy philosophies about women. Plus, the most poisonous seed planted was the losing of my virginity at the hands of a gangbang. This lead to my distorted misconceptions and rationalizations about my treatment of women. You can even add good old Cousin Reggie into this equation. His negative advice along with the pimps' and hustlers' crazy philosophies on women led my little mind astray.

Some of these characters were considered to be smooth ladies men because of all the women that gravitated to them. Why is it when a man sleeps around he is thought of as a player or a big baller, but if a woman does the same thing, she is considered a slut, a whore or a freaky bitch? Such a twisted double standard. Why is it that some men think that their manhood is found at the tip of their penis? Does the number of girls we physically or mentally abuse determine our manhood? Picture this scenario:

"Hey Man. Me and my homeboys fucked the shit out of this bitch."

How sick is that! Why is it that some men think they can gain some type of power at the behest of our women? Is it ego, insecurity, low self-esteem, stupidity or ignorance that makes us believe this? Please somebody tell me the answers to these questions.

I remember my former girlfriend, Misa, telling me about a big drug dealer in Harlem she dated because she was attracted to him. The guy took her to the movies, dinner and then they went to the hotel. When they got to the hotel room in New Jersey, he told her to take a shower while he went to the liquor store. She thought nothing of it, and went to take a shower. She got out of the shower buck naked and headed to the room. Five guys were there, naked and waiting for her. The drug dealer and his four homeboys raped her all night.

These same guys, would kill anybody that even thought about running a train on any of their mothers, sisters, daughters or female friends. They would think nothing of blowing some guy's brains out with a gun, for doing the same things that they do. How sick is that! One thing I will not try to justify is running a train on any woman. Even though there are some fast women, who are down for anything sexually, it still does not make it right. That is why every time that I ran a train on some woman, something bad always happened to me. You reap what you sow. No bad deed goes unpunished. I think that is why I was robbed twice, possibly set up at the hands of women. Mistreating women is one of the reasons I found myself in so much trouble from time to time. A woman brought me into this world, fed me, raised me, clothed me and provided for my every need in the best way she could. So, there is no way in hell that I can pay her back by running trains. I am wrong for what I have done. And, I cannot rationalize or make excuses for any type of physical or verbal abuse of a woman—not for me or any other man. What is wrong is wrong and what is right is right.

I watched men abuse my mother. Although no trains were run on her, she was still physically and mentally abused. I remember, when I was a little kid, watching her boyfriends abuse her. I wanted to protect her, but I was too small and these were grown men. I wanted to do some serious damage to those assholes.

So, now that I am older, I should know better than to disrespect any woman. When you give respect, you get respect. That is why I would like to offer a few words of advice and wisdom to all the men: *Let's try our hardest to treat all women the way that we want to be treated. Women are more than sex objects. They are our mothers, our sisters, our daughters, our family, our friends. They were not put on this earth for our devilish lusts and gratifications. And last but not least, I offer a few words of wisdom. If you ever see the last trains that I spoke about headed your way, run, jog, catch a cab, but do not get on that train because it is headed to a train wreck.*

46

Conscience Call

I said, "Two hundred more. Two hundred more. If I can bluff you, I can beat you. Two hundred more."

The nervous-looking lady said, "Okay, I got it."

Then she put up the other two hundred dollars and turned over the card.

I yelled, "Black—you lose!"

She screamed, "Oh my God! My husband is going to kill me! That was my rent money!"

Then she walked out of my game with a look of pure panic, crying uncontrollably. Everybody watched her as she staggered away. She made it halfway up the block then, *bam!* She fell on Fifth Avenue's hard cement sidewalk. People gathered around, trying to revive her. As soon as they helped her up, my lookout told me to "slide 'em up," because of what had just transpired. I told my team to meet me at the donut shop so we could split up the money.

As I headed down Fifth Avenue, I could not get my mind off of the woman. The anguish that I saw on her face when she lost her rent money bothered me. I knew when she got home, she was going to be in big trouble with her husband. I thought maybe she had kids and I had just taken her monthly expenses to feed and house her family.

I have no idea how many vics I had beaten throughout the years. Until then, it didn't bother me. I always figured that these were people who were trying to beat me out of *my* money—a fair exchange, not robbery. They deserved what they got. But, for some strange reason, my rationalization had not been working for me lately. I thought back to some recent occasions. Even though my pockets would be filled with money, I still could not get the vics' faces out of my mind.

This, was a drastic change, especially coming from a person who through the years could not wait to get downtown to beat all the chumps out of their money. My anticipation had been so great that I could not sleep the day before. I tossed and turned all night as my mind vividly played out the next day's events. I was like a boxer, the day before a championship fight—amped to the next level. When I arrived downtown the next day, I would make the vics pay for the previous night's tossing and turning. I was like an entertainer giving them entertainment, but for a hefty price. After beating them for every dime they had, they would be the ones tossing and turning. I did not care who I beat out of money—rich people, poor people, tourists, celebrities, crazy people, etc. I did not care. They were just faces in the crowd with money signs in their eyes.

But, now lately I was feeling sorry for the vics who lost their money. This was a very bad sign for a three-card monte player. When a monte player starts feeling sorry for the vics, he has lost his edge. He might as well tear up his cards and go home. Imagine a boxer feeling sorry for his opponent. That is something that could get him killed in the ring. I could get killed in the street. If a vic lost all of his money to me, and then detected that I was feeling sorry for him, there was no telling what he might try to do to get it back. Soft, sympathetic people cannot make it in the game of monte. You cannot have a conscience. Having a conscience on the streets can work against you, big time. If a monte player is scared to death of a vic, he better not show it. Weakness equals death. I have had vics pull out guns, knives, machetes and anything you can imagine, to try to get their money back. One guy I beat out of just forty measly dollars pulled out a real hand grenade, threatening to blow everybody up, if he did not get his money back.

Feeling sorry for the vics was affecting my mental state. Add to that the fact that China has been trying for the last few years to get me off of the streets. A lot of the things that she had told me through the years were starting to make a whole lot of sense. I did not feel a part of this scene anymore. That feeling I used to have about being so anxious to get downtown was gone. The bright lights and energetic atmosphere of Midtown did not impress me like before. I was no longer a curious, impressionable little boy. I was a man with a girlfriend and two kids. We both knew there was more to Michael Evans than Midtown Mike, the street hustler. The choices were now up to me. I was responsible for my own actions, and lately I felt that I was wasting my life.

I was tired of watching the effects of drug use, especially crack and cocaine, ravage the players. When drugs took control of some players, they did not care how they looked, dressed, smelled or even if they ate. Once they became addicted, drugs would take everything—their minds, bodies and souls. But, sadly, when these same players looked in the mirror, they still saw themselves the way they used to be. They saw the person who used to make all the fast money, looked good and got all the pretty women.

I was so glad that drugs scared the hell out of me. I knew if I started taking drugs, I would get hooked just like all the rest. I once tried to smoke some skunkweed with my homeboy, Kendall. It messed me up so bad that I forgot whatever we tried to talk about. I could not hear or think straight. When China saw me afterwards, she wondered what the hell had happened to me. She would not have guessed I was under the influence of drugs—not in her wildest dreams. She knew drugs were never my thing. That was the last time I tried drugs.

However, my temptation was money. You know like that O'Jays' song that goes, "Some people got to have it. Some people, really need it." That's me in a nutshell. Always looking for a way to make a fast buck—but, preferably through con. I was not a drug dealer; I was a con man. Some say the love of money is the root of all evil, but, what about the lack of money. I might not know everything, but one thing I do know, is that if you do not have money, you cannot eat and clothe yourself—let alone, have a place to live. It takes money to make things happen.

The hustlers had always told me, "No romance without finance." But, I was thinking differently about a lot of the things they told me. I knew that China and my kids did not love me because I was some rich dude. No, they loved me for the person that I was—the good, the bad and the ugly side of me. China knew I had character flaws, like anybody else. But, she accepted me for me, as Michael Evans or Midtown Mike. China told me that she sensed little subtle changes in me. She said that I did not talk about Midtown the way that I used to. The first few years that we were together, I came home with stories about Midtown and what had transpired during the day.

Maybe some of those same things are slowly bringing about this change in me. I have seen, done and heard too much. I have seen too many people die in this city of bright lights. I have witnessed too much on these streets. I have done so much dirt to people, that sometimes I feel there is no turning back. I have deceived and mistreated so many women that sometimes I find it hard to look at myself in the mirror. I was scared to look into my own eyes. I was afraid of what I might see. I had avoided making eye contact with other people when I was talking with them because I was afraid of what they might see. They might see all of my secrets. If the lady who lost her money in my game could have just looked in my eyes instead of at the cards, she never would have placed a bet.

My mother used to tell me, "Look into my eyes when you're talking to me." The reason she would say this was that she knew the eyes tell it all. If that lady had looked in my eyes, she'd have seen that I was up to no good. Eyes do not lie. When I heard her scream after losing her money, it was not only her voice I was hearing. I was hearing the voices and the pain of all the vics I had conned throughout the years. Some yelled, "That's all the money I had in this world!" Or, "That was the money for my kid's birthday party." Or, "That was the rent and food money for me and my family." The list went on and on. There was a time when I could not even hear their words of despair. All I cared about was their money, not their problems. I didn't care anything about their lives or their families. Their money is what bought all of my food, nice clothes, jewelry and cars. Their money is what bought all the materialistic things the girls liked. Their money is what I used to protect me from dealing with real-life issues—like getting a job, becoming a law-abiding citizen or even working towards becoming a better person, a better mate and a better parent.

During my days running the streets I felt that as long as I had money, no one could tell me anything. I once read a statement by a NBA basketball player, in which he said no one could offer him any advice unless they made a million dollars or more. When I read that statement, I thought, *Damn, his reasoning is kind of crazy.* But, as I considered my own thoughts about money, I could see it was a bunch of bullshit with flies.

Sometimes a person needs to be told something. How many times have you thought you were 100 percent right about something, then found out you were wrong? And, that same something the person schooled you on, may have saved your life.

Sometimes even a little kid can educate you about something that you think you are doing right. I remember one time Curtis and I were traveling in my car. I was reading the directions out loud, while he played in the backseat. Suddenly my son yelled out, "Daddy, you were supposed to make a left turn."

I was getting ready to tell him to shut up, but I looked at the directions and he was right. I had made a wrong turn. If I had kept on driving after that wrong turn, I would have been lost for hours. You never know who will be the one to help you with certain situations. It could be some drunk or bum on the street. Maybe if you tried to talk to him, he could tell you what not to do to avoid winding up in his predicament. That's why people always say, "Never judge a person unless you've walked a mile in their shoes." There are many things to be learned by watching the mistakes of others.

I knew my sons could learn a lot from me. They could learn never to get caught up in street life. They could learn to always be there for their own children. They could learn from my mistakes. They could learn to never let money guide their every move. There is a lot that I could tell my sons to help them not fall victim to the streets. I am their father and it is my job for the rest of my life to guide them in the right direction.

And, maybe China is the one who God put into my life to guide me in the right direction. I know that all things happen for a reason. Maybe something positive could come out of the dreadful scene of me beating that woman out of her money, then watching her fall. Maybe if I used that, along with the many other things that have gotten me in my present state of mind, maybe the lady's falling would not be in vain. She forced both of us to get up off these mean streets.

47

Street Addict

Have you ever been caught up in something you felt you had no control of? And you wanted to do something about it, but you did not have the know-how or the courage to solve the problem. I have had ringside seats to something like that a few times in my life.

The first time was during the years I spent watching Ma-Ma battle an alcohol addiction. Then the other times were the years I spent trying to deal with my addiction to street life. Yes that is truly what it was, an addiction. But, before I get into that, I would like to talk about Ma-Ma.

I had watched her battle the disease of alcoholism since I was nine years old. I saw the change in Ma-Ma's attitude even if she drank just one beer. The mental and physical transformation was like Dr. Jekyll and Mr. Hyde. One minute she was this sweet woman with a smile that could light up a room. Then, after drinking alcohol, she became this evil woman with a devilish scowl on her face. The first beer she would drink would then magically turn into another one, then another one. Before you could say "presto" it would turn into cheap Thunderbird wine. By this time she would have already transformed from Mrs. Resident Evil to mad and angry. I was Ma-Ma's firstborn, so most of the time I took the full brunt of the wrath of Mabel.

She would say, "You're just like your father. He ain't shit and you ain't shit and you look just like the bastard. And why are you always up in my face? Get your ass out of here!"

What's a little kid to do but just suck this all in? I wanted to go burn down the liquor store, or the bar she frequented up the block from our building. But, I thought if I did, I would go to jail, or even worse, get a beating from Ma-Ma. So, all I could do was sneak peaks from the other room—as the alcohol made her vision too blurry to see me. I call alcohol "poison in a bottle."

But even though she could not see me, she could hear loud-ass Winchester who was also pissy drunk. One time my sister, Carolyn, and I stopped her from throwing lye in his face. Sometimes she mixed an old Southern concoction of molasses, Pepsi and lye to throw on whoever she happened to be fighting with while drunk. I am glad we stopped her because that stuff would burn anyone's face right off. Just picture acid and something sticky together. So, after some of those episodes, she would stop drinking for about two weeks, then *boom,* right back to the scene of the crime. But, this time just a little bit thirstier.

This is the progressive part of the disease. It took increasing amounts to get the same buzz she used to get. Watching what this poison did to her was the equivalent of a little kid watching some big bully beat the living shit out of his mother, and not being able to do anything about it. Even though Carolyn, Kevin and I could not physically help Ma-Ma with her alcohol problems, we did manage to sometimes keep her abusive boyfriend, Winchester, a little scared.

Winchester seemed to sleep with one eye open, knowing we were going to do something bad to him for hitting our mother. We put anything we could find in his hidden bottles of alcohol: pills, liquid detergent, Ex-Lax, you name it. These concoctions made him very sick. He eventually caught us messing with his Thunderbird wine and he told Ma-Ma to beat us. But she didn't. Maybe she knew that in our own little way we were trying to protect her

I also had to watch alcohol destroy Ma-Ma's mind, body and soul. This poison messed up her health so bad that she developed high blood pressure, sugar diabetes and thyroid problems. All of these complications eventually led to a stroke and hospitalization. Ma-Ma's brother, Woodrow, also drank himself to death. I watched Ma-Ma battle addiction for so long that I should have been well prepared for any type of problems with my own addictions. Although, her problems with alcohol helped me to not fall victim to alcoholism and drugs, I failed to realize there were other things I could become addicted to: sex, money, gambling, and lust.

When I first arrived in Midtown, I was already aware of the addictive powers of drugs from watching what they did to the dopefiends in my neighborhood. I knew drugs were worse than alcohol, so I knew not to mess with them. At this time, I did not even drink beer because I had suffered that bad episode on Easter. I only drank a few beers or a little champagne after being downtown. So I had alcohol consumption under control. But, I found out after years of playing monte that I had become addicted to the con-man lifestyle. This held a grip on me so strong, even Hercules could not help me. This brings me to my predicament.

I used to think I had the street thing under control. When China told me to leave the streets, I was quick to say, "Whenever I find a good job, I will stop what I'm doing."

China's persistence, and the love of my boys, helped me tremendously when it came time to make the transition from monte player to law-abiding, working-class citizen. I was employed as a New York State officer. The inmates with whom I worked were what they call "730s," for the statute number. This means that the courts found them to be criminally insane and not responsible for their actions. For the first few months, everything was going smoothly and I was slowly adapting to my change in lifestyle.

Then Kendall, who lived in my building, came up to my apartment bragging about the money he made playing monte in Midtown. Whenever he flashed money, it took its toll on me. One day it just got the better of me and I snuck downtown and played monte. Without any question, I was dead wrong. How could I be so stupid? After telling China for so many years that once I got a good job, I would stop my nonsense. Deep down at the times I said these things, I really did mean them. When China and I first got together, she did not have a problem with my playing monte and running the streets because she understood I loved what I was doing. But, after we had two kids, China made me understand it was time to change my lifestyle and get a job.

She finally convinced me that when you become an adult you have to stop doing immature things and behave responsibly. But, it was wishful thinking on my part. I was risking everything, my job, family and freedom, all because of a sick need for fast money and street life. I was stuck in the mind-set of a hustler and still addicted to the street life. I thought I could get used to working a state job and getting paid every two weeks. But, I was having a hard time adapting. Talking about doing something, and actually doing it, are two different things. I came from a lifestyle of fast money and fast women. I either made money or I went to jail, there was no in-between.

I had been accustomed to making it fast and spending it fast. Have you ever seen the big-time hustlers around the neighborhoods doing things ass-backwards? You know, like buying a $60,000 car, but still living with their mother in the projects, or wasting money on fly-by-night fashions or material items that came and went. I call it materialistic-simplistic living for today, but not caring about tomorrow. The hustler wants to get rich, but stays stuck in a fantasy world, while the rich think stocks, bonds, and diversification. That is why the rich get richer and the poor get poorer. The rich man's way of thinking is to save and invest. The hustler's way is to get it fast, spend it fast. So hustlers always end up broke, in jail or dead.

It may seem like I am going off into a tangent, but believe me, this is all relevant to my present predicament. My stupid hustler's mind-set is what got me into the situation that I find myself in—playing three-card monte. Sort of like going backwards, when I should be going forwards.

I knew China was going to find out this stupid shit I was doing, and when she does she will be 100 percent right in leaving me. There would be no more stupid excuses for me to make because I had a good job.

It's funny how things work out. When I was younger, Ma-Ma used to tell me that my father was so smart, it made him crazy. She said that is why he committed suicide. Now I find myself working with unstable inmates. I guess it is God's way of telling me to help these people and pay homage to my father at the same time. They say God works in mysterious ways. Well, God, I think I need some more help.

China did find out. I gave myself away when I came to the apartment with new things, yet no money was taken out of our bank account. My stupidity was sort of like a little kid who comes home with expensive new clothes and items paid for through illegal activities, yet his mother knows he does not work. So, it didn't take a rocket scientist to know he was doing something illegal.

Here I was still making stupid hustler mistakes. I was still caught up in the make-money-fast, spend-it-fast mind-set. Maybe I had a monopoly on ignorance.

When China came home, she told me how ignorant and selfish I was for jeopardizing my job and family, and she promptly kicked me out of our apartment.

My world was turning upside down and I was devastated beyond belief. I was losing my family because of something I thought I had control of, but I was wrong—dead wrong. Now, because of my nonsense, are two more kids going to grow up without a father? When would the negative cycle get broken? Did I want my kids to endure the pain of not having a positive male role model? Who would guide my kids on their way to manhood? Not some strange man with ulterior motives who just wanted to have sex with their mother, by offering my kids dollar bills to go to sleep. Not some greasy Jheri curl-haired brother who was just looking for a place to shack until his woman took him back. Was this the life I wanted for my family? Why did I not think about these things before I decided to sneak downtown? Could reality be setting in or was it that I am just another stupid hustler thinking ass-backwards?

I sat in a dark empty room of Ma-Ma's apartment asking myself, *Why me?* My mind drifted back and forth: *China will take me back; no she will not. China will take me back; no she will not . . .* (A sad game of love-me-nots.)

It was time for me to go to work when I really did not feel like being around people. I could not tell the officers at my job what I was going through. Picture this: "Hey, Mike, why are you looking so down?"

"Oh, it's nothing. My family just left me because I decided to sneak downtown and play three-card monte for a little extra money."

No way, I just had to keep it all in, while I put up a façade. My three-card-monte game face should come in handy for this one. *Damn, if China would just call me before I leave, maybe I can ask her to marry me. Then she might take me back. No, that's not going to work. All she would say is "Why now? When all the years I wanted to get married, you always put it off." So, that will not work. Maybe if I tell her I am going to enroll in gamblers anonymous. No, China's not stupid. She would see right through that. Rrrrrring, rrrrrrrring. Oh, thank God the phone is ringing. It's got to be China.*

"Hello, can I speak to the head of the household?"

I said, "Who is this?"

"Well, we're the Salvation Army and we're looking for a small donation to help with . . ."

Slam. Fuck off. Don't those motherfuckers know I am the one in need of help right now? The nerve of those bastards! Someone must be playing a cruel joke on me. Maybe it is one of the many vics I beat downtown. Oh, shit, my mind is starting to play tricks on me. I guess I am in pre-bugout mode now.

Daddy if you can hear me, I need some help. Could you please have a talk with God and ask him to help your boy and grandkids? I know you hear me. I am not blaming all of this on you. It is no one's fault, but mine. I know my father is dead, but I still talk to him from time to time.

Man, if I play my cards right and China takes me back, then I can be in my sons' life and this scenario of a son talking to his dead father will not repeat again. Wait a minute. Did I just say, if I play my cards right? Hold up, that is a Freudian slip. There it is again, three-card monte sneaking back into my shit.

48

Head Crack

Kevin stole my hair clippers and I beat the living shit out of him. He had stolen from my family and me far too many times, and taking my clippers was the last straw. Like they say in the 'hood, "I beat him like he stole something." All through the beating he just looked at me with a blank look and didn't try to defend himself.

This was the first time I had hit him since we were little kids. I had tried everything to get him to stop using drugs, but to no avail. So, I lost it and let my actions speak louder than my words. I wanted to beat his crack addiction out of him. And, anybody who has dealt with a drug-addicted family member, knows that doesn't work. The person truly must want to stop. And, that takes their whole mind, body and soul. They can't do it for you, love, or even God. They have to do it for themselves.

After hitting my brother, I felt like I was the one who was abusing something. My love for him was so strong that I had let my emotions get the best of me. I became the judge and jury as I released my fury and acted out in the most negative of ways—resorting to physical abuse. I felt like an abusive husband who beats the shit out of his wife to get her to do what he says, knowing deep down that two wrongs don't make a right. Well, my brother is caught between a crack rock and a hard place and I don't know what to do. *Somebody please help my brother.*

Mama used to say, "Take your time young man."
Mama used to say, "Don't you rush to get old"
Mama used to say . . .

49

The Awakening

Three weeks have passed and China finally agreed to give me another chance. This was after three long weeks of pure hell. During that time, I had to really dig deep inside my soul as I asked myself if I was going to choose the streets over my family?

I took long walks at night by myself on my exterior jail patrols. During them, I asked God for help as I turned the searchlight inward. I told God, "I have tried to change my life on my own, but I have failed. Now the only way I will be able to do it is through the help of your guidance." I knew there was no other way. I prayed like I had never prayed before. I knew God was listening. I found this out one day when I was walking during my exterior patrols, feeling depressed.

I walked into a little empty church on the jail grounds and sat down in one of the pews. I really didn't do anything but stay there, sitting and looking around. I guess it was my way of meditating in God's house, and I experienced the most peaceful feeling since my breakup.

All of a sudden, the pastor was in front of me. He said, "How are you doing, officer? What brings you into the church on this quiet night?"

Then I said, "How's it going, pastor? I was just walking around the grounds doing my patrols, when something told me to come inside. So, I came in and took a seat."

Then, out of the blue, he said, "You know, son, God hears your prayers."

I said, "Thank you, sir. I needed to hear that."

Then he walked away. At that moment, I knew God was talking through him, telling me everything was going to be all right.

The first time I met with China after our breakup, I asked her, after a little small talk, if she would like to go with me to my mother's church that Sunday. She gave me a funny look and said, "Mike, it's not Easter this Sunday. What makes you want to go to church?"

"Well, China, there's no particular reason. I just want to go."

She said, "Well one day I will go with you, but not this Sunday." Then she smiled.

I immediately knew what was going through her mind. China just wanted to see how serious I was about this church thing before she got involved. One thing is, I do know my woman a little bit.

People always talk about a woman's intuition, but men have a little bit of that also, even though I feel a woman's perception is ten times stronger. And, while I'm on the subject of perception, something told me I was going to like being in God's house again on Sunday. But for this first get-together, China and I decided to go out to eat with our two sons, Curtis and Mikey. We headed to Yolanda's Restaurant on 149th Street, where we had a good time, eating and laughing. I told my sons about the time I took their mother on our first date to this same place and how I ordered Asti Spumante wine trying to act high class, but the wine wound up tasting like cheap Thunderbird wine. We laughed like crazy. I thought about the time my cousin George told China I had missed my calling—I should have been a comedian.

I was in rare form, telling joke after joke. On this day, comic Bill Cosby had nothing on me and, at that moment, we did not have a care in the world. As we enjoyed ourselves, I realized that I was nothing without my family.

* * *

Sunday came around and before I went to the church, I stopped to pick up my mother at her apartment. She was looking good in her favorite peach-colored dress with a big floppy white hat.

She said, "Mike, you know I'm going to be the sharpest lady in church and I'm gonna get me a new man."

Her boyfriend, Robert, yelled out, "You don't want me to come over there and bust somebody's ass, Mabel."

She said, "Ah, shut up, Robert, and take your drunk ass back to sleep!" As I chuckled, all I could think was *Ma-Ma don't take no mess.*

After a few minutes we left the apartment, and, on our way to the church, everyone told my mother how good she looked.

She said, "Ya'll know this is my oldest son, Michael."

"Yeah, Mabel, he looks just like you."

She smiled and said, "Ain't he handsome?"

The day was starting off well. My mother was happy, which made me happy. The pastor, Wendell Smith, preached a beautiful sermon on "It's Never Too Late," He talked about how it is never too late to turn to God. I liked his preaching. He made everyone feel like he was talking directly to them, including me. His sermon made me understand it was never too late for me to change my life around and come to God.

After the service we met the pastor and his family, plus the other churchgoers. After that day, I could not wait for Sundays to come around. Even if my mother was too tired to go to church, I still went anyway. Soon China and our boys starting attending. She took a liking to going to church from day one. But, my boys were another story. They only liked it if they could run around the church causing mischief. I understood because when I was a little kid, I used to do the same thing—running around church begging for peppermints and money.

When I was eight or nine years old, I got up in front of a church with a money basket, faking like it was my birthday so everybody would give me money. As soon as we got home from the church, my best friend's mother, Martha, told Ma-Ma what I did and she beat me like I had stolen something. This told me the pastor was right when he said, "If you play with God, you get burned in the fires of hell." But, this time around there would be no playing around with God.

After a few weeks in church, I asked God for a cross; I was ready to turn my life over to him. Not too long after asking for it, I was walking on the facility grounds at my job and I found a cross in two inches of snow. I knew right away God had granted my wishes. But, it did not stop there. And, what I am about to tell you, let God be my witness.

About a month later, when I was walking to the store near my mother's block, I found what looked like an ounce of cocaine in a plastic wrapping. I picked it up, took it upstairs to Ma-Ma's apartment and flushed it down the toilet. Deep down in my heart, I knew God was giving me a test to see if I was really serious about changing my life. If I was not, I would have taken those drugs and sold them like any other street hustler. So, as I watched the drugs going down the toilet, I knew I was on the road to redemption.

Not too long after this experience, my family and I joined the church. I was elated we had God in our lives. Two months after our religious transition, I asked China to marry me, and she said yes with a big Kool-Aid smile.

Yes, we were going to be married. I give all the glory to God. *Thank you, God. Thank you, Jesus.*

50

Quick Slides

Although I had stopped playing monte, somehow the game still found a way to creep back into my life. I started to have quick slides in my dreams. These dreams were sort of like a Vietnam vet having nightmares about his traumatic war experiences and waking up sweating and screaming. In mine, I would be playing on Fifth Avenue, beating all the vics out of their money, when all of a sudden my lookout would yell, "Quick slide," which made me take off running with the cops in hot pursuit.

In these dreams, I ran through stores, and parks into big office buildings. Some dreams even had me running through high-rise apartments, fixed up with nice furniture, artwork and exotic fish tanks. No one would be home and I, Mr. Resident Monte Man, hid behind the curtains in an apartment in which a black man most likely would never be allowed. I envisioned a rich white couple living there, throwing lavish parties serving champagne and caviar, while talking about which Ivy League college they graduated from and how much money they were making. After hiding from the cops, I would eventually leave and get busted by them as they waited for me outside. The cuffs would be placed on my wrist, waking me out of my crazy nightmare.

It would always take me a few minutes to gather my composure as I lay there nervously wiping sweat off my forehead. Just when I thought I was out of the game, these dreams always drew me back in. Could it be my inner being was telling me that I had more paying back to do for all those vics I had taken money from? I even dreamt about making so much money playing monte that I didn't have enough pockets to hold it all. Then I would wake up, mad as hell because my pockets only contained lint, and I had to go to work.

I guess it was my subconscious mind telling me: No more free rides at another's expense. Get your ass up and go make an honest dollar.

And, when I really think about it, there was nothing really wrong with that. I knew there were people who would not agree, using an illustration of a person they knew who worked twenty-five years, retired, then died—so-called proving hard work did kill him. But maybe the person died from too much kicking back and getting lazy during retirement, which in turn shocked his whole system and he croaked. But, if you had asked me that same question when I was running the streets, I, too, would have said working twenty-five years killed the person. The reason being, it would have been easier for me to think that way, because at the time I found it easier to beat people out of their money, than to work for a living. I was a lazy mother-fucker.

Why do people who are caught up in doing things they know are wrong, find it so convenient to rationalize and make it right? Could it be that sometimes it is hard to deal with the real answers to life's questions? Even a rapist can rationalize his acts. "Man, the reason I raped her was because she was wearing those tight pants. She wanted it." And a robber can rationalize robbing someone because he feels he could make better use of the money.

Grand Master Flash and the Furious Five had a song called "The Message," which had a line: "My brother's doing bad, stole my mother's TV. Said she watches it too much and it's not healthy," which was rationalizing stealing from one's own mother. If a person can justify stealing from his mother, he can do that with anything. When I beat people out of their money, I told myself that I was just a con man. I did not picture myself a robber. But I was just rationalizing beating vics out of their hard-earned money, which wasn't hard for me to do.

So, now that I am a so-called changed man, maybe I can change my old way of thinking and at the same time possibly change my crazy dreams. Quick slide.

51

Jersey Bound

I parked my car, got out and headed towards my building when all of a sudden I noticed a black guy with a bald head, wearing a wife-beater white tank top, heading in my direction with a 9mm silver gun in his hand. My heart pumped at a crazy pace as sweat trickled down my forehead. My whole life was flashing before my eyes. I thought, *Well, daddy I'm finally coming to see you in heaven (if that's where I'm going) and man, I did not even tell China and the kids that I loved them before I left for work today. Well, if I got to die at least I got a chance to change my life around. Man, here he comes. Whoa, thank God, he kept walking right past me.* By the time I made it to the front of the building *Bam! Bam! Bam! Bam!* The gunshots sounded like they were coming from the park in back of my building.

As I rode the elevator to my floor all I could think was that I had to get my family out of this neighborhood. It was even worse than when my family and I first moved there years earlier. I was not saying that it was all that good in the first place, but I do know there were no shootings and stabbings every night. Since the arrival of crack in the ghetto neighborhoods everything had taken a turn for the worse. It had become so bad that you couldn't let your kids look out windows for fear that they might be hit by gunfire. Kendall told me a girl had been raped and thrown off of one of the buildings around Twin Parks. Before I moved my family to this neighborhood, I used to love coming here after playing monte with CeeWee, Dante, Jaheim, and Kendall. People would be outside, kids would be playing and beautiful women were everywhere. Now there was so much violence every night that people were scared to go outside. Even my homeboy, Big Dee, who helped me with some ghetto street drama, had been killed because of some static involving the crack epidemic. This drug scourge was destroying the ghetto areas.

I remember when this crack epidemic first hit and three so-called thugs, who must have thought I was a big drug dealer, decided to start trouble with me. It was a humid spring day and I had decided to wash my new car by the Forest Projects, a few blocks from my mother's building. One of the guys standing on the sidewalk picked up one of my wheel rims. I told him to put it back and there would be no problems. Then one of his homeboys said, "What the fuck you mean? There will not be any problems?"

So, I got in my car and I said, "Wait here. I'll be right back."

When I pulled off, the assholes kicked the side of my car. I was heated to the next level, as I yelled, "These motherfuckers don't know who the fuck they are fucking with!"

In all the years that I ran the streets, I never claimed to be a thug, and I never carried myself like one. I was just a bona fide street hustler, nothing more, nothing less. But I did know how to crush a problem when it presented itself. So, I put the pedal to the metal as I rode to Twin Parks to get my homeboys.

I found Kendall, Dante, CeeWee, Big Dee and a bunch of guys from the block. After I told them about the trouble everybody got their guns and we jumped into our cars and headed to Forest Projects. We were a bit unorganized because when we got there, some of the guys beat up whoever happened to be outside. We caught one of the thugs who had caused the trouble and beat the living shit out of him. One thing you learn on the streets is, if you are disrespected by anyone, you must retaliate. Because if you don't, some other fool will think you are soft and will try you. This same attitude applies if you ever go to jail—squash the problem. Street justice dictates that you always fight back.

These things flashed through my mind as I headed upstairs in the elevator, thinking about the guy with the gun outside. I knew I had to get my family out of the ghetto. I did not want us to become one of the innocent bystanders who sometimes get killed in a drug dispute gone wild.

After telling China what had happened, I told her that maybe we should look into buying a home in the suburbs because the streets were getting crazier everyday. She said she had been thinking the same thing. I told her we needed to look for a house immediately. I was making good money as a state officer and she had a good city job. We contacted Realtors in New Jersey, and they set up appointments for us to look at some beautiful homes. I could not wait to get out of the ghetto.

The first time I had gone to New Jersey, it was to the Great Adventure Amusement Park with my uncle's family when I was about eleven years old. I fell in love with the state as my cousins and I looked out the windows from the back of my uncle's Cadillac. I can visualize the tall trees with all types of fruit on them: red apples, green apples, and peaches. The grass seemed to be greener than the grass at Fordham University. I saw horses, cows, goats, and other animals running through large grassy fields. And, the houses were bigger and better than some of the houses that I had seen on TV. At the time, my whole world consisted of a twenty-block radius. So, I had not known that such beautiful places existed, except on television. My eyes wandered everywhere as I visualized Ma-Ma, Carolyn, Kevin and me living in one of the immaculate houses and playing in the big back yards. My cousin, Bud, had asked me, "Man, Mike what are you thinking about?"

And I had told him, "Just daydreaming." I was hooked on New Jersey and all its scenery.

When I was a teenager, my homeboy Cham, from 169th Street, and I had taken two raving beauties from Harlem to the Courtesy Motel in New Jersey. While the girls got high off of skunk marijuana in the rooms, my homeboy and I sat in my car drinking champagne and getting deep about growing up without fathers in our lives. As the alcohol took effect, I became emotional and had told him if I ever got married, I would not raise my kids in the ghetto. I would make it my business to move them to a pleasant environment like New Jersey. I had told him I did not want my kids to grow up in the same types of places we lived in. We agreed that surroundings play a major part in how people turn out in life. After we finished talking in the car, we headed to our hotel rooms to get with the pretty girls. But the girl that I came with was paranoid and bugging out from the potent skunkweed they had smoked. As her eyes were bulging out of her head, she said, "Mike, are you and your friends going to try and run a train on me and then leave me for dead in New Jersey?"

I looked at her and said, "Have you ever smoked marijuana in your life?"

She said "No."

Right then, I knew it was the drugs talking. So, I let her go to sleep for a few hours. Then later, I did my duty, which was to please that booty.

52

Holy Ghost

We could not have asked for better summer weather on our wedding day. China looked like an angel in her long, beautiful white dress. And, I must say, my sons, Curtis, seven, and Mike, four, and I were not looking too bad ourselves in our black and white tuxedos.

While waiting for the limousine to take us to the church, I could not stop smiling as I looked at my family. Deep down I knew that without God and the church, this day would never have been possible. I knew now that a family that prays together stays together, something I did not know as a kid. I thought going to church was for squares, so whenever my mother took me there, I ran around like a fool. I laughed my little head off at parishioners who jumped and screamed as they caught the Holy Ghost. Ma-Ma's I'm-gonna-whip-yo'-ass-look was the only thing that would stop me.

But now, many years later, I took going to church more seriously. This was why not too long after arriving at the church on my wedding day, something strange came over me. A few minutes before the wedding started, I caught the Holy Ghost in one of the back rooms of the church.

My cousin, Bud, who was my best man, tried his best to calm me down as I sweated profusely, crying and rambling about my love for China, and my father not being there. Eventually, I gained my composure and married the love of my life in the church where I had been saved.

After the ceremony, everybody congratulated us and commented on how calm and relaxed I was during the service. Bud and I found this amusing because they didn't know about my Holy Ghost experience. But, we were not the only ones laughing on my wedding day.

The limousine company that China and I booked had its own little inside joke. They ran a bait-and-switch scam in which they showed us a picture of a brand-new white limousine, which we selected. But, on our wedding day, they sent an old 1950s, beat-up jalopy. The con man had gotten conned. Ha, ha, ha. We were mad as hell, but we didn't let it spoil our day.

Everybody who showed up to help us celebrate had a great time. Some of our friends skipped the service, but damn if they didn't come to the reception at Parkside Plaza, which was a beautiful place with big chandeliers and mirrored walls. My family, and about one hundred fifty guests, partied like we were acting out the R&B singer Prince's hit song "1999" as we ate, drank, danced, sang and talked.

Our son, Curtis, danced like he was ready for amateur night at the Apollo, while little Mikey ran around like he owned the place. After a few drinks I got on the microphone with my preacher's voice in full effect and let everyone know about my love for China. I told everyone that we had made it through the bad times and now we were enjoying the good. Everybody laughed when I said, "No pain, no gain. And, it's cheaper to keep her." The guests were happy knowing what we had been through. While I continued to go into blab mode, Bud yelled, "Preach, brother, preach," which tore the house down.

On this day I wasn't the only one catching the Holy Ghost. My uncle, Howard, even got on the microphone and sang one of his favorite church songs as Ma-Ma yelled, "That's my brother. He can sang, he can sang," just like she used to do when my sister and I were little. "My kids can sang. I tell ya'll they can sang."

Thinking about this made me want to jump and shout and tell the world how much I loved God and my family. At the end of the day, China and I left with a bag full of money. And you know how much I like money!

53

Wing Hing

"Daddy, Daddy, tell us the Chinese food story," begged my son.

"I cannot believe that you and your brother want to hear that same story again. How many times have I told it already?"

Little Mikey said, "Please, Daddy, please."

China giggled. She knew I loved it when my sons called me "Daddy." I thought, *Man, I am somebody's daddy.* China knew I was going to tell their favorite story again.

"Okay, boys, let me start it this way. One day I was at my job reading the *Daily News* when I ran across this story that caught my attention. The story was about this Chinese restaurant on St. Anne's Avenue in the Bronx that was busted for something I could not possibly believe was true. The writer of the story stated that this restaurant had been given multiple summonses for this certain something that I will get into later. First of all, what I was reading made me sick to my stomach. And, second, the name of this restaurant, Wing Hing, sounded very familiar. I said to myself, *I know I have seen this name before. Wait a minute. This cannot be the same restaurant where my sergeant goes to buy all of the officers something to eat sometimes. Nah can't be. The restaurant he goes to has the best Chinese food in the Bronx.* (I had not even finished the story and my boys were already rolling with horse laughter.) *So, this can't be it. But this name, Wing Hing, sounds a bit too familiar to me.* I said to myself, *I know what I can do, let me go to the sergeant's office and get the menu for the Chinese restaurant that he goes to.* So, I ran to his office, looked in his desk and found one of the Chinese restaurant's menus. When I looked at the name at the top of the menu, *bam*, it read Wing Hing Chinese Restaurant in big red bold letters. I could not believe what I was reading. So, I ran to the command room and picked up the newspaper I had been reading. Officer Martinez noticed I looked real sick and said, 'Mike, are you all right?' (The kids are howling.)

"I paid him no mind as I looked at the address of the Wing Hing Chinese Restaurant. It said, St. Anne's Avenue. When I looked at the menu and the address said St. Anne's Avenue.

"I yelled, 'Those dirty, nasty bastards!'

"Officer Martinez, who had also eaten food from this restaurant asked, 'What's going on, Officer Evans?'

"I said, 'I don't think you want to know what I just found out.'

"He said, 'Tell me.'

"Man, you know that restaurant where the sergeant goes to get our food?'"

"He said, 'Yeah, the Wing Hing with the good chicken fried rice?'

"I said, 'Well, officer, I hate to disappoint you, but it ain't chicken, we were eating . . . it was cat.'

"The story says the Wing Hing Chinese Restaurant has been busted fifteen times for cooking cats. After reading everything, I was so sick to my stomach I had to go to the bathroom. Officer Martinez was so shocked he had to read the story numerous times. After we told all of the other officers, they all had sick expressions on their faces. We all could not wait to get our hands on Sgt. Wing Hing, who had recommended this Chinese restaurant."

While I was telling the story, China and my sons were convulsed with laughter. Every time I told it, it seemed they laughed harder and harder. After enjoying this precious time with my family I told everyone to get dressed. We were going to the Wing Hing Chinese Restaurant. China cracked a smile and said, "Not this family," and we laughed again as our kids ran around the house saying, "*Meow, meow.*"

She said, "Honey, I just love it when you tell your stories. That is why I fell in love with you."

I laughed and said, "Oh, so that's the only reason you fell in love with me?"

"Nah, Mr. Bill Cosby, I fell in love with all of you."

I said, "Come here sweet buns," as I grabbed her booty.

"Yeah, honey, I fell in love with all of you, too," and we reveled in our happiness. While we stood there kissing, hugging and enjoying the moment, I whispered in her ear, "China, I got four tickets for the Mother's Day concert at the Beacon Theater."

She screamed, "Man, you're full of surprises," and kissed me and said, "That's another reason I love you so much."

Then I said, "You know there's nothing I wouldn't do for my baby."

"Mike, why did you buy four tickets?"

I said, "We both have mothers don't we?"

She said, "Boy, you are so thoughtful."

I said, "Everyday, all day."

My son's yelled, "Daddy, can we go to the concert, too?"

I said, "Nah, I'm taking you and Mikey to the Wing Hing Chinese Restaurant on St. Anne's Avenue."

That shut them up right away; they wanted no part of that.

* * *

The Mother's Day concert was to feature The Temptations, The Intruders, and a few other groups.

Mother's Day could not arrive fast enough for my mother, Mabel, and China's mother, Maria. They must have reminded us a hundred times not to forget about the concert. China and I were happy to be doing something for them. It was not often that we all got together to have a good time. And because we were planning to move to New Jersey soon, I knew we would not get to see them as frequently.

China looked lovely in the beige and white pants set I bought her for Mother's Day. The beige coordinated superbly with her light-skinned complexion. She looked as ravishing as the first day I laid eyes on her. I was not looking too bad myself with my beige linen suit and green lizard shoes. We both could not take our eyes off of each other. I was so happy that I had changed my life around and now China and I were enjoying married life. Midtown Mike was history.

For every strong man, there's a strong woman beside him, and that woman was my wife, China. I planned to do everything humanly possible to provide a happy home for my family. I could not wait to see our two boys playing in the back yard of our new house. We wanted out of Twin Parks housing in the worst way. But, for now, we just had to wait until that day arrived.

My wife and I were ready to go pick up our mothers so we could all celebrate their day. Strong mothers are a positive elixir for a lot of problems in the ghetto areas. When men do not step up to the plate to be role models in their kids' lives, strong mothers are there to pick up the slack. I am not saying that all fathers are bad, but that we need more positive fathers to become constructive members of their families. Women, for far too long, have been raising kids by themselves, giving their all to their families. They find a way to provide shelter, food, clothing and love through the hardest of times.

That's why I love it when I hear the song "I'll Always Love My Mama." When I heard The Intruders were going to be performing at the Beacon Theater for Mother's Day, I knew I had to get tickets for my family. Every time I hear that song on the radio, it always sends a chill through my body—it makes me think about my mother and all she has done for me. When I was a little kid, I used to hear another song on the radio with the lyrics "Please Don't Take Her, She's All I Got." I would get this crazy visual in my head of my mother lying in a casket. I wanted to cry; I could not picture life without her.

That just tells me that the power of music has no bounds. Music does different things to different people. It has the power to make you laugh, cry, dance and sing. Music can be inspirational. What better way to show our mothers a good time than to take them to a concert.

As we hoped, The Temptations and The Intruders tore the place down with all their classic hits. The Temptations sang "My Girl," "I Wish It Would Rain," "Ball of Confusion." When Eddie Kendricks sang his hit "Keep on Truckin' Baby," the audience went wild. He jumped into the crowd and sang it to all the mothers. It wasn't just the young women who let it all hang out, but older ones, too. My mother was acting like she was going to lose her mind when The Temptations sang "Ain't Too Proud To Beg."

Maria, was trying to sing the English words to the songs, even though her first language was Spanish. I loved her accent, and she cooked some of the best Spanish food I had ever tasted—rice, beans and beef stew. Maria always treated me like a son and she and my mother got along well.

Watching the two of them enjoying themselves made me feel dandy. When The Intruders sang, "I'll Always Love My Mama" there was not one dry eye in the whole theater. Everybody was crying real tears, even me. Yes, I cried.

When I was young and immature, I would not have admitted to crying about anything. But, I would admit to making someone else cry. There were the times I broke a woman's heart with my deceit and deceptions and all the days I beat vics out of every dime. Even until this day, I have a lot of damage control to do. But, God's got my list. Some day I will have to answer for everything I have done wrong.

But for now, that was why I gave so much praise to China for helping me with my transition from street hood to a law-abiding positive adult. So, the same way I could joke and laugh around my wife, I could also cry around her. Yes, big boys do cry.

54

Scared Straight

Traumatic experiences have a way of playing with your mind. A person can go through something that is too much for his brain to handle, so he tries to block it all out, acting like it never happened. But in turn it always finds a way to creep back into his life.

My own experience dealing with this plays itself out in the strangest of ways. Sometimes I become shaken up when I think about the time I was robbed and had guns to my head. I have irrational thoughts wondering if maybe I was killed when it happened and that I am just fooling myself into thinking I am alive. Sort of like refusing to be dead as I go through life caught in a dead zone doing things that should have happened had I not died.

Just a dead person hanging around the living.

I once saw a movie in which the main character had the ability to see people's murders before they took place, so he went around trying to prevent them. Toward the end he saw his own murder and tried to do the same, but he found out he was already dead.

Just a dead person hanging around the living.

Maybe the only difference between us was that I was mentally dead. Through all of my years running the streets, I continued to go through life making the same "stupid" mistakes without learning from them. I was constantly finding myself getting caught up in dumb situations, all because I continued to use women for my own selfish needs. And everytime I did this, it always backfired and I became the person who was used.

The player getting played. Sometimes after having sex with a woman I had tricked into doing the nasty, I would say to myself, what does it all mean?

I guess it was my conscience telling me that no matter how many women I had used for my devilish pleasures before I married China, it was never going to make me a real man. If anything, it made me a user. Deep down, I knew the right thing to do was to stop the negative cycle of manipulating women. But the sad part about it was, these types of thoughts only entered my brain after sex, not before it.

Sometimes during my life I have impulsively gone about doing things, then later I regretted what I did. This is something I have had a problem with my whole life. When I think about it, this is the reason for a lot of my problems, doing things without thinking.

What if all the criminals of the world thought about the consequences of their actions before they commit crimes? Like *If I get busted I might go to jail and get raped.* That alone should be enough to make them not break the law.

I once took my sons to a Scared Straight program at the Rikers Island jail. I wanted to give them a vivid visualization of what a real jail experience was all about. I did not want them to fall victim to some fool on the street who bragged about how he was in jail living the good life and knocking chumps out, when, in reality, he was getting beaten up and taking it up the ass.

A lot of people who go to jail come out lying about what really went on there. You never get the truth. This is one of the reasons why I wanted my sons to see with their own eyes what really goes on in jail. So I surprised them one morning and, instead of dropping them off at school, I took them to the Scared Straight program.

All the way there they kept asking, "Daddy, where are you taking us?" And I said, "Shut up and be quiet." When we made it to the jail we were greeted by a sign that said: WELCOME TO RIKERS ISLAND. My sons' eyes lit up. Little Mikey nervously said, "Daddy, why are you taking us to jail?" And I said, "Shut up, get out of the car and get on that damn bus." They both were shocked as they got out the car and on to the bus. A few hours later I arrived back at the jail and waited for the bus to bring them back to the parking lot. When the bus pulled up and the doors opened, my two sons ran out like they were being chased by monsters, making me roar with laughter, as they raced towards the car. Then Mikey got in and said, "Daddy, I never ever want to go to jail. The inmates got arms like tree trunks and they took our sneakers a bunch of times. They said if we ever came back to jail, they was going to beat us up and turn us into girls." Meanwhile Curtis sat in the car so upset he was unable to talk.

Traumatic experiences have a way of playing with your mind.

55

Encounter at the Bridge

While sitting at this bar called The Bridge on 149th street in the Bronx, a guy by the name of Rick Vance, whom I had not seen since we both were members of the Boys Club, tapped me on my shoulder. "What's up Mike, long time no see?" When I saw who it was, I beamed.

"Man, if it ain't fly-ass Rick Vance. How ya doing, brother?"

"Well, Mike, I just got out of jail about a month ago from doing ten years for selling and transporting drugs. I'm just trying to get back on my feet and one of my homeboys just hit me off with a few kilos of coke, so I'm about to do my thing."

I said, "I can see that from just looking at you. Man you always been a fly motherfucker ever since you was a kid. Remember when you showed up at the Boys Club with those blue 'gator shoes? You had a nigga fucked up because I was starving like Marvin and you always had the fly shit."

"Yeah, Mike, I was a fly motherfucker but I heard about how you was doing your thing while I was in jail. Niggas told me that three-card monte shit was paying you off lovely. Man your name was ringing bells."

Yeah, Rick, I was doing my thing, but I been out the game a couple of years. I'm married now and I got two kids named Mikey and Curtis. Plus I'm working."

"Ain't that something. What you do for a living?" asked Rick.

I said, "Oh, I'm a state officer."

"That's good you got a good job, but I can't do that job shit. A nigga like me needs fast money, but more power to you."

Listening to him talk made me start to wonder if Rick Vance had become institutionalized in the prison system? Not too long ago I ran into his cousin Rudy who told me Rick's last bid was his third stint in jail. Now here Rick is telling me about things that can put him right back. Even though physically, he was not in jail, internally he was still there. This made me wonder if his pampered childhood played a part in him winding up in the prison system.

As a child, his parents made things easy by giving him every-thing he wanted. Silver spoon syndrome. Maybe when he grew up, he found out the hard way, that no one was going to give him shit, so he thought selling drugs would be the easy way out. This was really not true because when you choose that route, you eventually wind up in jail or dead.

Or, could Rick's going to jail, in some strange way, have played into his wanting things made easy? In jail you get three hots and a cot, plus they tell you what to do. A person who goes in and out of jail can eventually get used to being there. Then, the prison system programs you into unconsciously doing something to get locked up again—in Rick's case, doing the same crimes that already cost him ten years of his life.

Even though I also had been caught up in street life, I never ex-pected anything to come easy. Nothing was ever given to me and there sure weren't any silver spoons in my household. But, still I wonder how I managed to break the chains and unlock the locks that had me in the streets all those years? What made me any different from a lot of the people I grew up with who are still caught in the mix? I guess in the law of averages, someone has to make it out. But why me? What did I do to deserve to be among the few who get a chance to turn the tables?

Lord knows I have done some bad things in my life and I've still got some paying back to do. I've paid dearly for every bad deed that I did all through my life. In the streets, you learn you have to pay to play and sometimes the player gets played. And Rick was no excep-tion.

Not too long after talking to him in the bar, I heard he killed someone and he was facing twenty-five years to life in jail. Every time I hear something like this, I thank God for giving me a chance to change my life around.

56

Moving on Up

As the slippery ice and snow on the steep road pulled the car with the force of an eighteen-wheeler Mack truck, I yelled, "Oh my God, China, I can't stop the car!" I furiously applied forceful pressure on the brakes, but my little Ford car continued to pick up speed.

China yelled, "Mike, a car is headed straight towards our direction. Move the car over!"

I tried, but the steering wheel was locked and the speedometer read 98. I tried again and again but I could not stop the car. My sons woke up in the backseat and Curtis said, "Daddy, what's going on?"

As soon as he mouthed those words the car spun around, and I didn't know where it was headed. It was like we were caught in the twilight zone and on our way to sudden death. Then the next thing we knew, *bam! boom! crack!* The car went straight into a tall, wooden power pole covered with snow at the side of the road. I immediately looked at China and the kids, and in my dazed, plus shaken-up state, I asked nervously if everyone was okay.

China mumbled with tears in her eyes, "I'm dizzy, but I think I am all right."

Then she looked in the back at the kids. They seemed okay, but they looked scared by what had just happened. The front window of the car was shattered. Glass was everywhere and I had a few cuts on my hands. I tried to get out of the car but my door would not open, so, I told China to open hers.

We both got out on the passenger's side. The back of the car was so mangled that my sons had to get out from the front. When I looked at the banged-up vehicle, I could not believe we made it out of the accident alive. Every part of the car was bent up and pushed in. The pole that the car had hit was cracked and leaning over like it was getting ready to fall; we moved away from it.

In shock, we did not utter a word. The car that had been headed toward us before the accident had pulled over. The driver got out and asked us if everybody was all right and we all nodded, dazed. Then he looked at the car wreck and said, "Man, God must have been in that car; I don't know how anyone made it out alive. That car is demolished."

When he spoke those words, I looked at China, who was still crying, and hugged her tightly. Our sons stood by us, trembling and looking frightened and confused. I thought about what the man had said about God and there was not a doubt in my mind that he was 100 percent right. Just looking at the smashed-up car told me all I needed to know.

Another reason I knew he was right was because of something that happened to me a week prior to the accident. I had helped a man and his family whose car had broken down on the highway, Route 80 East leading to New York. I was leaving New Jersey after dropping off some things at our almost-finished house. While en route to the tollbooth, I noticed a man standing by a station wagon on the side of the highway. He was trying to flag down cars for help, but no one stopped on this cold November afternoon. So, I pulled over next to his station wagon, which was occupied by a lady and some kids whom I thought maybe were his family.

I got out of my car and offered some assistance and he gladly accepted. We stood on the side of the highway trying to get the car started for about a half hour, but to no avail. So, I told him to put his car in neutral and I would push him to wherever he was going, which he told me was the Bronx. When he looked at my little car, I could tell he was thinking we were about to perform an impossible task. He had a big blue station wagon and I had my little car. It was going to be similar to a tugboat coming to the rescue of a large ship. None of this deterred me as I pushed the man and his family all the way to their destination.

When we got to the Bronx, the man and his family could not thank me enough, and they offered me money, which I refused. They could not believe I did not want any money for helping them.

They told me, "May God bless and guide and protect you."

I say all good deeds come back to you tenfold, which is why I feel God did just that. He helped my family and me make it out alive from this car accident. If you have ever looked at a totaled car after a crazy accident and wondered how anyone could have made it out alive, then you know what I am talking about. China and I were so glad we were all right that we didn't care about the car.

Our moving date was a week after the traumatic accident, still fresh in our minds. But, we tried our best to forget about it. If you let something like that occupy too much space in your head, it can drive you nuts. We were happy that we were finally moving to our big beautiful house in West Milford, New Jersey.

I, with my friend, Mitchell from 169th Street, and another guy, had already moved the furniture, and my family and I got into our new Ford Bronco we had bought after the accident.

It was a cold brisk November day, when I drove my family to our new home. I took my time driving to West Milford, about an hour away from New York City. China and I listened to music and enjoyed the scenery as the kids played in the back seat of the Bronco. When we arrived, the boys could barely wait for me to open up the car doors. When I did, they got out and ran toward our big, ranch-style house with a tan stucco exterior. Just looking at it made my heart beat a mile a minute as a crazy adrenaline rush took over my whole body. It reminded me of that same feeling I had when I first wore my expensive jewelry at fifteen years old. I looked at China, who had joyful tears in her eyes as she stared at our home.

While standing there something hit me like a bolt of lightning. *Man, we were so much in a rush to move to our new house that it almost killed us.*

It was a three-bedroom house with a living room, kitchen, and dining room that led to big outside deck. It had two bathrooms and a basement downstairs that led to a spacious back yard with lush green grass and trees. Not bad for a young married couple from the Bronx. After we took the kids all around the house and showed them which bedrooms were theirs, we shopped for food at the local supermarket.

When we returned, many of our neighbors who lived in the other beautiful houses came by to welcome us. All of them were white; we were the only minority couple in the neighborhood. But, no one seemed prejudiced; they all were real friendly. The funny thing was everybody who showed up brought Rolling Rock beer, which China and I had never tasted before. We grew to like it even though it tasted more like water than beer. Some of our neighbors even offered to take us fishing.

One guy stopped by fairly frequently, offering to take our little boys fishing. But he never offered to take us with them, which I found very odd. We eventually found out from a few of the neighbors that the guy was not to be trusted because he was a pervert who molested kids. It brought back memories of the perverts who preyed on the little kids in Midtown. And, even then I knew that some of them came from neighborhoods just like these. Like my mother used to say, "Don't let the green grass fool you." Pedophiles are everywhere.

I remembered when I was a little kid hanging with my cousins and friends around the 169th Street projects, when little twin girls were raped and thrown off a roof. Everybody wondered who could do such a terrible thing. The cops eventually arrested a guy who used to hang out with the girls' brothers.

Another time cops found a girl murdered in one of the building's staircases. She had been raped and stabbed all over her body, and then burned alive. Eventually the cops arrested someone who used to go to Fordham camp with us. So, I knew all too well about people like this so-called fisherman who went fishing for little kids. That's why I always told my kids the things they should be on the lookout for. I never sugarcoated anything. I gave it to them raw. I told them the good, the bad and the ugly about this world we live in. I knew if I didn't tell them, someone would show them and not always the right way. I wish when I was little that the adults had not hidden so many things from me. Maybe if they had told me about a lot of things that could be detrimental to my upbringing, I would not have had to learn the hard way. But despite my concern about the "fisherman," I still found New Jersey a pleasant place.

The atmosphere and scenery were peaceful. The schools were better than in the Bronx, and my family and I loved living there. My favorite part of the house was the deck. I liked listening to music and watching the boys play in the back yard. Once while we were doing this a song by Janet Jackson called "Save the Children" came on the radio. As the song played, my sons climbed our big trees with the green leaves and apples. Her song is about helping our children survive this cruel world. It made me reflect on my whole life and what I had had to go through to finally be able to sit down and watch my kids play in a back yard in the suburbs. I started to think how much my life was turning full circle to the positive. I knew where I had come from and where I was now. I had taken a long hard journey but God had brought my family and me to a better place.

* * *

It was show-off, or flossing, time for my family and me. This is the time when you get something new and you want everyone to know you got it. If you grew up poor, like we did, then you know exactly what I am talking about. I did not get too many times to show off anything, because there was not a lot of money in our household. Whenever I got something new, like clothes, footwear, or toys, I ran outside to show everybody. One day my mother bought me a new pair of Pro-Ked sneakers. I was so happy I could not keep my little feet planted on the ground. I was in ghetto heaven as I showed off my new sneakers to all of my friends. I ran around the block like a speed racer, thinking the new sneakers made me run faster.

China and I decided to have a housewarming because, like "The Jeffersons" on TV, we were moving on up. The only difference was that our move was not to the eastside, but to New Jersey—the place of beautiful houses, green grass and pleasant scenery. And, of course, moving into a new house gave us a perfect opportunity to show our friends and family that we were trying to give our kids a better way of life.

When I was younger, I always wondered why people invited friends and family to their new houses and called them housewarmings. Still to this day, I am sort of confused. Could it be the fact that it gives the guests warm feelings being inside someone else's new house, even though they themselves might still live in apartments? I might not know much about this housewarming business, but what I did know was that I was inviting all of my family and friends. But, I hoped no one would act a fool. Every family has one member who likes to show his or her ass at family functions. Ma-Ma used to be that person.

She would come to a family get-together with every intention of having a good time, as she looked fly with her nice pantsuit, shoes and a new wig. Everything would be all right until she got a little alcohol in her system. Then it was on. One minute she would be dancing up a storm and then the next minute she was cursing everybody out. Her older brother, Howard, always tried to calm her down, but then he would feel the wrath of Ma-Ma, as she yelled, "You think you're better than everybody because you make all that damn money with your roofing business, but I can buy it and blow it up." Whoa! Could you picture my mother at a housewarming with matches? Not a pretty sight. Ma-Ma has calmed down a little bit, so I didn't have to worry about that.

All of my family and friends knew about the trials and tribulations in our relationship, so they only want the best for China and me. This is why, when we got married, everyone showed up to the wedding, even some that we forgot to invite. In the 'hood, one of the first things you learn is no pain, no gain. Everyone was also happy for us when I said that we bought a house. That is why when we invited everyone to our housewarming, a lot of people showed up.

The day of the housewarming was a pleasant one. It was nice and warm with the sun beaming on the property. Our kids got up bright and early and ran through the house bursting with energy. China watched them while I went to the supermarket to purchase the food and drinks. Then I went to the department store and bought a miniature blow-up pool for the kids and a volleyball set. Guests started arriving by the carloads. My mother and my brother, Kevin, came with my uncle and his family in their custom van. (My sister, Carolyn, could not make it because she was living in California at the time.) A lot of my friends from 169th Street showed up, like Joey, Renny, JB, Denny Jackson, Sticky Hines, Will, Ced-Gee, from the legendary rap group, Ultramagnetic MCs, and many others. My friend, Spence, did not come because I was mad at him for not coming to my wedding, so we were not talking. Years later we made up after he apologized to me through a jail house window.

Every time I looked, another car with family and friends appeared. Everyone complimented us on our beautiful new house. My mother and all my aunts, Mamie, Betty, Nell and Mary, were all happy for us. We took everybody on a tour of the house. Aunt Mamie became so emotional that I thought she was going to cry. Ma-Ma told everyone I was a man amongst men and she was proud I changed my life around. Mothers never give up on their kids.

While giving them a tour, I asked Aunt Mamie and Bud when George was coming and they told me he was on his way. I could not wait to see him because the love that I had for him could not be expressed in words. George was such a likeable person. I never heard anyone say anything bad about him. He was what people call an "old soul," because despite his age, he always had the wisdom of an older person. Everybody loved him, including babies. He was my oldest cousin, but more like my big brother, and I could not wait to see him. I had heard that George had been sick lately, but I knew he was stronger than any virus, so I knew he was going to be all right. After asking them about him, I finished up the tour. Everyone played volleyball, listened to music, ate and drank. We all had a good time and no one acted up.

Meanwhile, Curtis and the other kids played in the mini pool. Mikey went around getting dollars for his birthday, nine months in advance. Good ol' Cousin Reggie would have been proud of his little birthday scam.

While Bud, Greg, Bryant and I stood in front of the house talking, George's car pulled up. When he got out, my whole world felt like it had been turned upside down. He looked like he only weighed about one hundred pounds, soaking wet. I was devastated, but I had to act like I was all right. He walked up to me and gave me a big hug as we exchanged greetings. His brothers knew I was trying to keep my composure, so they cracked a joke about George's old car and we all started laughing, which was all I could do to keep from crying.

I showed George around the house and then we went in the back yard to play with the kids. When China saw us, she gave George a big hug and made small talk. Then she looked at me and noticed I was not acting like my normal self. She pulled me to the side, and told me I had to be strong for George. So, I put on my best game face and acted like nothing was wrong. It was hard.

When everyone left, I stared at the sky from my deck. I thought, *No one may have showed up at the housewarming, acting the fool, but there was an uninvited guest. His name is the grim reaper and he showed up with George.* Death was knocking on my family's door and we needed some help. So, as I sat there on the deck staring at the sky, I talked to my dead father:

Daddy, being that you are up there with God, can you ask him to help George? Pray for us, Daddy. Pray for us.

57

The Breakup

Okay, here was my dilemma. How do I make anybody understand the numerous reasons for the deterioration of a relationship and the breakup of a marriage of two adults who have been together since they were teenagers? How do I explain it in such a way that I do not come across as blaming the other person for everything? These were just some of the obstacles that I faced before I put pencil to paper. The reason I say pencil is because numerous times while attempting this traumatic mental endeavor, I had to erase what I wrote and start all over. I guess maybe the best way to explain it all is to talk about it in a hypothetical context.

What if two people get married after experiencing numerous trials and tribulations due to the fact that they both were too young and inexperienced to understand what it really took to make a relationship work? Then, what if those same two individuals think that the love they have for each other will be enough to conquer anything? Then factor in, both of them not having the proper guidance and instruction in dealing with male-female relationship etiquette, which may include trust, loyalty and respect for the other partner's opinions, along with not knowing how to deal with the issues of sex, jealousy, self-esteem, and insecurity. Normally parents are the ones to help with this, but anyone with experience, knowledge and wisdom in how to have a successful relationship could guide them. But what if this hypothetical couple's parents and so-called role models do not have the answers themselves in how to deal with such issues?

I found out for myself that a lot of times when I asked an adult questions about something I did not understand, grownups would yell, "Stay out of grown folks' business." Or, the classic, "Grown folks are talking, so get out of here." This was just another way of saying, "I don't have the slightest idea of what to tell you." In other words, can teachers help students with problems that they themselves don't know how to solve? This brings me to my present situation.

A lot of times, young people in relationships never learn how to go about dealing with important things like sex, relationships, money and problems of the heart. As you can tell by what you have already read about my street drama, anyone who attempted to have a normal relationship with me was destined to fail.

When I first met China, I did not have the slightest idea about how to treat a woman. I knew how to use and abuse them for all of my selfish needs. I learned that from the negative role models I hung around, starting with Reggie, the pimps, prostitutes and other unsavory characters. When I met China, I already had a lot of skeletons in my closet and I was already going through many different emotions when it came to women. Our relationship was doomed from the start. I was too blind to see that a confused, conflicted, deceitful, and deceptive individual like myself would break a woman's heart. This was at the time I had been set up, and I did not know if Misa was the one who had set me up. I did not know if I wanted to hate women, love them, or destroy them.

If you add to that all of my misconceptions about manhood and womanhood, it was a recipe for disaster. Just like alcohol was poison to my mother's system, I was poison to China's whole mental state. By the time we married, it was already too late. I was no angel and I never pretended to be. I am responsible for all of the sins I have committed against God, women and humanity. Of course, I can try to make a case that China should have been able to forgive and forget my indiscretions. But sometimes that is easier said than done. Even though I feel I had changed a lot of my negative behaviors and actions, with the help of God and her, maybe my transformation was a little too late. They say God is always on time, but maybe, I was not. Add to this the new ownership of a house, plus bills coming from every angle, the change was too much. We tried to sustain a good, normal, healthy relationship as we both continued to work odd hours to afford this type of lifestyle. We had bills for mortgage, car notes, phone, insurance, gas, electric, kids, food, and clothing.

When China and I married I had already sown my wild oats and I was more mellowed out and laid-back. I was content with the lifestyle my family and I were trying to lead. Deep down I knew that I would never be a perfect person, but I was a whole lot better than I used to be. I was content with no longer being a street hustler and was happy with my transition to law-abiding citizen. I felt our marriage was headed in the right direction. But that can take time. Being married and staying married take a whole lot of work, and when problems come up, you have to be able to deal with them head on. You can't ever think problems will just go away. Life does not work that way.

A couple cannot stay married just to please their kids. If the couple is not happy, it will affect their children. If the parents are miserable, their children will become miserable. I am not saying that my wife and I had not shared some good times, but maybe the bad times outweighed the good times. I also feel that our relationship and marriage never got a chance from the start. Deep down I will always believe that my past destroyed any chance of a good life we could have had together. We were just not mentally equipped to deal with so many problems. I do not blame my wife for our breakup. I blame the "Mike" of old.

I tell everyone even today that God and China played a major part in my turning my life around. God does not make any mistakes. He put us together for a reason. Even though our marriage did not work out, we still have two wonderful children. Every time I look into little Mikey's eyes, I see her and I know every time she looks into Curtis' eyes she sees me. Although we are not together, we still both play major parts in our sons' lives. They have more than what I had growing up as a young kid. They have two parents who love and care about them. I am 100 percent certain that our children love us unconditionally.

I know there were times I preached too much to my kids about getting their education and staying away from drugs. Every opportunity that I got to tell them something positive, I did. I taught my sons not to be followers, but to be leaders. I also told them to use their own minds, and not to let somebody lead them down the wrong road.

I pushed them hard because I wanted to protect my sons from falling victim to the streets. I knew if they were not strong enough to withstand the streets' temptations, they would be eaten alive. Their mother once told me she caught my boys making fun of some of my advice. They imitated me by saying in my preacher's voice, "Whatever the brain can conceive, you can achieve, keep hope alive; stay away from drugs; go to school; get your education, be all you can be." I knew they were just two little kids joking, but I felt I had to tell them that my advice could one day save their lives. I would have loved to have had a father who preached to me.

One time at my apartment, my sons asked, "Dad, why do you have so much African artwork with women in it?"

I told them, "Because a woman helped me change my life around."

So, they asked, "What woman?"

I told them, "Your mother."

I tell my sons all the time, to never disrespect a woman, because a woman is the one who brought them into this world. A woman is not a bitch, a whore or a slut. Women are to be treated with the utmost respect. Treat women the way you would want a man to treat your mother or your sister. And I must say, I have never seen my sons disrespect anybody, let alone a woman. If I can help it, there will not be any more "Midtown Mikes" in my family. The only bright lights I want to attract my sons' attention to, are those from a Christmas tree.

58

I Cried

I woke up late after being up all night, stressed about my problems. I was depressed and I felt I needed some female companionship. So, I called Tiffany, someone I had met recently. She lived on Crescent Avenue in the Fordham section of the Bronx. I showered, got dressed, and then jumped into my car and headed to her apartment. It was raining hard, so I took my time on the twenty-minute drive.

Tiffany was a nice, single, thirty-three year-old woman, with an eleven-year-old daughter. I liked her a lot. She had a pleasant demeanor and she carried herself like a woman with class. Plus, she was educated and had a nice positive vibe.

I liked visiting her because we always had good conversation and she helped me deal with issues involving my breakup with China. She helped me to avoid getting involved too quickly with the first person I met after an emotional breakup, which often happens. Tiffany knew I was not ready for a relationship, but she understood my need for companionship. So, there we sat talking in her living room listening to a Marvin Gaye CD.

While we sat there vibing to "Mercy, Mercy Me," my beeper went off. It displayed my cousin's number with 911 next to it. When I dialed the number, Greg told me with a somber tone in his voice that George had died in his bed at the house, and I should come quickly. He also said his mother, my aunt Mamie, was at the mall with her best friend, Mary, and knew nothing yet. The crazy thing about it all was that this was the first time my aunt had left the house since George became sick with AIDS. Mary had to practically beg her to go out so she could get a little peace of mind. Now she was at the mall and did not know her firstborn son, George, was dead. I felt like I had been

304

hit with a bolt of lightning. Tiffany could tell something was wrong and said, "Mike, is everything all right?"

I tried to talk, but my mouth was having a hard time saying the words. This was the man who I had known and loved all of my life. This was the man who used to pick me up from my mother's apartment and take me all over town, buying me everything. This was the man who took me to see my first Rocky movie, when I was a snotty-nosed kid. So, when I eventually mouthed the words, Tiffany tried to offer sympathy.

A few minutes later, I gained composure, and left her apartment, headed to Long Island in the pouring rain so I could be there with the rest of my family when my aunt came home. Uncle Howard eventually got in touch with Mary by calling the mall security and they located her via the intercom system. She called the house and, he told her what had happened, and advised her not to tell Mamie, but to make up something to get her home.

As we waited for them to arrive, I could see by the looks on everyone's faces, they were upset. I tried to keep my composure; I knew I had to be strong for my aunt and all of my family. Thirty-five long minutes later, they arrived and she said, "What's going on, Howard?"

He grabbed her hand and walked her towards their room. But as soon as she got next to George's room, she let go of his hand and ran inside. She screamed, "Where's George?" Then she passed out. My cousins, Stan, Bryant, Bud and I carried her to her room. She woke up after a few minutes, got up and walked right back to George's room. No one could stop her. *Bam*, she fainted again. We carried her back into her room. After about two hours, we calmed her down a little bit. Mary and my uncle stayed upstairs providing comfort for what must have been the most traumatic event in her life.

When I found out the situation was a little under control, I headed downstairs and sat in the dark and for the first time in about two years, I cried like a baby. The tears came down like waterfalls. I cried for my aunt and uncle who lost their son. I cried for my cousins, who lost their eldest brother. I cried for China for enduring all of the pain I put her through all those years. I cried for my sons for not being with them everyday of their young lives due to my breakup with their mother. I cried for having to endure all the stress of my mother's sickness, and George's death without the comfort of my wife. I needed to cry.

59

Pre-Bugout

After my breakup with China, it took me about a year to get over the fact that our marriage was really over. I call this period my pre-bugout days. If you don't know exactly what I'm talking about, let me break it down.

Pre-bugout is the period right before you go crazy. You know it's setting in when your mind is so preoccupied with something stressful, you just cannot think about anything else. You walk around in a daze, oblivious to everything and everyone around you. Have you ever witnessed someone blindly crossing the street with a blank look on his or her face? Then someone yells, "Hey, watch where you're going you stupid ass!" What you fail to realize is the person might be going through pre-bugout. Their minds are so warped, they cannot see or hear anything, unless it pertains to whatever is occupying their thoughts.

At the time I was going through this, I remember there was a certain song that was played on the radio called "I Wanna Sex You Up." Every time I heard it, I would cringe, thinking that some slimy guy was boning my ex-wife. If the song happened to come on when I was lying down in bed, I covered my ears with pillows trying to drown out the words. "I wanna sex you up. I wanna sex you up . . ." I could not take the lyrics to that song. I hated it.

Then pre-bugout had me going through the crazy stages of meeting women and talking about my ex-wife. When the women picked up on the fact that I was living in the past, they got on the first train smoking out of there. Then pre-bugout had me listening to Keith Sweat songs; one, in particular was "It's Just One of Them Thangs." I listened to it over and over again. Sometimes pre-bugout had me over

306

at my cousin Bud's house on Long Island spending the night talking to him and my family about my ex-wife. And, of course, playing that same song over and over again. Until one time Bud yelled out, "Hey, Mike, I understand what you are going through, but I just can't take it anymore!" Even now, we laugh about that one.

The funny thing about it all was he had just broken up with his woman of many years and he was bugging out too. Boy, ain't that something; two cousins bugging out at the same time in the pleasant surroundings of the suburbs!

Eventually after getting over this stage, I ran into this buck wild rap star that my cousin, Bud and I knew from 169th Street. We both moved in with him at his mini-mansion in New Jersey. It was a beautiful place with three floors, four bathrooms, and three bedrooms, one of which was a large master bedroom with a sliding door to a deck, which overlooked a spacious back yard. We were like the hillbillies living in Beverly Hills. This rapper had a few major hits and was living the life of a star.

I was over pre-bugout, and I felt that I never wanted to be involved with anyone again. I had tried the relationship game and I was finished. Oh, I still dated, but I told every girl I met that we could hang out and have good times, but if they were looking for a boyfriend, I was not the one. I treated them with the utmost respect, so they understood my straightforward approach. Every so often, one would try to push the issue, but after she saw that I was serious about staying single, she left that idea alone.

The buck-wild rap star sometimes went on tour and left us at the mini-mansion. When he returned, he had different types of videotapes with groupies having sex with him and his posse. Some of the girls would be having sex with ten guys. Not everything you see in rap videos is real, but some of it is. He used to try to get me to go on tour with him, but I had my job; plus, I wanted no part of any after-the-show nonsense. I had already sown my wild oats during my crazy Midtown Mike street days, which is why I was trying to go forward, not backwards. I knew all too well that the mistreatment of women leads nowhere.

Sometimes the rap star asked me to tell him stories about my wild street days. Instead, I chose to tell him what all my nonsense had gotten me—trouble and more trouble. I tried to make him see the error in his ways. His rationale was payback. He said that before he became a rap star, he could not get any girls. But, being that he was popular and had money now, all the beautiful girls wanted to be with him. To him, this meant, they were trying to use him, so he used them first.

I tried to explain that two wrongs didn't make a right. Just because someone had a negative agenda, didn't not mean you had to resort to being negative, too. The way to solve the problem was to stop dealing with those types of women. Listening to his trying to justify his actions only made me want to try even harder to help him.

I knew as a rap star, he held a lot of power with impressionable youth. This is the same guy who could expose a young kid to his negative philosophies by way of exploitative rap videos, radio and magazines. I had already watched the power that he yielded with his nerdy producer, Jerry, who moved in with us for the same reason I had—his wife left him.

Jerry wore buttoned-to-the-top shirts, khaki pants and penny loafers. And, by the looks of him, maybe he could do a great rendition of singer Michael Jackson's popular dance called the "Moon Walk." He spoke proper English and carried himself in a dignified manner. Meanwhile, the buck-wild rapper, who also knew how to speak proper English, chose to talk ghetto slang, wore black sweatshirts, baggy jeans and Timberland boots.

The producer had a hard time coping with the breakup of his marriage. Every time he tried to become involved with a woman, she realized that he was going through pre-bugout. Boy was I glad to be over that shit! As a result, he was having major problems finding another woman.

The odd thing about it all was he had to watch the rapper act out all his devilish fetishes with a different lovely lady every night. The rapper even had sex with one of the girls with whom the producer talked on the phone. This woman picked up on the fact that he was bugging out, so she got involved with the rap star instead. Boy, when the producer had to listen to them having sex, it almost killed him!

After he experienced numerous setbacks in his quest for a girlfriend, the producer decided to take drastic measures. No more nerdy outfits and Michael Jackson penny loafers for him. He changed the way he dressed, acted and talked. One morning I came home from work and he was dressed up in a sweatshirt, baggy jeans, Timberland boots and a NWA hat (rap group: Niggers With Attitudes). I was shocked beyond belief as he said, "What's up my nigga?"

I could not believe what I was seeing or hearing. So, I said, "What's up, Jerry? What's with this drastic change?"

He said, "Mike, they say, if you can't beat 'em, join 'em."

After I finished laughing at his stupid statement and what stood before my eyes, I sat him down and had a man-to-man talk with him. I told him not to feed into the negative nonsense of a studio rap gangster. I told him he was fine just the way he was, and that after he went through his pre-bugout stage, he would be all right. We both laughed, because I had gone through the same thing. He spent another few days perpetrating this façade, before returning to the person he was before.

But, the pure craziness of it all made me really see, what I already knew—that the rapper yielded a lot of power, to influence other individuals' minds. If he could do this to a grown man, you knew what he was capable of doing to an impressionable kid. This makes me ask, *What can we do as a people, to help save the children?* I do not have all the answers to this question, but I do have some suggestions.

If we want to try to help save our children, I think first it starts with the person you see in the mirror, you. And, if you happen to be a mother or a father, you need to get more involved in your kids' lives. Latch on to your kids instead having your kids latch on to house keys. I know a lot of us work, but our kids should be our number one priority. Tell your kids you love them. Show them you love them, don't just tell them. And please, do not drink, smoke or do drugs. Kids imitate what they see. Cut off the television. Cut off the radio. Open up the books.

There is a whole other world in books. My love of reading played a big part in helping me to change my life around. If a child cannot read, he or she will not stand a chance in this world. You know what they say about television. *Tell-lie-vision.* Children need to read. Do not let your kids come home from school without telling you about their day. Help them with their schoolwork and homework, and if you cannot help, then find a tutor.

We need to teach our children to speak proper English. Our kids cannot succeed in this fast-moving world, talking ghetto slang. (i.e. "Know what I'm saying," "Know what I mean," and "I was like.") Picture them talking like that during a job interview.

The buck-wild rap star thought the people from the 'hood would think he was a nerd if he spoke proper English. This is pure nonsense. It always amazes me when someone from my neighborhood was this stupid. I say there is nothing wrong with being versatile, when it comes to learning how to communicate in different situations.

We, as parents and adults, should talk to our kids, but also listen to our kids because they have opinions, too. When they are doing well, let them know. And, if they are slacking, also let them know. You should always know where your kids are, and what they are doing when they leave your presence. Never should we take the approach of out of sight out of mind. I remember this message on TV that said, "Do you know where your children are?" Well, if you don't know where your kids are—find out! I feel if we can just try to accomplish some of the things I expressed, then maybe our children of today will at least stand a chance.

60

Brother's Keeper

I was sitting in a barbershop waiting to get a haircut when I received a call on my cell phone from a person who was telling me something that was bringing me to tears. Noticing my expression, my barber asked if I was all right and I nodded my head and went outside.

It was not only what the person was saying that had me in this state of mind, it was the emotion and sincerity behind the words. The person spoke about how his life was changing for the better due to the fact he was in a drug treatment program and had been clean for two years. He also told me he was training to become a chef. This made me smile because this brother could cook and I don't mean crack.

This was not the first time I had heard him speak about cleaning himself up, but I knew this time was different. In our conversation he stated it took him a long time to realize that staying clean was all up to him. They say people do things in their own time. And it took this particular person twelve years to see the light. The reason I had gotten so choked up is because this person was my brother, Kevin. During the time he was caught up in abusing drugs he put my family through pure hell. His lying and stealing had taken an emotional toll on us for too many years. Two years had passed since the last time we had spoken, after I kicked him out for stealing meat from our mother's freezer. Afterwards I told him until he got his life together in my eyes he was dead. Learning that Kevin was getting clean and trying to change his life around was like having a dead person come back to life.

I remember when I changed my own life, the sun and the sky seemed brighter and the air seemed fresher. I felt like a new man and no longer had to worry about going to jail or being robbed or killed. It was like life was starting over for me and I knew if I applied myself to a new way of living, everything was going to be all right.

Maybe my brother was feeling the same way because street hustlers and drug addicts both have to deal with street drama in some form or another. They always have to look over their shoulders. But, if they change their life around, they no longer have to do this. This makes a big difference in their lives.

I told my brother to take it one day at a time and things would work out for the better. He told me he understood why I took a tough-love approach when dealing with his drug addiction and that it helped him a lot. After we finished talking and I got off the phone, I thought about our conversation, and it made me reflect on the things my brother and I had been through since we were kids.

I realized it was always my duty as a big brother to look after him. We both grew up without fathers. After all, I am my brother's keeper.

61

No Sellout

There are a lot of people who choose to go shopping when they feel depressed. There's just something about going out and buying something nice that makes a person feel real good. I, myself, fit into this category. When I am feeling down, I often get in my car and go shopping.

My relationship with my seventeen-year-old son, Mikey had been stressed since he moved to Florida with his mother. It seemed that our relationship had become one-sided and I was the only one making the phone calls. But, when we talked, he acted like he saw me all the time. I know the feeling of not having a father in my life and I never wanted my sons to feel that sort of pain. But I became so mad that I decided to try a tough-love approach and not call him unless he called me.

The other thing that had me depressed was having to watch my mother's health deteriorate while she was in a nursing home. I felt like I was watching her die right before my eyes. She needed the twenty-four-hour nursing care because she had a class-three stroke.

Ma-Ma is the one person in this world who has always been proud of me, even when I did not deserve it. Every time I visited her, she proudly told the nurses, "That's my son." She has been there for me. That is why I will always be there for her.

This was the second time she had been admitted to a nursing home. The first time I did everything in my power to get her out. The doctors and staff told me she was too sick and she would never be able to go home, which did not sit too well with me because every time I visited her, she seemed to be getting better. She cried through the whole visit, begging to go home.

My mother always said, "If I ever get sick, never let them put me in a nursing home. I would rather die." So, when I visited her, she gave me a pointed look that said: *Why did you let them go against my wishes?*

Sometimes after visiting her, I became so mentally drained, I could not think straight. After a whole year, I did everything humanly possible to get her out of there. She was out for about two years and everything was fine until she had another stroke. So, she had to be admitted again.

Sometimes when I look at my mother lying in bed, I have visions of her dying: I am at work and I receive a call on my cell phone telling me she has passed away. At that moment my whole world turns upside down and I know I have lost the most important person in my life.

A lot of parents say they would prefer to die before their children do. My mother always said, "I just want to live long enough to see my kids become adults." But, I say I want her to live to be one hundred years old.

Sometimes when I ride in my car, a Marvin Gaye record comes on the radio and I think about her. When I was little, my mother and Reggie always listened to his music in our apartment. I remember them sitting in the living room drinking alcohol and blasting our floor-model TV and record player component.

Cousin Reggie has been dead a long time now. I watched him drink himself to death. His drinking caught up with him and he got cirrhosis of the liver, which made his stomach swell up like he was nine-months pregnant. His eyes turned yellow and puss came out of them. Watching him die was not a pretty sight.

Now, my mother was the one who was sick. Deep down, I knew if she ever were to die, it would be hard for me to listen to any Marvin Gaye songs especially, "What's Going On," and "Mercy, Mercy Me." Even now, every time I hear them, I get a shiver through my body.

It's funny how listening to music brings back memories. My sister and I used to sing "Lean On Me," by Bill Withers, when it came on the radio. My mother and Reggie had us thinking we were really good singers, even though we sounded more like chipmunks on helium than the sweet sounds of hummingbirds. One time they told us they were going to take us to the Apollo Theater in Harlem and put us in their amateur contest. The next day we told all our friends we were going to be big stars. Just picture two snotty-nosed kids practicing in a living room for their big day.

So, when I looked at my mother in her nursing home bed, these memories flashed through my mind. And, one thing I knew was, *when my mother dies, shopping will not make me feel better. There will be too many memories to deal with.*

As soon as I left a Fordham Road jewelry store, after buying a $475 diamond earring, I happened to run into a couple of my former Midtown three-card monte homeboys who were playing monte. This was not the first time that had happened. Sometimes when I saw them playing, a sad feeling came over me. I knew things must not be going good for them if they had to play on Fordham Road instead of in Midtown where the real money was.

I spotted my cousin, Dennis, who was always secretly jealous of me and started playing monte after I left the game. He decided to stir up some shit when I stopped to talk to my monte homeboys. As we reminisced about the good old days, you know, the remember-when-we-used-to type of stuff, the green-eyed monster reared its ugly head.

He interrupted our conversation and said, "Hey, Mike, niggas say by writing a book, you're selling out the game. But I told them my cousin was a legend with this shit."

When he finished talking, I knew immediately what he was trying to do. He was trying to make me look bad in front of everybody.

I was fuming and I said, "Who told you that?"

He replied, "My springer, Steve, across the street said it."

This surprised me because although the guy was not down with us back in the day, he knew of me from the streets and we always were cordial to each other. So, when Dennis told me he was one of the people who said it, I was surprised.

Then I said, 'No matter what you do in life, there are always going to be haters."

After expressing my feelings, my homeboy, Mike Soto, who was standing there said, "Boy, back in the days when we played monte in Midtown and little Mike was the man, sometimes I would come down late and everybody would be talking about how Mike took it today. I would walk around with my head up all day, telling all the players who didn't know which Mike, 'Yeah, I took it today.'" This had us in stitches.

Deep down I knew Mike Soto did that because he knew what Dennis did was wrong. Mike understood 100 percent about people saying something about selling the game. Back in the days when I first came to Midtown and started playing monte, Mike was one of the top springers in the game. But, he started getting high and wound up on the "David Letterman" show, revealing to everyone how the game of three-card monte actually went down. The next day when he went to Midtown, everyone treated him like he had leprosy, saying, "Yo Mike, you sold the game." After that he became known as the guy who sold the game. So, he understood exactly how Dennis's comment made me feel.

When I started writing my book, I knew it would be a hard task trying to tell my story without giving away some of the game's secrets. But, I could not let it deter me from writing a book, which I have wanted to do since I was about twelve years old, and way before I even knew what three-card monte was. It just so happened that I became a monte player and of course being that it was a part of my life, it would have to be written about. But, this book is more about me, than monte—not so-called "selling the game." And most of the monte players who really know me, understand that my story, our story, has to be told. When Johnny Ranks, Chelsea and Peanut died, their murders did not get one paragraph in a newspaper. It was like they never even existed. Just another hustler killed out in the streets. They may have not meant anything to the masses, but they meant something to me.

Deep down I know there are going to be some people who do not give a rat's ass about my life story or anybody else's. If the writers that I read about when I was a little kid had not written for this same reason, I would never have been inspired to write. Maybe by telling my story, truthfully and honestly, I can prevent some kid who happens to read from making the mistakes I made and may even be inspired to write his or her own life story. A positive cycle starts with something positive. So, if someone out there thinks I so-called "sold the game," it will not bother me one bit. I know the only game I am selling is the game I played on myself for far too long.

Epilogue

China and my son, Mikey, are living in Florida, enjoying the sun, beaches and blue skies. They deserve it. My oldest son, Curtis, lives at Ma-Ma's apartment. He loves to read books, rap, write poems and poetry. And, I want to let him and everybody in on a little secret— one day he is going to write a book. He's truly gifted. Like father, like son, he shares my passion for words.

Money Gus is in jail upstate. Someone told me his woman, Pinky, died.

Some of the hustlers told me Little Glenda died in a mysterious car accident.

About a year ago I ran into Lady Day on 169th Street, and even though she had put on a little weight, she was still looking good. She told me she was working and drug-free, dealing with life one day at a time.

Big Head Louie, after many years, finally left the streets and got a job upstate.

Honey Combs is either somewhere pimping or dead. His motto— pimp or die.

The last time I heard about Misa, somebody told me she was living in a different state, but still running the streets and getting high. We both were just two poisoned souls who met on Hell Street.

My sister, Carolyn, lives in sunny California, and works with wayward kids. She's doing her part to help save the children. Sis, I am so proud of you. Love always!

My cousin, Bud, is running two businesses and one of them deals with music. One day he's going to be the next Berry Gordy. You are my brother from another mother. Love ya!

My aunt Mamie, Uncle Howard and the rest of the Evans' family are doing well and living large on Long Island. Without them in my life, there would be no me. Thanks for believing in me! "What up Deputy Evans!"

Kevin is in a drug program trying to get his life together. Keep the faith.

Sad to say, Spence, and a lot of my Midtown family are still caught up in the struggle and trying to find a way off of those mean streets. They are all proud that I, one of their own, made it out. I love them with all my heart and I have paid homage to them by getting the only tattoo I have on my body—three cards and a cross. Love is love.

Glossary of Street Terms

Bitch ass: A person of weak character; soft.
Boosters: Shoplifters, people who take things without paying.
Boned: Had sex, fucked.
Buck wild: Crazy, nuts, loony.
C-notes: $100 bills.
Ceelo: A street gambling game played with three dice.
Dimepiece: Pretty woman at the top of the scale of ten.
Doing the nasty: Having sex, stroking, sexual relations.
Drop a dime: To snitch, tell on someone.
"Fifty-two block": Fifty-two defensive blocking techniques used in street fighting.
Floss: Showing off, wanting to be seen.
Fly: Looking real good, top-notch, eye-catching.
Fronting: Showing off, perpetrating a fraud
Game tight player: A good manipulator, who is well-versed in his or her particular hustle, or craft.
Get over: To con, use, or take advantage of.
Get down: To play three-card monte; to be a part of, to do something.
Hoes: Whores.
Holding down: Looking out for the cops, protecting, shielding from harm.
Homeboys: Friends, comrades.
House medallion: A silver or gold jewelry piece that is shaped like a house. Normally it has a religious figure sculpted in the middle, such as Jesus or a saint.
Jostlers: Pickpockets, thieves.
Kick game: Persuade someone to see things your way through lying or cheating.
Knocked: Busted by the cops; caught doing something wrong.

Lames: Suckers, stupid people.

Lay some pipe: Slang term for having good sex, sexual relations.

Lick: Three-card monte game.

Lug: Bend in a card.

Mack game: Smooth slick talk.

Murphy: Con game.

Munchies: Big appetite, hungry.

No Nervous: Don't be nervous.

Props: Giving proper due, showing respect for.

Radar, radar: Calm down, or chill out, or stop whatever you are doing.

Redbone: Light-complexioned woman.

730s: Crazy, insane inmates. The courts have deemed them not responsible for their criminal acts.

Scared money: Money that a person is scared to lose or spend.

Shield: The stick or fake bettor.

Shorty: A young kid, or a name used for someone of small stature.

Skid bids: Short jail stay.

Skunk: Potent marijuana.

Slide: Lookout man.

Springer: The guy who flips the cards in three-card monte.

Sticks: Fake bettors; shield.

Train: More than one guy having sex with a woman at one time.

Tush: A monte trick. (Only the best know how to do it!)

Two deep: Two people.

Vics: Victims of a con or crime.

Wife-beater T-shirt: A slang term for a men's white tank top